Console-ing Passions

Television and Cultural Power

Edited by Lynn Spigel

Haunted Media

Electronic Presence

from Telegraphy to Television

Jeffrey Sconce

Duke University Press

Durham & London

2000

to my parents, Jerry and Evelyn

Contents

Acknowledgments

Many people have contributed significant advice, time, and assistance to the research, ruminating, and writing phases of this book. I would like to thank especially Julie D'Acci for her guidance of this manuscript at a particularly difficult time in its genesis, as well as John Fiske, Michele Hilmes, Don Crafton, and Jack Kugelmass for their many useful comments on this work while it was still a dissertation project at the University of Wisconsin–Madison.

Friends and colleagues around the country have also provided valuable commentary on various parts of this manuscript. I would like to thank in particular Chris Anderson, Mark Alvey, and Hilary Radner for their years of advice, friendship, and support on this and other projects. William Boddy, Micheal Curtin, and Tom Gunning have also offered valuable advice on the manuscript. I would also like to thank my colleagues at the University of Southern California, and in particular, Dana Polan, Michael Renov, Marsha Kinder and Tara McPherson for their comments on this work. I am grateful as well to Jan Olsson for the opportunity of editing a special issue of the journal *Aura,* an experience that helped focus many of the arguments during the completion of this book.

This book is indebted as well to the community of scholarship in Madison during the early 1990s, and I would like to thank in particular Dave Brean, Steve Classen, Robert Dawson, Kevin Glynn, Lisa Parks, and Sally Ross for their direct and indirect influences on this manuscript. I would especially like to thank Moya Luckett and Sean Feeney for being great friends and intellectual partners who always inspired me to produce better work, both in the land of badgers and beyond.

Much of this manuscript was revised while I was teaching at the University of Wisconsin–Oshkosh, and I would like to acknowledge the valued friendship and support of Dan Streible, Teri Tynes, Karla Berry, and Franca Barricelli during my years there.

I am also grateful to the early encouragement of faculty at the University of Texas–Austin, including Janet Staiger, Tom Schatz, and Horace Newcomb. Mark Fenster, Jim Wehmeyer, and Barbara Burton remain valued friends from my time in Texas as well.

Finally, this book would not have been possible without the advice, wisdom, patience, and support of Lynn Spigel, who was a great inspiration for this project both in its earliest inception and in the final days of its revision.

A shorter version of chapter 2 appeared as "The Voice from the Void: Wireless, Modernity, and Distant Death" in the *International Journal of Cultural Studies* 1, no. 2 (1998). Chapter 4 appeared in a different version as "The 'Outer Limits' of Oblivion" in *The Revolution Wasn't Televised: Sixties Television and Social Conflict,* edited by Lynn Spigel and Michael Curtin (New York: Routledge, 1996).

Introduction

Amid daily newspaper coverage of national politics, foreign policy, and local crime, readers of the *New York Times* in the early fifties encountered three bizarre and seemingly unrelated stories concerning the then emerging medium of television. On the night of 20 October 1952, Frank Walsh went to bed in his Long Island home while his wife and children watched an episode of *Abbott and Costello* on the television set downstairs. Disturbed by the volume of the program and unable to sleep, Walsh got out of bed, found his handgun, and started down the staircase. Halfway down the steps, Walsh paused, aimed, and in the words of the *Times* reporter, "stilled the television with one shot from his .38 caliber revolver." After a few moments of stunned silence, Walsh's wife called the police to report the incident, but, as the paper observed, "Since there is no law against shooting television sets, the only charge against Mr. Walsh will be a substantial one from the repairman."[1] Walsh was able to avoid even this charge, however, by converting his newfound status as a television assassin ("They should give him back his gun; his work has barely started," quipped columnist Jack Gould) into an opportunity to appear on a quiz show. As a contestant on *Strike It Rich,* Walsh won a new television set.[2]

On 30 June 1953, Richard Gaughan, an unemployed shipping clerk who would later describe himself to police as a "professional justice man," rushed past the guards at CBS studios in New York with two newly purchased kitchen knives. Gaughan made his way onto a set where a rehearsal was taking place for the series *City Hospital.* In a scuffle with actors, technicians, and security personnel, Gaughan managed to stab a CBS cameraman and smash a pitcher of water over an actor's head before finally being apprehended. Gaughan confessed at the police station that he had "purchased the knives for the specific purpose of killing someone connected with television." Later he told the police that he hated television because its shows were "scandalous." More important, he also felt he was being personally "slandered by the programs."[3]

Finally, on 11 December 1953, readers of the *Times* met a family from Long Island that had been forced to "punish" their TV set for scaring the children. As Jerome E. Travers and his three children were watching *Ding*

Dong School one day, the face of an unknown woman mysteriously appeared on the screen and would not vanish, even when the set was turned off and unplugged. "The balky set," which "previously had behaved itself," according to the *Times,* "had its face turned to the wall . . . for gross misbehavior in frightening little children."[4] The haunted television finally gave up the ghost, so to speak, a day later, but not before scores of newspapermen, magazine writers, and TV engineers had a chance to observe the phenomenon. Visitors to the Travers' home also included Francey Lane, a singer from the episode of the *Morey Amsterdam Show* that had preceded *Ding Dong School* on the day of the initial haunting. Lane was thought to be the face behind the image frozen on the screen, and her agent apparently thought it would make for good publicity to have the singer meet her ghostly cathode-ray double.[5]

Something less than newsworthy, these odd incidents from the early days of television are nevertheless of interest as diverse examples of a common convention in representing television and other electronic media. Each of these stories draws on a larger cultural mythology about the "living" quality of such technologies, suggesting, in this case, that television is "*alive* . . . living, real, not dead"[6] (even if it sometimes serves as a medium *of* the dead). The "living" quality of television transcends the historically limited and now almost nonexistent practice of direct "live" broadcasting to describe a larger sense that all television programming is discursively "live" by virtue of its instantaneous transmission and reception. Central as well to the initial cultural fascination with telegraphy, telephony, and wireless, such liveness is at present the foundation for a whole new series of vivid fantasies involving cyberspace and virtual reality. At times this sense of liveness can imply that electronic media technologies are animate and perhaps even sentient. Although the various parties involved in the peculiar episodes detailed above may not have actually believed their TV sets were "alive," the reporters who needed to make sense of these assignments certainly wrote as if their readers would make, or at least understand, such an assumption. These stories are either amusing or alarming to the extent that the reader shares in a larger cultural understanding that television and its electronic cousins are, paradoxically, completely familiar in their seemingly fundamental uncanniness, so much so that we rarely question the often fantastic conventions through which we conceptualize and engage these media.

Perhaps initially only a product of Frank Walsh's insomnia, for example, shooting the T V set has become over the years a familiar gesture in the nation's hyperbolic loathing of television as an intruding house guest. Although it would be difficult to document exactly how many people really do shoot their sets in a given year, it is easy to gauge the symbolic importance of this act by how frequently it appears in films, books, and even in television programming itself. In this scenario, the television figures as an obnoxious, deceitful, cloying, banal, and/or boring visitor within the home whom must be dispatched with extreme prejudice. The intrusive, imperious and, above all else, living presence of television is such that it cannot simply be turned off or unplugged—it must be violently murdered. The *Times* headline for Walsh's ballistic tirade reinforced the pseudo-sentience of the doomed set, justifying the act as "Obviously Self-Defense" (a sentiment that echoes in contemporary bumper stickers that implore surrounding drivers to "Kill Your Television"). Owners of personal computers make similar animating investments in their media, of course, but here the interactivity and intimacy of the computer more often transform the machine into a friend and confidant (albeit one with which we occasionally have a stormy relationship).[7]

Gaughan's paranoid attack on the T V studio, meanwhile, exemplifies another familiar theme involving the media's awesome powers of animated "living" presence: the delusional viewer who believes the media is speaking directly to him or her. A common symptom among schizophrenics,[8] this delusion also foregrounds in exaggerated but obviously compelling terms the powers of "liveness" and "immediacy" experienced by audiences of electronic media as a whole. With the delusional psychotic, the media assume a particularly sentient quality, figuring as a seemingly candid and intimate interlocutor engaged in direct contact with its (psychotic) audience (of one). The television industry, in particular, would no doubt like for its entire audience to consist of such schizophrenics (as long as they remained functional consumers), since it continually tries to maintain the illusion that it is indeed speaking directly to us. Some might argue that the home computer has allowed this long-latent psychosis to at last come true: the computer (and other operators) can now speak directly to us (and we to them) in an immediate electronic interface. Such interactivity, of course, has led to new stories of electropsychopathology, centering this time on "addicted" operators who find this living electronic connection so alluring as to shun the real world in favor of cyberspace. Here too "liveness" leads to a unique compulsion that ultimately dissolves boundaries between the real and the electronic.

The haunting of the Travers family, finally, highlights an uncanny and perhaps even sinister component in "living" electronic media. What exactly is the status of the worlds created by radio, television, and computers? Are there invisible entities adrift in the ether, entire other electronic realms coursing through the wired networks of the world? Sound and image without material substance, the electronically mediated worlds of telecommunications often evoke the supernatural by creating virtual beings that appear to have no physical form. By bringing this spectral world into the home, the TV set in particular can take on the appearance of a haunted apparatus. The concerns of the Travers family should be familiar to those who watched televisions with older model picture tubes in the fifties and sixties. Early viewers will always remember the eerie presence of the slowly fading dot of light appearing at the center of the screen once the set had been turned off, a blip that suggested something was still there in the cabinet even after the image itself had vanished. In media folklore past and present, telephones, radios, and computers have been similarly "possessed" by such "ghosts in the machine," the technologies serving as either uncanny electronic agents or as gateways to electronic otherworlds.

Tales of imperious, animate, sentient, virtual, haunted, possessed, and otherwise "living" media might seem at first no more than curious anecdotes at the fringes of American popular culture. And yet metaphors of living media also structure much academic thought on electronic telecommunications — albeit in a more specialized jargon. Perhaps the most visible scholar of the century, Marshall McLuhan, pronounced telecommunications media to be nothing less than an extension of humankind's "nervous system." Even those who stop short of such cybernetic propositions often operate from a similar assumption that electronic telecommunications have somehow forever and irretrievably altered human consciousness itself, if not as a prosthetic enhancement then as a form of narcotizing hypnosis. One could argue, for example, that a thin line divides the knife-wielding Richard Gaughan and his psychotic delusions from the hapless subjects posited by much social-scientific media effects research. Frequently portrayed as a public enmeshed in an immediate, interpersonal, pathological, and ultimately unmediated relationship with electronic media, these subjects, like Gaughan, are doomed to misapprehend the living artifice of television as the basis for their own social "reality" and personal behavior. Zombified cola drinkers, Bobo-punching kindergartners, and clueless Susan Lucci fans have thus, in their time, all been depicted by social scientists and journalists alike as slaves to a particularly persuasive electronic master, an almost malevolent entity whose powers of control are somehow believed to eclipse those of all previous nonelectronic media.

Other avenues of media theory, meanwhile, have taken the imagined powers of electronic simultaneity and "liveness" to increasingly apocalyptic heights through ever more complex improvisations on the concept of "simulation." In this postmodern vision of the media occult, the postwar period has represented the supernatural "dissolution of TV into life, the dissolution of life into TV."[9] From this perspective, the ubiquitous circulation and constant mediation of television imagery have contributed to an accelerated evaporation of reality into "hyperreality." For critics of postmodernity ranging in temperament from Jean Baudrillard to Fredric Jameson, television's constant transmission of instantaneous representations makes the medium both the prime catalyst and most pervasive symptom of an age marked by the increased dissolution of all referentiality. In the past decade or so, however, we have seen a major shift in these arguments. Whereas critics of television and postmodernity at first decried the electronic erosion of reality in harrowing parables of affective dissipation, more recent scholarship in the fields of cyberspace and virtual subjectivity frequently embraces these phantom landscapes and synthetic identities. Once the object of critical scrutiny and ideological debate, the "subject" of cybertheory now frequently reigns in academic discourse as a self-evident, emancipated entity free to reinvent itself in the new electronic frontier. Simulation, in turn, once a lamentable cultural condition, is now our beatific future, one so seductive that many current media theorists readily and routinely collapse previously meaningful distinctions between "subjectivity," "fantasy," and "identity" in order to forge the intrepid cybersubject — an autonomous being at last purged of annoying contact with history, the social order, and even the material world. For now and the foreseeable future, cyberspace and virtual subjectivity remain constructs more imaginary than technological, yet pop culture and pop academia often regard them as sovereign principalities somehow more "real" than the terrestrial geography and human subjectivity they are said to replace. Such are the conjuring powers of this seemingly most "live" of living technologies.

Variously described by critics as "presence," "simultaneity," "instantaneity," "immediacy," "now-ness," "present-ness," "intimacy," "the time of the now," or, as Mary Ann Doane has dubbed it, "a *'This-is-going-on'* rather than a *'That-has-been . . . ,'* "[10] this animating, at times occult, sense of "liveness" is clearly an important component in understanding electronic media's technological, textual, and critical histories. The sheer proliferation of such vague terminology around this phenomenon and the necessary imprecision with which it is often used, both in popular and academic circles, testifies to the need for a more sustained examination of this seemingly "inalienable" yet equally "ineffable" quality of electronic telecommunications and textuality. This book undertakes such a project by examining a variety of historical questions surrounding the issue of "presence" in electronic media, exploring how this basic quality of "liveness" has been conceptualized and creatively elaborated in American culture over the past century and a half.[11] Under what social and historical circumstances did electronic media come to be seen as "living" and "alive"? How have ideas of an animating sentience in electronic telecommunications changed across history and media? How have metaphors of living electronic technology impacted cultural debates over telecommunications technology? I will argue that electronic presence, seemingly an essential property of telecommunications media, is in fact a variable social construct, its forms, potentials, and perceived dangers having changed significantly across media history. This project, then, is a cultural history of electronic presence, an interpretive examination of the fields of electronic fiction socially generated around telecommunications technologies. I am interested here in the overall persistence of such expressive speculation over the past century and a half, as well as the sociohistorical specificity of individual articulations of media presence from telegraphy to virtual reality. In exploring the development of such media metaphysics, I wish to analyze the expressive functions of electronic presence, both as a historical phenomenon and as the foundation for our own era's continuing fascination with telecommunications media. Why is it, after 150 years of electronic communication, we still so often ascribe mystical powers to what are ultimately very material technologies?

Currents, Streams, and Flow

The elaboration of electronic media's capacity for "simultaneity" into a more expansive ideology of presence dates at least as far back as the advent of electromagnetic telegraphy in the mid–nineteenth century. The telegraph not only inaugurated a new family of technologies, of course, but also produced a new way of conceptualizing communications and consciousness. Whereas messages had previously been more or less grounded in the immediate space and time of those communicating, the wondrous exchanges of the telegraph presented a series of baffling paradoxes. The simultaneity of this new medium allowed for temporal immediacy amid spatial isolation and brought psychical connection in spite of physical separation. The central agent in these extraordinary exchanges was electricity. The focus of much popular scientific interest in the eighteenth and nineteenth centuries, electricity was for many a mystical and even divine substance that animated body and soul. When harnessed by the telegraph and the media that were to follow, this "life force" seemed to allow for a mechanical disassociation of consciousness and the body. Telegraph lines carried human messages from city to city and from continent to continent, but more important, they appeared to carry the animating "spark" of consciousness itself beyond the confines of the physical body. Electricity remains a somewhat uncanny agent in popular thought even today, making it a prime component in the continuing metaphysical presence attributed to contemporary media. From the initial electromagnetic dots and dashes of the telegraph to the digital landscapes of virtual reality, electronic telecommunications have compelled citizens of the media age to reconsider increasingly disassociative relationships among body, mind, space, and time.

Although the exact form that "presence" is imagined to take may vary greatly from medium to medium over the past 150 years, a consistent representational strategy spans these popular perceptions of electronic media. Grounded in the larger and more long-standing metaphysics of electricity, fantastic conceptions of media presence ranging from the telegraph to virtual reality have often evoked a series of interrelated metaphors of "flow," suggesting analogies between electricity, consciousness, and information that enable fantastic forms of electronic transmutation, substitution, and exchange. In the historical reception of each electronic telecommunications medium, be it a telephone or a television, popular

7

culture has consistently imagined the convergence of three "flowing" agents conceptualized in terms of their apparent liquidity:

(1) the electricity that powers the technology
(2) the information that occupies the medium
(3) the consciousness of the viewer/listener

Electricity, for example, has for over two hundred years been conceived of as a "current," despite physicist Robert Maxwell's early admonitions as to the limited explanatory value of such a term.[12] Writing in the age of Victorian electrification, meanwhile, psychologist William James coined the now familiar phrase "stream of consciousness," arguing that "river" and "stream" are the metaphors that "most naturally describe" the human thought process.[13] Most recently, Raymond Williams provided media studies with the concept of *flow,* a term now in general critical circulation to describe the unending and often undifferentiated textual procession of electronic media and their reception in the home.[14] The cultural articulation of "presence" around electronic media thus depends in large part on how the public imagination of a given historical moment considers these flows of electricity, consciousness, and information to be homologous, interchangeable, and transmutable. In the more fantastic discourses of presence, these varieties of flow frequently appear as interrelated and interdependent, casting the media and audience as an interwoven and at times undifferentiated complex of electricity, consciousness, and textual data. This "flowing" imagination presents the possibility of analogous exchanges, electricity mediating the transfer and substitution of consciousness and information between the body and a host of electronic media technologies. Such electrical possibilities for fusion and confusion, of course, remain central in describing both the wonders and horrors of an emerging cyberculture.

As we will see in the following chapters, the shared electrical basis and apparent electrical transmutability of the body's flow of consciousness and flows of information in the media have produced a remarkably consistent series of cultural fantasies involving the telegraph, radio, television, and computer. Three recurring fictions are especially central to the development of telecommunications technology, familiar stories that appear in new incarnations with the advent of each new medium. In the first fiction, these media enable an uncanny form of disembodiment, allowing the communicating subject the ability, real or imagined, to leave the body

In the story "Sam Graves' Electrical Mind Revealer," telepathy, telephony, and television combine for a particularly vivid fantasy of transmutable flow. (*Practical Electrics,* 1924)

and transport his or her consciousness to a distant destination. In more extreme versions of this technological fantasy, the entire body can be electronically dissolved and teleported through telecommunications technology, a convention at least as old as the imaginative adventures of Baron Munchausen in the mid–nineteenth century. Closely related to this fantasy of disembodiment is a second recurring fiction — the familiar premise of the sovereign electronic world. In this scenario, the subject emerges into an enclosed and self-sustaining "electronic elsewhere" that is in some way generated, or at least accessed, by a particular form of electronic telecommunications technology. Awestruck projections about the future splendor of virtual reality are perhaps the most familiar examples of this fiction today, but this fantasy of utopian electronic space also flourished as far back as the nineteenth century. Finally, a third common fiction based on the transmutable powers of electricity involves the anthropomorphizing of media technology. Perhaps most visible in the contemporary fascination with androids and cyborgs, this particular fiction is also more than a century old and, as the stories from the *Times* suggest, figured centrally in representing television during its earliest years.

Although the longevity of such fantastic accounts of the media may suggest an ahistorical "deep structure" to these tales, as if these stories were somehow the founding mythemes of the media age, I would argue that apparent continuity among these accounts is actually less important than the distinct discontinuities presented by the specific articulations of these electronic fictions in relation to individual media. In other words, although the process of elaborating electronic simultaneity into fantasies of disembodiment, teleportation, and anthropomorphization—all achieved through the common conceit of electronic transmutability—has remained constant over the last 150 years, there are tremendous differences in the actual social, cultural, and political "content" of these stories within differing historical and technological contexts. For this reason, the analysis of such fantastic media stories must recognize that the cultural construction of electronic presence is always inextricably bound to the social application of a technology within a given historical moment. Tales of paranormal media are important, then, not as timeless expressions of some undying electronic superstition, but as a permeable language in which to express a culture's changing social relationship to a historical sequence of technologies.

Through the analysis of five distinct moments in the popular history of electronic presence, I will argue that an early fascination in American culture with fantastic media technology has gradually given way to a fascination with forms of fantastic textuality. Whereas discourses of presence were once dominated by the varieties of contact and communion to be achieved through the discorporative powers of telecommunications, such discourse is now most often concerned with the extraordinary and seemingly sovereign powers of electronic textuality in and of itself. In the age of telegraphy and wireless, in other words, many believed telegraphs and crystal sets could be used to contact incredible and unseen yet equally "real" worlds, be they extrasensory or extraterrestrial. The ethereal "presence" of communications without bodies suggested the possibility of other similarly preternatural interlocutors, invisible entities who, like distant telegraph and wireless operators, could be reached through a most utilitarian application of the technology. As we shall see, the telegraph and early wireless held the tantalizing promises of contacting the dead in the afterlife and aliens of other planets. Fantastic accounts of media presence in this case emphasized the extraordinary powers of the technology itself and suggested that its rational application would eventually lead to crossing ever more incredible boundaries of time and space. The miracle of electronic simultaneity thus portended the possibility of "live" contact with distant frontiers, making early media presence an avenue of wonder bound to the exploratory social deployment of these early technologies.

The centralization of network radio and the subsequent hegemony of television broadcasting, on the other hand, led to a quite different account of electronic presence. In the gradual transition from point-to-point communication to mass broadcasting, presence became less a function of engaging an extraordinary yet fleeting entity across frontiers of time and space and instead assumed the form of an all-enveloping force occupying the ether. No longer a mere conduit for extraordinary exchange, electrical presence became instead an extraordinary world in and of itself. With the rise of the networks, "liveness" in radio and television meant joining a vast invisible audience as it occupied the shared, electronically generated worlds of national programming. The most fantastic accounts of such presence, both then and today, have gone so far as to grant this electronic shadow world a strangely tangible autonomy, where "reality" itself has in some mysterious manner been eroded by its electronically circulated analog. This is the strange virtual terrain that sustains both the high theories of hyperreality and the similar yet more prosaic notion of "televisionland." It is an electronic maelstrom where a ceaselessly mediated and ultimately phantom public sphere exists interwoven with the eternally unfolding diegesis of a thousand worlds in television's ever expanding universe of syndication. In the playful and infinitely reversible binaries of television (or at least television theory), *The Brady Bunch* and CNN are equally real/unreal — each sealed in the common electronic space of televisionland's unending metadiegetic procession.

This book provides a historical preamble to this now familiar technologic, examining the articulation of electronic presence in five important cultural moments in telecommunication history: the advent of telegraphy in the nineteenth century, the arrival of wireless at the turn of the century, radio's transformation into network broadcasting in the twenties and thirties, television's colonization of the home in the early sixties, and contemporary debates over television and computers as virtual technologies. This series of technologies describes the gradual emergence of an expanding electronic sphere, one initially accessed at the other end of a distant wire but whose presence is now seemingly all pervasive. A historical analysis of this transformation, I believe, will answer why, in our contemporary fascination with television, cyberspace, and other worlds of digitized, mediated, and increasingly displaced consciousness, "presence" now exists as either the beatitude of an electronically liberated subject or as the incarcerating mirages of an encroaching electronic subjectivity.

From the Telegraph to the Telesubject

Soon after Samuel Morse publicly debuted the electromagnetic telegraph in 1844, America was swept with a tremendously popular social and religious movement that would come to be known as "Modern Spiritualism." Constructing a "spiritual science" from the doctrines of mesmerism, electrophysiology, and reformist Christianity (among other sources), the Spiritualists believed that the dead were in contact with the living. Through séances conducted under the direction of gifted "mediums," they believed the material world could receive transmissions from the dead through what they called the "spiritual telegraph." More than a metaphor, the spiritual telegraph was for many an actual technology of the afterlife, one invented by scientific geniuses in the world of the dead for the explicit purpose of instructing the land of the living in the principles of utopian reform.

Chapter 1 examines the "spiritual telegraph" as an initial popular response to the baffling new electronic powers presented by telegraphy. Inspired by the truly revolutionary capabilities of a technology that could defeat time and space by sending messages hundreds or thousands of miles at the speed of light, the Spiritualists conceptualized an even more fantastic technology that could defeat the seemingly unassailable temporal and spatial void of death itself. But Spiritualism was more than a fantastic superstition or an idle parlor game. As many historians have noted, the Spiritualist movement provided one of the first and most important forums for women's voices to enter the public sphere. The majority of "mediums" were women, and mediumship itself was thought to be a function of the unique "electrical" constitution of women. While in a state of mediumistic trance, these women were able to comment (through the "telegraphic" voices of the dead) on a variety of contemporary social issues of concern to women, including marital equality, reproductive rights, and universal suffrage. As an increasingly high profile and profoundly gendered political movement, Spiritualism quickly became a target of attack by the male-dominated paradigm of "scientific rationalism" in

A nineteenth-century "uplink": spirits in the heavens
above contact a medium in the house below through
the "spiritual telegraph." (Andrew Jackson Davis,
The Present Age and Inner Life, 1853)

medicine, psychology, and physics. In contrast to the Spiritualists' vision
of an electrically charged spirit world communicating utopian social principles through the "spiritual telegraph," neurologists and alienists of the
period put forth equally fantastic yet more socially legitimated theories on
the electrical etiology of "insanity," an illness they believed to be produced by an unbalanced telegraphic relationship between the female mind
and body.

The advent and subsequent contestation of Spiritualism provides a powerful early example of the cultural construction of "presence" in elec-

tronic media. Conceptually energized by Morse's new technology, spiritual telegraphy gave voice to previously "invisible" beings, be they ghosts or women, whose consciousness could flow through the medium's magical wire and into the public world's material arena. For many women of the period, telegraphic presence was an important electrical space that disassociated the gendered body from the patriarchal realm of thoughts and ideas, thereby making possible new forms of political expression. Medical science, on the other hand, imagined an equally politicized form of presence by arguing a direct and most literal homology between the telegraphic network and the central nervous system. Consequently, medicine operated according to quite different theories about the transmutable flows of electricity and consciousness, its goal to employ electricity as a means of reinscribing women in their traditional Victorian social roles. In effect, both the Spiritualists and their antagonists elaborated the electrical mysteries of the telegraph into a theory of woman as technology, demonstrating that media "liveness" was from the very beginning a concept understood through a compelling complex of arterial metaphors linking body and consciousness with technology and information.

The advent of wireless at the turn of the century heralded a radically different vision of electronic presence, one that presented an entirely new metaphor of liquidity in telecommunications by replacing the concept of the individuated "stream" with that of the vast etheric "ocean." Disembodied consciousness of the living and the dead no longer traveled a fantastic wire that connected the mundane "here" with the transcendental "there." Wireless replaced this comforting and often utopian ideal of extraordinary interconnection with a more bittersweet presence, one that evoked a no less marvelous yet somehow more melancholy realm of abandoned bodies and dispersed consciousness. In this respect, wireless was not a technology that stood as an analog to the body, but an apparatus that possessed the power to atomize and disperse both body and consciousness across the vast expanses of the universe. Although most accounts of wireless celebrated the technology as an exciting gateway to a new electronic community of the airwaves, other stories answered these tales by recasting the electronic presence of wireless hovering in the ether, not as a community, but as a lonely realm of distant and estranged consciousnesses, a vast ocean where the very act of communication reminded the operator of his or her profound isolation.

In chapter 2, I concentrate on the historical development of this more melancholy and alienating sense of presence, examining both its general emergence in the vast social transformations of modernity and in specific moments that inextricably linked wireless technology with death. Whereas telegraphic presence had suggested new possibilities of contact, presence with wireless was as much concerned with the impossibility of such communion; that is, although it provided the miracle of distant contact through the open atmosphere, wireless also threatened a sad estrangement that could occur even within the most intimate of communications. Capturing the medium's discorporative wonders while also evoking a more terrifying vision of absolute isolation, tales of wireless in the first three decades of the century frequently centered on lovers separated by death but reunited through wireless, paranormal romances that were bittersweet meditations on the radio subject's electronic inscription and mediation. Such tales captured the newfound sense of wonder accompanying the possibilities of long-distance communication through the atmosphere, and yet at the same time conveyed a related sense of loss, alienation, and despair as they explicitly equated the wandering radio signal with telepathy, clairvoyance, and other forms of lost discorporated consciousness. Equating the medium's electrical dispersal of consciousness with modernity's increasingly profound social atomization, these stories portrayed wireless, not only as a medium of mass communication, but as a marker of personal isolation where the loss of the wire allowed for extraordinary yet potentially terrifying forms of electrical disembodiment.

Chapter 3 continues considering the emergence of a new sense of electronic presence with radio, examining in this case its development during the rise of the networks. The twenties, of course, were a pivotal period of transition in radio history. As many radio historians have noted, the gradual entrenchment of the centralized, unilateral broadcasting of the networks during this decade displaced the lone "radio bugs" who had explored the mysteries of the ether for the first two decades of wireless. With the rise of the networks, the voice of radio was no longer a fleeting and mysterious presence in the ether. Instead, it became an omnipresent telecommunicative blanket uniformly covering the nation. As the term *network* implies, listeners who once "fished" for stray signals in the ether were now caught themselves by the sweeping nets of NBC, CBS, and other national broadcasters.

Using period interest in the prospects of extraterrestrial communication by radio as a case study, I follow the trajectory of this transformation in electronic presence from an initial fascination with capturing the "DX" (distant) signal to the eventual normalization of radio reception through the network broadcast schedule. This account begins with efforts at the turn of the century to devise working radio transmitters for contacting Mars and follows this "alien" strand of radio history to its culmination in what is perhaps the most notorious parable of the oppressive qualities of network presence — Orson Welles's 1938 adaptation of *War of the Worlds.* I will argue that the infamous "panic broadcast," taking place in a medium where the lure of "DX fishing" had so recently given way to the routine controls of cyclical consumption, was as much a panic over the new and rather suffocating presence of mass communication as it was a panic over extraterrestrial invasion. The *War of the Worlds* incident is emblematic of an entire series of tales from this period that portrayed broadcasting, not as the utopian realization of a new mass community, but as a form of forced patriation in an unsettling and uncertain public arena, one made terrifyingly immediate through the medium's strength of seemingly omnipotent presence. *War of the Worlds* presented a panic to the extent that listeners had successfully internalized this new model of media presence as a seemingly omniscient consciousness in the air, one capable of bringing together an invisible mass audience while at the same time "watching over" them electronically as a higher authority. The symbolic power of *War of the Worlds* as a favored parable of media studies resides in its ability to make this relationship explicit only to then provide an account of its absolute destruction. Significantly, *War of the Worlds* remains fascinating not so much as a story of the end of the world, but as a story of the end of the *media.* Listening to the simulated live dismantling of the network voice and the authority it implied, the *War of the Worlds'* audience heard the empire of the air collapse into rubble through a foregrounding and then decimation of this network presence, an experience both terrifying and exhilarating.

With the advent of electronic "sight," television represented another significant change in the cultural perception of media "presence." Chapter 4 considers how this extra dimension in broadcasting produced new fantasies and anxieties of discorporation, as it depicted the apparent transmutability of human consciousness and electrical transmission in a more palpable form. Television brought with it a new form of "visual" program flow, making it more than an extraordinary medium linking the invisible voices of the living and the dead, the earthling and the alien. With its illusion of fully formed realities of sound *and* vision adrift in the ether, narrative worlds to be accessed and realized through the antenna, television came to be conceived, not only as an electrical extension of human sight, but as an uncanny electronic space in and of itself. Fantastic discourses of televisual presence frequently portrayed the new medium as generating its own self-contained electronic world, a depiction that has its legacy in the now familiar premise of the television viewer who is somehow transported into this virtual realm within the TV set. As a box in the living room, the dimensionality of television has been particularly conducive to indulging fantasies of technological incorporation. Such stories of "absorbed" viewers certainly have a precedent in the cinema (in films ranging from Buster Keaton's *Sherlock Jr.* [1924] to Arnold Schwarzenegger's *Last Action Hero* [1993]), but televisual versions of this convention are distinguished by the more permeable relationship they establish between the imprisoned viewer's subjectivity and the unending electrical flow of textual information. Building on this history of transmutability in electronic media, the subjects of these stories are not confined to a single diegetic world (as often happens in the cinema), but within the more ambiguous boundaries of a flowing metatextual empire. While entrapped in these worlds, formerly flesh-and-blood viewers find themselves subject to the logics of electricity and program flow, their subjectivity and experience rudely switched from channel to channel by some form of divine remote control.

Concentrating on television's public profile in the early sixties — a full ten years after its initial arrival in the American home — this chapter examines how this fantastic electronic space of television had by then come to be imagined as a form of "electronic oblivion." In this topographical era of President Kennedy's "new frontier" and FCC commissioner Newton Minow's "vast wasteland," television was often thought of as a sinister space within the home, capable of transporting viewers to a vast electronic "nowhere." This popular image of oblivion had strong links to the period's growing intellectual critiques of television as a site of patently "unreal" reality. After settling in as a public institution, television came under frequent attack in the late fifties and early sixties for producing a distorted and duplicitous world. A realm of saccharine sitcoms, dishonest game shows, and superficial news coverage, television forged its own reality, a world related to real life and yet strangely removed and distorted. In this case, presence served as a gateway into this self-sustaining and wholly enclosed electronic elsewhere, a phantom double to the real social world where one faced the danger of being absorbed and assimilated into a static "nowhere." Here presence came to be figured somewhat ironically as a form of negation; that is, even as television made this idea of an electronic elsewhere more palpable, it increasingly represented it as an electronic limbo, a zone of nothingness, a "vast wasteland." Even more ominously, for critics of the medium on both the left and the right, television's lurking presence of electronic nothingness threatened to one day spill out and consume the real world, colonizing and destroying real culture, real politics, real life. Once only a bridge between worlds real and fantastic, electronic media in the age of television became a crucible for an uncanny electronic space capable of collapsing, compromising, and even displacing the real world.

Such rhetoric, of course, portends the equally fantastic discourses of postmodernism, especially in their attention to the prospects of simulation and virtual subjectivity. Chapter 5 considers the striking similarities between popular stories of paranormal television and the discourses of contemporary postmodern theory. As a system of belief dissolving boundaries between self and screen, reality and representation, postmodern media theory has been equally concerned with the transmutability of electricity, information, and consciousness within electronic telecommunications. Many critics have attempted to historicize this transmutability by locating photography, cinema, and television as the privileged technologies of realism, modernism, and postmodernism, respectively. In this trajectory, the solid reality behind nineteenth-century photography (or at least imagined behind photography) has gradually given way to a world of electronic surfaces in the twentieth century, a social realm mediated by images and evacuated of any sense of depth, whether such "depth" is conceived in terms of "consciousness," "history," or a once stable realm of "signifieds." Where there was once the "real," there is now only the electronic generation and circulation of simulations. Where there were once whole human subjects, there are now only fragmented and decentered subjectivities. Considered in this context, certain varieties of postmodern criticism can be placed within this larger tradition of fantastic fictions about the disassociative properties of electronic media; indeed, what postmodern critics more recently describe in metaphors of "simulation" and "schizophrenia," popular culture has long anticipated in stories associating televi-

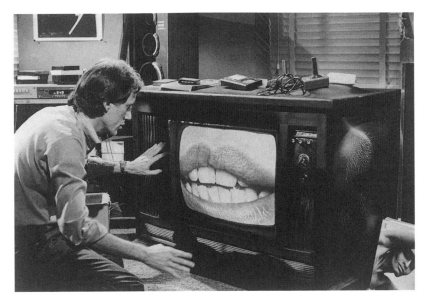

David Cronenberg's *Videodrome* ponders the line between television and reality, a common theme in both popular cinema and postmodern criticism. (© 1983 Universal City Studios)

sion with counterfeit realities and psychosis. In postmodernism's fascination with the evacuation of the referent and an ungrounded play of signification and surface, we can see another vision of beings who, like ghosts and psychotics, are no longer anchored in reality but instead wander through a hallucinatory world of eternal simulation where the material real is forever lost. Although some see this emerging electronic subjectivity as an ironic coda to the processes of alienation ("In the image of television," writes Baudrillard, "the surrounding universe and our very bodies are becoming monitoring screens"),[15] others have celebrated emerging techno-identities as a potentially progressive engagement of the social world ("I'd rather be a cyborg than a goddess," notes Donna Haraway).[16] In either case, emerging accounts of cyberspace, virtual reality, and other modes of electronically mediated subjectivity represent the most recent, and certainly the most baroque fantasies of transmutability yet encountered in electronic media. Imagined since the age of the telegraph, dreams of a complete absenting of the body and entrance into a more rarified plane of existence have definitively shifted from the metaphysics of the church to those of the computer chip. As we shall see, some even feel that the key to immortality itself is to be found in the telecommunications networks of the future.

By examining shifting accounts of electronic transmutability and media presence, *Haunted Media* provides an important sense of historical context for what many take to be a wholly "postmodern" debate. I will argue that current debates over the electronic mediation of consciousness necessarily incorporate this longer history of converting electronic simultaneity into more fantastic fictions of media presence. Although some might argue that the technology finally does exist (or will soon) to realize such discorporative fantasies, this book argues that such dreams have always been vivid and seemingly eminent but are, of course, ultimately impossible. In the end we are always left with a material machine at the heart of such supernatural speculation, a device mechanically assembled, socially deployed, and culturally received within a specific historical moment.

1 Mediums and Media

Within a five-year span in the 1840s, the American public witnessed two of the most remarkable moments in telecommunications history. On 24 May 1844 friends and observers gathered with Samuel B. Morse at the Supreme Court in Washington, D.C., to participate in the first official test of an electromagnetic telegraph line. Miss Ellsworth, the daughter of the commissioner of patents, had the honor of choosing the first words to be transmitted by this new technology. Morse sent her chosen message, "What hath God wrought?" to his associate, Alfred Vail, in Baltimore, who then sent the message back to Washington for confirmation. In the ensuing years, the telegraph rapidly expanded as a commercial operation, and in the following decade its lines quickly crossed the continent. By 1861 the telegraphic network had outraced the transcontinental railroad to California. By 1866 a reliable cable reached across the Atlantic to England and beyond.

For a world that had waited weeks to receive messages from across the ocean, and days to receive messages from across the nation, the ability to contact London from New York in only seconds must have truly tested the limits of credulity. Even more astonishingly, the electronic circuitry of the telegraph made possible the instantaneous exchange of messages in the complete absence of physical bodies. Reporting on a meeting conducted by telegraph employees over the company wire in 1857, an awestruck commentator provides a typical account of the baffling new "telepresence" created by this technology: "We publish the following novel and interesting account of a meeting of the employees of the American Telegraph Company on the 3d instand, at — what place? that is the question — at no place, or at all places where there were Telegraph offices, within the circuit of seven hundred miles. A large room, that — seven hundred miles in diameter — for a meeting to convene. . . . The members together in spirit — in communication, and yet in body seven hundred miles apart!"[1]

This sense of disembodied communion was an unprecedented and most provocative quality of the celebrated new medium, inspiring many commentators to declare Morse's invention the most momentous innovation in human history. In the first of a series of such glowing predictions about electronic media, many believed telegraphic technology would lead to nothing less than a utopian age. "The world, it has been said, will be made a great whispering gallery," wrote one telegraph enthusiast; "I would rather say, a great assembly, where every one will see and hear everyone else. The most remarkable effect, if I may judge from my own narrow thought, will be the approach to a practical unity of the human race; of which we have never yet had a foreshadowing, except in the gospel of Christ."[2]

In the midst of such utopian technophilia — only four years after Morse's public debut of his remarkable invention — the family of John and Margaret Fox went to bed for the evening in their small cottage in Hydesville, New York, a tiny village just southeast of Rochester. For a number of months previous to the night of 31 March 1848, the family had endured many sleepless evenings punctuated by a series of unexplained disturbances in their home. Previous tenants had also complained of the incessant rappings and knockings in the cottage, but despite frequent attempts to discover and eliminate the source of these sounds, the noises continued unabated. On this particular night, John, Margaret, and their two young daughters slept together in the parents' bedroom. The rapping sounds were particularly violent that night, and although Mr. and Mrs. Fox tried to get their children to ignore the noises and go to sleep, the daughters amused themselves by imitating the commotion. Finally, the youngest daughter, Kate, said aloud, "Here, Mr. Split-foot, do as I do." Kate then clapped her hands three times, which instantaneously triggered three of the mysterious raps in apparent response. Kate's sister, Margeretta, did the same and also elicited three of the mysterious knocking sounds. Suspecting an unseen intelligence behind the rappings, the children's mother engaged the invisible entity in dialogue. Eventually, by rapping its answers in response to the questions of Margaret Fox, the spirit correctly counted to ten, identified the ages of the Fox children, and numbered how many of the Fox family were still alive and how many were dead. Later the spirit responded to more complex questions by rapping once for "yes" and twice for "no."[3]

Recounting this apparently supernatural encounter in the numerous articles, books, and pamphlets that appeared in its wake, many believed that with this exchange of words and knocks Kate Fox had opened a "telegraph line" to another world. During the first week of this contact, more than five hundred people are said to have gathered at the house to witness

A portrait commemorating Kate Fox's initial "telegraphic" contact with the spirit world in 1848. (*History of Spiritualism,* Cassell and Company, London, 1926)

this extraordinary series of communications, an event that became a topic of national conversation and controversy.[4] Shortly after the mysterious rappings in Hydesville, the Fox daughters were separated and sent away to visit relatives. Removed from the "haunted house" and from each other's influence, the two girls nevertheless continued to attract the inexplicable rappings in their new homes. Quickly, those around the girls also began to manifest the strange rapping phenomena, including their older sister in Rochester, Leah Fox (who would soon become the first to charge interested parties money to witness the rappings). Communication via this first link of the "spiritual telegraph" gradually became more complex. Moving beyond simple yes-no answers, the spirits began to "speak" in sentences by rapping in response to a recited alphabet. Curiously, those who visited these homes often returned to their own towns to find that the knocking spirits had followed them home as well.

Occurring in an era of vast social and technological change for the nation as a whole, the mysterious rappings in upper New York State helped spark a religious and political movement that would become known as Modern Spiritualism. Within a decade the movement would attract thousands of avowed believers, souls searching for spiritual truth who now turned to the century's other most remarkable telecommunications device — the clairvoyant medium. Inspired by Kate Fox's ghostly "telegraphic" exchange in her parents' home at Hydesville, Spiritualism eventually included among its members Harriet Beecher Stowe (who claimed that *Uncle Tom's Cabin* had been dictated to her by "spirit" authors), Horace Greeley, James Fenimore Cooper, and even President and Mrs. Lincoln (who are said to have conducted séances in the White House).[5] As Spiritualism expanded into a national and international phenomenon, it assumed many forms and intersected with many other practices and beliefs, so much so that providing a brief overview of the movement is almost impossible. In its most basic form, however, Spiritualism was a philosophy that proposed the dead were in communication with the living through mediums who "channeled" the spirit world. From their abode in the "seventh heaven," the spirits reassured those on earth that their loved ones lived on in the afterlife. In séances across the country, the telegraphic spirits proclaimed "the joyful tidings that they all 'still lived,' 'still loved,' and with the tenderness of human affection, and the wisdom of a higher sphere of existence, watched over and guided the beloved ones who had mourned the dead, with all the gracious ministry of guardian angels."[6]

Within this five-year period, the United States thus saw the advent of both the "electromagnetic" and "spiritual" telegraphs, technologies that stand as the progenitors of two radically different histories of "telecommunications." Most technological time lines credit Morse's apparatus with ushering in a series of increasingly sophisticated electronic communications devices over the next century, inventions developed in the rationalist realm of science and engineering that revolutionized society and laid the foundations for the modern information age. The "Rochester knockings" heard by the Fox family, on the other hand, inspired the modern era's occult fascination with séances, spirit circles, automatic writing, telepathy, clairvoyance, Ouija boards, and other paranormal phenomena. The historical proximity and intertwined legacies of these two founding "mediums," one material and the other spiritual, is hardly a coincidence. Certainly, the explicit connections between the two communications technologies were not lost on the Spiritualists themselves, who eagerly linked Spiritualist phenomena with the similarly fantastic discourses of electromagnetic telegraphy. As Spiritualist belief crossed the country along with the unreeling cables of the telegraph companies, Spiritualist books such as

The Celestial Telegraph and periodicals such as *The Spiritual Messenger* frequently invoked popular knowledge of Morse's electromagnetic telegraph to explain their model of spiritual contact. "You send a telegraphic dispatch from New York to London through the medium of the Atlantic Cable," wrote one Spiritualist. "Break the Atlantic Cable, and all communication must stop through that medium. Break the laws that are favorable to mediumship in spiritual affairs, and all communication through that channel must likewise cease."[7] One account even suggested that electromagnetic telegraphy itself was the result of spiritual intervention. Said a "spirit" from the other side when channeled through a medium in 1874, "Morse, of himself, could not have fashioned the magnetic telegraph. His mind was reaching out for thought that would help him in his work, and, as the mental action of your sphere is visible to the denizens of this, those who had been watching the workings of his mind suggested, through a familiar process of mental impression, that which enabled him to shape the invention into a form of practical utility."[8]

American Spiritualism presented an early and most explicit intersection of technology and spirituality, of media and "mediums." Enduring well beyond a fleeting moment of naive superstition at the dawn of the information age, the historical interrelationship of these competing visions of telegraphic "channeling" continues to inform many speculative accounts of media and consciousness even today. I would argue that many of our contemporary narratives concerning the "powers" of electronic telecommunications have, if not their origin, then their first significant cultural synthesis in the doctrines of Spiritualism. Although the idea of a spiritual telegraph may seem ludicrous today, the contemporary legacy of the Spiritualists and their magical technology can be found in sites as diverse as the "psychic friends" network, Baudrillard's landscape of the hyperreal, and Hollywood's current tales of virtual reality come alive and run amok. A century and a half after Kate Fox's initial exchange over a ghostly wire, American culture remains intrigued by the capacity of electronic media to create seemingly sovereign yet displaced, absent, and parallel worlds.

In suggesting the limitless possibilities of flowing electrical information, telegraphy's apparent ability to separate consciousness from the body placed the technology at the center of intense social conjecture, imaginative cultural elaboration, and often contentious political debate. In these at times volatile struggles, the disembodying power of telegraphy and the liberating possibilities of electronic telepresence held a special attraction for women, many of whom would use the idea of the spiritual telegraph to imagine social and political possibilities beyond the immediate material restrictions placed on their bodies. Significantly, from the earliest moments of the movement, Spiritualists associated the powers of "mediumship" most closely with women, and especially with teenage girls. Through a unique convergence of social, scientific, and spiritual logics, women appeared to be "naturally" suited for the mysteries of mediumship. As Ann Braude writes in her history of the movement, "Americans throughout the country found messages from spirits more plausible when delivered through the agency of adolescent girls. . . . The association of mediumship with femininity was so strong that it was not dispelled by the contravening evidence of the existence of male mediums."[9] When men did manifest mediumistic powers, they were said to embody the "feminine" qualities that made such otherworldly contact possible. As one Spiritualist noted, "It may be observed that ordinarily the feminine mind possesses, in a higher degree than the masculine, two important requisites of elevated mediumship: first, it is more religious; and, secondly, it is more plastic."[10]

As difficult as historiographic questions of agency and belief are to begin with, the questions raised by Spiritualism are even more perplexing. Did these mediums and their acolytes actually believe in the reality of spirit communications? If not, did mediums willfully deceive those in search of spiritual contact? Did followers realize the phenomenon was not supernatural yet enjoy the social interaction of the séances so much that they played along in an elaborate *folie en masse?* The "truth," such that it is, would no doubt consist of a variety of Spiritualist practices and experiences, ranging from the most devout belief to the most cynical deception. Although it would be impossible to reconstruct the exact motivations of those who embraced a paranormal explanation of Kate Fox's communications (and who would then cultivate spiritual communications beyond simple knocks and raps to include table tipping, spirit voices, spirit trumpets, trance speaking, and even full body materializations), it is certainly true that Spiritualism would have quickly vanished from the national scene had it not possessed some form of wider popular appeal. Clearly, those who believed in Spiritualist phenomena "wanted" to believe in some respect, and although many would dismiss such interest as mass gullibility, it might be more productive to consider the movement as a particularly esoteric form of popular culture. As a movement centered primarily on the spiritual power of women, Spiritualism became "popular" not only as a widespread and publicly visible sensation, but also as a means of articulating the often highly radical aspirations of a subordinate political formation. As we will see in the following pages, the Spiritualists elaborated telegraphic principles into an intriguing and politically engaged theology of telepresence, weaving complex fantasies of gender and technology around the century's most celebrated electronic marvel.

Several excellent histories of Spiritualism have discussed the complicated politics of gender involved in the movement's rise and fall during the nineteenth century. There has been relatively little discussion, however, of Spiritualism as a popular discourse on gender *and* telecommunications, one that produced the modern era's first fantasies of discorporative electronic liberation. Long before our contemporary fascination with the beatific possibilities of cyberspace, feminine mediums led the Spiritualist movement as wholly realized cybernetic beings — electromagnetic devices bridging flesh and spirit, body and machine, material reality and electronic space. Then as now, such fantastic visions of electronic telecommunications demonstrate that the cultural conception of a technology is often as important and influential as the technology itself. As James Carey argues, the telegraph not only served as the material foundation for a new communications network but also "opened up new ways of thinking about communication within both the formal practice of theory and the practical consciousness of everyday life. In this sense the telegraph was not only a new tool of commerce but also a thing to think with, an agency for the alteration of ideas."[11] In contrast to Morse's material technology of metal, magnets, and wire, the spiritual telegraph could only exist in the mortal world as a fantasy of telegraphic possibility. In an era when the technology of the telegraph physically linked states and nations, the *concept* of telegraphy made possible a fantastic splitting of mind and body in the cultural imagination, demonstrating that electronic presence, whether imagined at the dawn of the telegraphic age or at the threshold of virtual reality, has always been more a cultural fantasy than a technological property.

Understanding our own culture's continuing interest in fantastic forms of electronic telecommunications requires examining more closely the historical context of telegraphy's technological advent and conceptual influence. What was the cultural environment at midcentury that allowed spiritual telegraphy to thrive? How did the women mediums channeling this telegraphy use the mysteries of telepresence as a means of social empowerment? Finally, what became of both the technological and cultural power of the medium by the end of the century? I believe such an analysis of this founding spiritual technology will demonstrate that our own era's fascination with the discorporative and emancipating possibilities of the looming virtual age is in many ways simply an echo of this strange electronic logic, a collective fantasy of telepresence that allowed a nation to believe more than 150 years ago that a little girl could talk to the dead over an invisible wire.

Electromagnetic Mysteries

When Samuel Morse and Kate Fox opened contact with Baltimore and the Beyond in the 1840s, they did so at a time when there were few distinctions made between what would shortly become the antithetical domains of physics and metaphysics. Lacking this modern distinction, the Spiritualists' initial conceptualization of "celestial telegraphy" was not so much a misapplication of technological discourse as a logical elaboration of the technology's already "supernatural" characteristics. Talking with the dead through raps and knocks, after all, was only slightly more miraculous than talking with the living yet absent through dots and dashes; both involved subjects reconstituted through technology as an entity at once interstitial and uncanny. Spiritualism attracted the belief of many converts because it provided a technically plausible system of explanation for these seemingly occult occurrences, transforming the supernatural into the preternatural. People had claimed to talk to ghosts before 1848, of course, but as interest in spirit phenomena spread in the wake of the Rochester knockings, the first apostles of the movement, whether attempting to legitimate and thus conceal an elaborate hoax or, more innocently, genuinely searching for a credible system of explanation, sought a logic and language appropriate to understand rationally this seemingly irrational phenomenon.

In a bid for such authority, Spiritualism attempted to align itself with the principles of "electrical science" so as to distinguish mediumship from more "superstitious" forms of mystical belief in previous centuries. It was the animating powers of electricity that gave the telegraph its distinctive property of simultaneity and its unique sense of disembodied presence, allowing the device to vanquish previous barriers of space, time, and in the Spiritualist imagination, even death. More than an arbitrary, fanciful, and wholly bizarre response to the innovation of a technological marvel, the spiritual telegraph's contact with the dead represented, at least

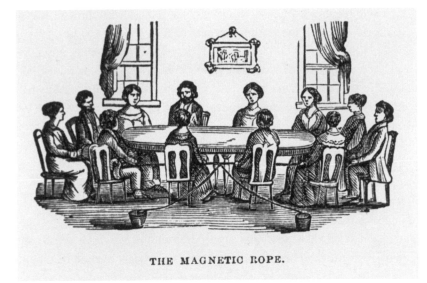

THE MAGNETIC ROPE.

The séance as "spirit battery." Here a medium hopes to improve contact with the spirit world by asking her guests to hold a magnetized rope, its ends dipped in copper and zinc buckets of water. (Andrew Jackson Davis, *The Present Age and Inner Life,* 1853)

initially, a strangely "logical" application of telegraphy consistent with period knowledges of electromagnetic science, the experimental frontiers of physics/metaphysics, and the vicissitudes of a highly unstable (and highly gendered) force known as "nervous energy." The following blueprint for a "spirit battery" (as the séance was often termed in the electrodiscourse of Spiritualism), testifies to the movement's desire to bridge science and spirituality:

> The males and females (the positive and negative principles) are placed alternately; as so many zinc and copper plates in the construction of magnetic batteries. The medium or media have places assigned them on either side of the junction whereat the rope is crossed, the ends terminating each in a pail or jar of cold water. . . . But these new things should be added. The copper wire should terminate in, or be clasped to, a *zinc* plate; the steel wire should, in the same manner, be attached to a *copper* plate. These plates should be *dodecahedral,* or cut with *twelve* angles or sides, because, by means of the points, the volume of terrestrial electricity is greatly augmented, and its accumulation is also, by the same means, accelerated, which

the circle requires for a *rudimental aura* (or atmosphere) through which spirits can approach and act upon material bodies.[12]

Elsewhere, this spiritual scientist observed, "We are *negative* to our guardian spirits; they are *positive* to us. The whole mystery is illustrated by the workings of the common magnetic telegraph. The principles involved are identical."[13]

Such theories and proclamations were common within Spiritualist literature, and demonstrate why any discussion of the movement's interest in electronic presence must necessarily engage the more general cultural profile of electricity and magnetism in the early nineteenth century. Although it would be impossible to isolate the precise beginnings of the electrical science that eventually produced both the telegraph and its attending mysteries of telepresence, interest in electrical phenomena, be it lightning or lodestones, dates back to antiquity. The innovation of the "Leyden jar" in 1745, however, proved a key moment in advancing electrical science into the modern era. Developed by Pieter van Musschenbroek in Holland, the Leyden jar allowed scientists to accumulate for the first time large amounts of electricity in a storage container. Before the development of this crude battery, scientists studying electricity had to confine themselves to spontaneous electrical phenomena — brief manifestations of electricity generated by machines (or cats) engaged to produce small amounts of static electricity. As a fairly reliable source of continuous and larger flows of this ephemeral substance, the Leyden jar enabled a whole new era of electrical experimentation.

Significantly, this ability to produce electricity on command soon made this mysterious force a source of popular spectacle and amusement, especially in relation to the body. In an ingenious display of scientific and political power, Jean-Antoine Nollet debuted the Leyden jar in Paris by simultaneously "shocking" 180 members of the royal guard in the presence of the king. At the convent of Carthusians, Nollet constructed a two-and-a-half-mile chain of monks connected by wire who were then given a simultaneous shock. One clever experimenter concealed a Leyden jar for practical jokes, giving the world its first "joy buzzer." Amplifying this concept, another used a Leyden jar as a prototype "taser," electrifying a walking stick that could be used to stun an attacker. Unlucky experimenters soon discovered that substances such as ether could be ignited by the Leyden jar to make a fiery spectacle.[14] Others used the newly harnessed electricity to stun and kill small animals. In the United States, Benjamin Franklin organized an entire social gathering around newly fashioned electrical appliances. "A turkey is to be killed for our dinner by the *electrical shock,* and roasted by the *electrical jack,* before a fire kindled by the *electrified bottle:* when the healths of all famous electricians of England, Holland, France, and Germany are to be drank in *electrified bumpers,* under a discharge of guns from the *electrical battery.*"[15] Franklin also created electrical toys and curiosities, including a spider whose legs moved when in proximity to a Leyden jar and a portrait of the king of England wearing an electrified crown that "shocked those who had the temerity to touch it."[16] Yet even in these early and often amusing stages of electrical research, deeper and more profound connections endured between this evanescent substance and the enigma of life itself. Franklin's helpful attempts to install lightning rods in Philadelphia, for example, met with much opposition from the local clergy, who no doubt still believed lightning to be an expression of God's will and therefore best left to strike according to its own designs.[17]

A more scientific study of the relationship between electricity and the divine "spark of life" began with research by the Italian scientist Luigi Galvani. Historians are unclear as to the exact date of Galvani's discovery (sources cite 1771, 1780, and 1790). It is also ambiguous whether the momentous discovery belongs to Galvani or his wife. In any case, someone in Galvani's household at sometime in the late eighteenth century noticed that a pair of frog legs, sitting on a table near an electrical generator, twitched violently when touched by a metal knife. Inspired by this odd phenomenon, Galvani immediately began his famous experiments on muscular motion and "animal electricity." Although scientists had earlier speculated about the relationship of electricity and organic energy, Galvani's book, *Commentary on the Effects of Electricity on Muscular Motion,* inspired a flurry of related research in the early part of the next century.[18] Even when their theories were in disagreement, scientists and physicians were convinced that electricity was in some way related to the "vital force" of life.

Experiments concerning electricity and muscular motion became increasingly ambitious and baroque in the new century. In 1803 Galvani's nephew, Giovanni Aldini, performed galvanic experiments on beheaded criminals and amputated human limbs. His most spectacular demonstration occurred in London when, in front of a large crowd, he performed

A conceptual foundation for both spiritual telegraphy and Mary Shelley's *Frankenstein:* Luigi Galvani's experiments with electricity and organic media. (Luigi Galvani, *Commentary on the Effects of Electricity on Muscular Motion*)

many such experiments on a criminal who had just been hanged. "A powerful battery being applied, very strong contractions were excited, the limbs were violently agitated, the eyes opened and shut, the mouth and jaws worked about, and the whole face thrown into frightful convulsions."[19] Aldini was eventually able to compel corpses to lift heavy weights, roll their eyes and extinguish candles with their breath, all through the animating principles of electricity. Others mounted similarly gruesome public exhibitions.[20] It was within the context of such public spectacle showcasing electricity's relationship to the body that Mary Shelley wrote *Frankenstein,* the most famous literary account of electricity and life's "vital force." The novel's preface describes the genesis of Shelley's literary creation and the now infamous pact made among her, Lord Byron, Polidori, and her husband to write competitive horror stories. "Many and long were the conversations between Lord Byron and Shelley, to which I was a devout but nearly silent listener. During one of these, various philosophical doctrines were discussed, and among others, the nature of the principle of life, and whether there was any probability of its ever being discovered and communicated."[21] "Perhaps a corpse would be re-animated," continues Shelley; "galvanism had given token of such things: perhaps component parts of a creature might be manufactured, brought together, and imbued with vital warmth."[22]

A particularly alarming manifestation of "animal electricity" and its "vital warmth" could be found in period reports of "spontaneous combustion," a phenomenon wherein a person would suddenly and inexplicably burst into flames. The emerging science of forensic medicine took great interest in this topic during the late eighteenth and early nineteenth centuries, and Charles Dickens forever emblazoned the subject in the public imagination by dispatching a character in *Bleak House* through such a fantastic explosion. Many theorized that an imbalance of electricity in the body was to blame for these tragic conflagrations. "Some conceive that certain persons possess the power of generating within themselves a state of electric tension, and quote relations of individuals who emitted sparks at the suggestion of the will," noted a medical encyclopedia of the period.[23] Doctors theorized that gases in the body could be ignited by such sparks to produce a spontaneous combustion of the torso, a process greatly facilitated if the victim happened to be drunk and thus saturated with alcohol.

Similar mysteries and experimental activities surrounded the phenomenon of magnetism. The figure who would prove most influential in this regard for the Spiritualists was the German physician Franz Mesmer. In the late eighteenth century, Mesmer was interested in the therapeutic possibilities of magnets. After witnessing the dynamics of priest and patient during a Roman Catholic exorcism in 1776, Mesmer became convinced of the theory of "animal magnetism." This theory maintained that magnetic fluid, much like electrical fluid, pervaded the world. By altering this invisible substance through looking, touching, and a passing of hands, the diseased body of a patient could be brought back into alignment with this force. Patients under therapy applied water taken from large "magnetized" tubs, and as "mesmerized" subjects some reported religious visions and even contact with the dead.

Such intense interest in mesmerism was not limited to France. Theories of animal magnetism, often combined with theories of animal electricity, occultism, and phrenology, were also common in England and the United States during this period, as reported in journals such as *The Magnet* and *The Phreno-Magnetic Vindicator*.[24] Edgar Allan Poe's gruesome story,

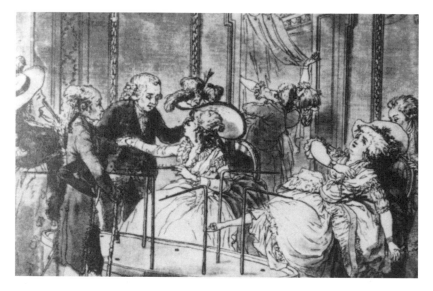

Working in the mysteries of "animal magnetism," Franz Mesmer applies magnetized water to swooning subjects. (Bibliotèque Nationale, Paris)

"The Strange Facts in the Case of Monsieur Valdemar," exploited this fascination with mesmerism as a power both factual and fantastic that somehow linked science and spirit. In this tale a man is mesmerized at the point of death and then kept in a state of limbo for a number of weeks. After the man begs to be allowed to die, the trance is at last broken, and the man's body instantly decomposes into a pool of "liquid putridity." The shocking conclusion of this tale depended on the reader's familiarity with the cryptic links hypothesized between "invisible" yet palpable forces such as electromagnetism and the greater mysteries of life itself.[25]

Perhaps the most revealing document of this period's vibrant electromagnetic imagination comes from the annals of the United States Congress. When Samuel Morse appeared before this body in 1838 to seek funding for his experimental telegraph line, his request proved so "fantastic" that certain congressmen, partly in jest but mainly in confusion, introduced amendments to the allocations bill that would have provided funds for research into mesmeristic phenomena as well. The difference between the two "sciences" was not immediately clear, and many judged Morse's material technology in light of the by then largely discredited doctrines of Mesmer. "It would require a scientific analysis to determine how far the

magnetism of mesmerism was analogous to the magnetism to be employed in telegraphs," wrote the chair of the committee. Morse's belief
that electromagnetic energy could be harnessed to send long-distance
communications was a topic that generated much interest and dialogue
while testing the limits of belief. The very concept of telegraphy portended the unknown and the occult, especially when linked to the intangible yet quite palpable forces of electricity and magnetism. As Braude
notes, "When the bill finally came to a vote, seventy congressmen left
their seats, many hoping 'to avoid spending the public money for a machine they could not understand.' "[26]

Thus was electrical science the quantum physics of its day, a frontier of
inquiry bordering science and spirit that raised more questions than it
answered. In this age of accelerated discovery, invention, and hypothesis,
an increasingly sizable reading public not only learned of new technologies and scientific principles (some often quite dubious), but also participated in more sweeping speculation about the constitution of the body and
its relationship to the material and spiritual worlds. This is the context in
which the American public theorized Kate Fox's enigmatic rappings. Already a fertile terrain for the speculative adventures of popular culture, the
mysteries of electromagnetism would become in the Spiritualist mind a
foundational science in a grand theory of technology and consciousness.
Conceptually energized by the example of the telegraph, Spiritual science
would promote the wonders of physical discorporation and a dream of
social emancipation, all to be realized through the telecommunicative
wonders of electronic presence.

The "Science of the Soul"

In his seminal study of nineteenth-century American culture, *The Machine in the Garden,* Leo Marx describes in detail the period's unending
fascination with technology and its faith that mechanization would produce a utopian balance between industry and nature. Writers of the period,
argues Marx, frequently engaged in "the rhetoric of the technological
sublime," rhapsodizing over the "unprecedented harmony between art
and nature, city and country" to be found in the Edenic nation's rapid
technological development.[27] But this utopian rhapsody soon came under
attack. James Carey and John Quirk argue that by the mid-nineteenth
century this utopian faith in technology began to shift from the machine to

electricity: "As the dreams of a mechanical utopia gave way to the realities of industrialization, there arose a new school of thought dedicated to the notion that there was a qualitative difference between mechanics and electronics, between machines and electricity, between mechanization and electrification. In electricity was suddenly seen the power to redeem all the dreams betrayed by the machine." Carey and Quirk term this new attitude, after Marx, "the rhetoric of the electrical sublime."[28]

The strange technologies of Spiritualism, both the flesh-and-blood medium in her parlor and the celestial telegraph in the invisible spirit world, were perhaps the most literal and dramatic expressions of the century's "electrical sublime." Importantly, Spiritualist faith in mediums and celestial telegraphy went beyond a mere utilitarian application of the telegraph as a metaphor. Critical to articulating a convincing technological (and thus "scientific") fantasy of mediumship, Spiritualist doctrine clearly stated that the spiritual telegraph was in fact a "real" (albeit invisible) technology. Writing in 1869, medium and Spiritualist historian Emma Hardinge described Kate Fox's initial contact with the spirit world in decidedly technological terms:

> From the first working of the spiritual telegraph by which invisible beings were enabled to spell out consecutive messages, they ["the spirits"] claimed that this method of communication was organized by scientific minds in the spirit spheres; that it depended mainly upon conditions of human and atmospheric magnetisms, and pointed to the ultimation of a science whereby spirits, operating upon and through matter, could connect in the most intimate relations the worlds of material and spiritual existence.
>
> They referred to the house at Hydesville as one peculiarly suited to their purpose from the fact of its *being charged with the aura requisite to make it a battery for the working of the telegraph.* (original emphasis)[29]

Elsewhere Hardinge wrote that the spirits who made the initial contact with the Fox family at Hydesville were "philosophic and scientific minds, many of whom had made the study of electricity and other imponderables a specialty in the earth-life."[30] Anyone who doubted the reality of the spiritual telegraph *as a telegraph* needed only to look at the example of Samuel Morse himself, who, once dead, became a frequent and proficient interlocutor from the spirit land, turning his mind back to mortal earth to continue uplifting the world that his material technology had already revolutionized.[31] Perhaps the most sincere testament to the technology's con-

The Fox cottage of Hydesville, New York, "charged with the aura requisite to make it a battery for the working of the telegraph." (George Adams, Aldus Books, ca. 1930)

crete existence in the heavens came from Horace Greeley, editor of the *New York Herald.* An early supporter of Spiritualism, Greeley offered two thousand dollars a month to any medium who could furnish him with news from Europe in advance of the more terrestrial modes of communications (this being, of course, in the days before the Atlantic cable).[32]

Significantly, within the century's general celebration of technology, the Spiritualists concentrated almost exclusively on electronic technologies of telecommunications. Inspired by the example of the telegraph and convinced of its parallel existence in the world of the dead, many Spiritualists described a host of ever more elaborate yet completely functional "spiritual technologies" that could be found in the afterlife, each of them centered on the wonder of telepresence and disembodied electrical contact. Some even claimed to have seen these extraordinary technological wonders firsthand. A letter written in 1852 to *The Shekinah,* one of the country's premiere Spiritualist journals, tells of a man's most unusual visitation in the night. Just as he was about to go to sleep, five apparitions appeared in his room dressed in "ancient costume" and carrying a familiar technology imbued with astounding new electrical properties.

One of them had what appeared to be a box about 18 inches square and some nine inches high; it seemed to be an electrical apparatus. They placed the box on the table, and then, electrical emanations, like currents of light of different colors, were seen issuing from the box. One of the company placed a piece of paper, pen and ink, on the lid of this box. The luminous currents now centered around the pen which was immediately taken up and dipped in the ink, and without the application of any other force or instrument, so far as I could perceive, the pen was made to move across the paper, and a communication was made which I have since learned was in the Hebrew language.[33]

A psychic circle tried a few months later to contact the spirit authors responsible for these messages. They received the following reply: "My dear friends — I am happy to announce to you that the project which has engaged our attention for some years has at last been accomplished. I am, Benjamin Franklin."[34] The purpose of this project, as with most spirit endeavors, was to inspire and edify humankind in preparation of a new social order on earth.

Other Spiritualist researchers worked diligently to create new and wondrous technologies here on earth, devices that would also invoke the mysteries of electromagnetic presence as a means of linking science and spirit, our world and the next. On 1 April 1853, for example, a Universalist minister turned Spiritualist, John Murray Spear, notified a Boston Spiritualist journal that he had received communications from the dead announcing the formation of a philanthropic organization in the spirit world. This group, "The Association of Beneficents," claimed as its members such illustrious figures as Socrates, Seneca, and Thomas Jefferson. The group proclaimed that other philanthropic committees would soon be announced. Spear later informed readers of an organization called "The Association of Electricizers," a group devoted to "teach of electric, magnetic, and ethereal laws, and of heretofore unknown mechanical forces."[35] Spear had long been interested in the relationship between electrical science and spiritual practice. Hardinge notes that Spear had at one point attempted to combine minerals with "vital electricity" in order to increase his powers of mediumship. In the process, Hardinge writes, he "subjected himself to the most scathing ridicule from his contemporaries by seeking to promote the influence and control of spirits, through the aid of copper

Often cited as a contributing inventor of the spiritual
telegraph, Benjamin Franklin was also a frequent
contact of mediums throughout the century. (Emma
Hardinge, *Modern American Spiritualism,* 1869)

and zinc batteries, so arranged about the person as to form an armor, from
which he expected the most extraordinary phenomenal results."[36]

In July of 1853, Spear and his supporters began work on a machine
based on communications given to them from the spirit world. Reported in
the pages of *New Era,* this machine was to be "God's last, best, gift to
man," a perpetual-motion device that embodied the principles of a "new
motive force." Composed of wood, metal, and magnets, the machine was
to be infused with the "life principle" by bringing it into contact with the
"personal magnetism" of a number of human subjects. Once operating,
the "new motor" (and others like it) would power a "circular city," a
"perfect earthly home" built on principles of "symmetry and peace" and
incorporating temples of art, science, and worship.[37] A convergence of
electromagnetisms, both physical and spiritual, Spear's machine was to be
a source of infinite, self-generating energy to power a new utopian age on
earth.

But Spear's device was more than a magical motor. Conceived by minds
in another world with blueprints communicated through spiritual telegraphy, Spear's earthly device was an attempt to develop nothing less than a
"living" machine. "Immediately after the announcement of the birth of

the 'electric motor,' " writes Hardinge, "the columns of the *New Era* were filled with descriptions of the mechanism, which, it seemed, was designed to correspond to the human organism and perform the functions of a living being."[38] As A. E. Newton comments in his summary of the experiment, "In short, the various parts of the model were alleged to *represent* (not in outward *form,* but in *function*) the essential vital or motive organs of the human or animal system, — that is, what is necessary to constitute a *living* organism."[39] Andrew Jackson Davis, a well-known visionary in Spiritualist circles, visited the machine and its creators during the summer of 1854. "They invest the very materialism of the mechanism with principles of interpretation which give out an emanation of religious feeling altogether new in the development of scientific truth," reported Davis. "Each wire is precious, sacred, as a spiritual verse. Each plate of zinc and copper is clothed with symbolized meanings, corresponding throughout with the principles and parts involved in the living human organism."[40] Eventually Spear himself was encased in the apparatus and surrounded by "metallic plates, strips and bands," as well as "precious metals, jewels, and other minerals alleged to enter prominently into the constitution of the human body."[41] As Spear entered a trance, observers noticed "a stream of light, a sort of umbilicum, emanating (from the encased person) to and enveloping the mechanism."[42]

Spiritualist fantasies of disembodied communication and living technologies such as Spear's proto-robot greatly resembled the fantastic devices of the then emerging genre of science fiction, another arena of popular culture that demonstrated an interest in the discorporative powers of telegraphic technology. Indeed, in many cases it would be difficult to differentiate between these two discourses of scientific possibility. Within later Spiritualist literature, for example, mediumistic accounts of adventures on Mars and Venus were not uncommon, while science fiction throughout the century frequently imagined the astonishing possibilities to be realized through the telegraphic liberation of mind and body. A particularly interesting author in this regard was Robert Milne, a Scottish writer born in 1844 who settled in San Francisco, where he penned a number of extraordinary tales detailing seemingly "paranormal" telegraphic phenomena. Some of Milne's stories merely exploited the culture's general conflation of Spiritualism and electrical science, as in "A Mysterious Twilight; Being a Dip into the Doings of the Four-Dimensional World," where Milne's narrator finds himself electrocuted by vengeful spirits who engineer a short circuit in a home's electrical wiring during a séance.[43] In "An Experience in Telepathy; in which Clairvoyance and Spiritual Telegraphy Play a Part," two men have out-of-body experiences as they telepathically "visit" with a friend in Mexico.[44] In what is perhaps Milne's most prescient story, written in 1879, his narrator happens on a wire that extends from a rooftop and up into the clouds. The narrator discovers that a scientist has learned to send messages anywhere in the world by tapping into the "electric diaphragm," an atmospheric layer that conducts electromagnetic messages across the planet.[45]

One tale in particular is of interest as a vivid fantasy of telegraphic disembodiment. In "Professor Vehr's Electrical Experiment" a young man visits the famous Professor Vehr, who has been experimenting with electronic telepathy. Vehr tells the young man that he has invented an apparatus that allows one to "see" anywhere in the world. Worried because he has not heard from his fiancée in many months while she travels in Europe, the young man asks if he can use the device to find her. Vehr agrees and places the mental traveler inside a complicated electronic apparatus, bearing a "marked resemblance to the known characteristics of a Leyden jar" with what looked like "ordinary telegraphic wires."[46] Once in the device, the young man holds a telegraph wire in each hand. Vehr then taps the wires into a telegraph line outside his window. The professor explains the process to the young man's friend in a passage that explicitly links the century's technological and spiritual fixations:

> "That is the first effect of [a] moderately strong charge of static electricity in the human frame," explained the professor. "It induces a highly wrought condition of the nerves, which in their turn act upon the ganglion of the brain; that, in its turn, reacting again, through the duplex series of nerves, upon the wire held in the left hand, which brings the holder into communication with whatever object enthralls his attention at the time of the trance. The experiment is, in effect, clairvoyance reduced to an art, the mesmeric trance accomplished by scientific means and conditioned by the recognized and accepted laws of electrical science."[47]

Through the machine he sees another man courting his fiancée in New Orleans. His telegraphic consciousness returned to the room of Professor Vehr, the young man is despondent about his imminent romantic loss and his sense of helplessness. Vehr then agrees to debut his latest innovation. This time by attaching his apparatus to the telegraph line, Vehr is able to discorporate and transmit the young man to New Orleans, where he quickly defeats his rival. But, in an ending much less utopian than most Spiritualist literature, when Vehr tries to bring the reunited couple back across the wires, they disappear into the vast electronic elsewhere never to be seen again.

While authors such as Milne depicted the era's telegraphic fantasies in science fiction, a number of respected scientists sympathetic to the Spiritualist cause developed theories and performed experiments in an attempt to provide empirical proof of Spiritualist principles. Dr. Robert Hare, an American physician and electrical engineer who devoted much energy to investigating Spiritualist claims, argued that a form of "spiritual electricity" powered the raps, knocks, and materializations of the séance. Just as the mysterious substance of electricity pervades our mortal world, Hare reasoned, "so the spirits ascribe *their electricity* and *their light* to the undulation and polarization of an analogous ethereal fluid."[48] Hare also designed several devices to test scientifically the power and veracity of the spiritualist medium.

Hare's work, which garnered much respect due to his established reputation in more "legitimate" science, intersected with a host of other scientific theories of the spirit world to articulate nothing less than a "science of the soul." This was an attempt to understand the soul through scientific inquiry while also mapping its location in relation to the material world. "The most external portion of the spirit being electricity, is the agent of life and motion," noted one spiritual cartographer; "the next interior portion being magnetism, is the agent of sensational power; and the inmost germ, which is properly the soul itself, being the divine principle of intelligence, is the expansive receptacle of celestial wisdom."[49] Some theorists imagined the spirits inhabiting a series of celestial spheres emanating around the earth; others believed that the spirits, unfettered by time and space, had unlimited access to the universe as a whole. One writer even posited a simultaneous existence of the material and spiritual worlds within the human body, arguing that the soul itself was an electromagnetic phenomenon trapped by material flesh:

> It is easy to conceive, then, that the magnetic essence of *all* the particles and compounds of the body, associated together, must necessarily form *an interior, magnetic and invisible body,* in the same manner as the association of the particles themselves forms the outer and visible body. Moreover, as the

pervading and surrounding essence of each of these particles must correspond in nature to the particle itself, and may be called the spirit of the
particle; so this interior, magnetic body, if it could be tested by spiritual
chemistry, would be found to consist of what may be termed spiritual
carbon, spiritual nitrogen, spiritual calcium, and so on to the end of the
category composing the *physical* body. At death the particles of the visible
body collapse, and this interior, vitalizing and magnetic body, exhales forth
in its united form, its various parts maintaining their mutual affinities as
before; and could we then see it as it is, we would find it to possess spiritual
bones, muscles, heart, lungs, nerves, brain, &c., and that it still preserved all
the *general* features of its original mould, though in a vastly improved
state.[50]

The author proposed that this "spirit body," or what we commonly think of
as the "soul," would then recognize itself in a new spirit world, "abound-
ing with scenery, organizations and other objects corresponding to its own
essence and affections; and then would commence a life sevenfold more
intense than that enjoyed while in the flesh!"[51] Just as Mary Shelley had
thirty years earlier conceived of a material body stitched together from
limbs stolen from the grave and then animated with jolts of electricity, this
Spiritualist constructed his own Frankenstein's Monster, one powered by
Spiritual electricity that eerily resided within each person as an invisible
doppelgänger waiting to emerge at the moment of death. Thus did heaven,
the afterlife, and the soul become theorized, spatialized, and concretized
phenomena subject to scientific inquiry and validation.

History prepares us, then, for the opening comments in physicist Frank
J. Tipler's 1994 book, *The Physics of Immortality*. Tipler introduces his
book by arguing that "theology is a branch of physics," and even more
provocatively, "physicists can infer by calculation the existence of God
and the likelihood of the resurrection of the dead to eternal life in exactly
the same way as physicists calculate the properties of the electron."[52]
Replacing telegraphic metaphors with those from the computer age, Tipler continues, "it is necessary to regard all forms of life — including human beings — as subject to the same laws of physics as electrons and
atoms. I therefore regard a human being as nothing but a particular type of
machine, the human brain as nothing but an information processing device, the human soul as nothing but a program being run on a computer
called the brain."[53] Tipler's theories, of course, are conceptual cousins to

the long-standing fantasy in science fiction and contemporary cyberculture that human consciousness (and presumably the soul as a by-product
of that consciousness) might one day be downloaded into a powerful
computer. For many, then as now, metaphysics are apparently most convincing when supported with some form of mathematics.

I note these parallels, not so much to ridicule such theories, as to demonstrate how enduring this dream of electronically evacuating the body remains even today. As in much science fiction, utopian, and religious literature, Tipler and the cyber-enthusiasts invoke an invisible future as a
compensatory vision for the problems of the present, imagining a "spiritual" technology as a means of bodily escape and deliverance from the
troubles of a material and depressingly finite universe. The Spiritualists
were the first to imagine such electronic technologies as a link to an
unseen world of phantom subjects, spirits who "transmitted" word of a
future utopia much brighter and more promising than the often dismal
realities presented by nineteenth-century industrialism and Victorian society. Operating within a larger general fascination for the possibilities of
electronic telecommunication, the Spiritualists found the telegraph a most
logical and appropriate instrument of social and even material deliverance.
The miraculous "disembodying" presence evoked by Morse's technology
suggested the tantalizing possibility of a realm where intelligence and
consciousness existed independent of the physical body and its material
limitations, be they social, sexual, political, mortal, or otherwise.

The Negative Female

As one might imagine, such "emancipating" possibilities were of particular interest to women, who from Kate Fox onward served as the ideological and technological core of the movement. Communication with the
spirit world required more than a mere telegraph, be it electromagnetic,
celestial, or otherwise. Spiritual contact also depended on the equally
enigmatic technology of the "medium," a complex receiver who channeled the mysteries of spiritual electricity through the circuitry of another
unfathomable entity in nineteenth-century science — the female body.
Like the telegraph, women presented many Victorians with "a machine
they could not understand," making "feminine" physiology and psychology an equally imaginative field of scientific speculation, especially when
such conjecture intersected, as did seemingly all aspects of nineteenth-

century life, with theories of electromagnetism. Exploiting the scientific ambiguities surrounding both electromagnetism and their own bodies, female mediums would make strategic use of "telepresence" as an avenue for empowerment and emancipation.

Electrical theories of femininity were almost as old as electrical theory itself. As with most other totalizing accounts of cosmos and consciousness, electromagnetic principles of the early nineteenth century gradually informed the study of ever more complicated phenomena, moving beyond galvanism and biology to pervade emerging disciplines such as psychology and anthropology. More important for the tenets of Spiritualist belief, electromagnetic theory also entered increasingly into debates over sex and gender. In *Animal Electricity; or the Electrical Science,* for example, published the same year that Morse debuted the telegraph in Washington, James Olcott proposed that "electrified" women were the agents responsible for the evolution and diversity of the world's races. Evolutionary progress, he argued, resulted at certain key historical moments when "a series of violent electro-magnetic disturbances in the womb" pushed evolution to new heights. In this decidedly racist branch of electromagnetic speculation, "the Negro [was] far back, and the Mongolian the more near, and the Circassian the last formation of the last great change."[54] Describing these periods of evolutionary transition, Olcott wrote, "Millions of females would at that moment be enceinte. They would, the more delicate and amiable, swoon away, and in this semi-living state, soon become emersed in electric menstruums, soft and energetic enough to crush, and at the same time warm enough slowly to evolve the embryo."[55]

While Olcott engaged in abstract theorization, others tested the mysteries of gendered sensitivity and electromagnetism in a more "empirical" manner. An important figure in the Spiritualists' eventual electromagnetic model of mediumship was Baron Charles von Reichenbach, whose work seemed to provide experimental proof of enhanced feminine sensitivity. His earliest experiments involved placing "cataleptic" and "feeble-brained" teenage girls in dark rooms and then exposing them to a magnet. After performing this experiment on some twenty-two young women, Reichenbach concluded that "those sensitive persons, who are so in a high degree, perceive in the dark, at the poles of powerful magnets, a luminous appearance of a waving, flame-like nature, less or more according to the degree of their diseased sensibility, or more or less perfect degree of darkness."[56] In other words, Reichenbach believed that girls with a "diseased sensibility" could perceive a flickering aura around magnets, a force that was neither wholly electrical nor magnetic (interestingly, "disease" in this scenario led to an increase rather than a diminution of this allegedly feminine trait, suggesting that femininity in itself was regarded as a diseased state). Reichenbach continued his experiments with other luminous objects and suggestible subjects, eventually developing a theory of a new universal force that pervaded all matter. Reichenbach called this newfound substance, Odyle, and referred to its presence in the universe as the "Odic force." Dismissed as a lunatic in later histories of electromagnetism, Reichenbach's experiments in the early part of the century nevertheless had a formative impact on Spiritualists seeking a credible scientific explanation for their incredible telecommunications with the dead.

Olcott and Reichenbach incorporated electrical theory into the related and more widespread patriarchal belief in Victorian society that women, although physically and mentally "inferior," were in some sense more "sensitive" than their male counterparts. Surveying the Darwinian tradition in gender psychology that dominated the century, Cynthia Russett observes that women were routinely distinguished from men by their "powers of intuition, of rapid perception, and perhaps of imagination."[57] Women also displayed their strength of emotion, as well as a " 'refinement of the senses, or higher evolution of sense-organs,' and rapidity of perception and thought, expressed in 'intuitive insight' and 'nimbleness of mother-wit' " (42). It should be noted, however, that these seemingly "positive" traits related to perception were, at the time, "held to stand in inverse ratio to high intellectual development, since the latter induced reflection and this in turn retarded perception" (42). Stunted in their physical and mental growth, women retained only a childlike wonder, a fragile constitution, and volatile emotionality. With his vivid image of "delicate" women "swooning away" under the influence of "electrical mentsruums," Olcott presented a familiar portrait of Victorian women as defined by an intrinsic and at times debilitating "sensitivity," an ultimately "passive" quality attending their primary purpose in life as the sex " 'sacrificed to reproductive necessities' " (43). Ironically, these "negative" qualities attributed to women were to become the foundation of their spiritual authority. As Judith Walkowitz notes, "Spiritualists deemed women particularly apt for mediumship because they were weak in the masculine attributes of will and intelligence, yet strong in the feminine qualities of passivity, chastity, and impressionability."[58]

Spiritualism and its eventual antagonists in medical science shared a brief but crucial moment of common intellectual heritage in these early accounts of feminine physiology. Although their theoretical concerns would eventually diverge, both the Spiritualists and the pioneers of scientific neurology, inspired by the electrifying examples of galvanism, attributed much importance to the "nervous principle" that governed a telegraphic model of the nervous system. Both paradigms thought mediumistic women particularly vulnerable to the vicissitudes of the mysterious forces of "nervous energy," a form of organic electricity one commentator described as "an intermediate agent by which mind acts on matter, and which is itself neither mind nor matter."[59] The nervous principle, he continued, operated much like other forces of nature. "In many modes of its operation, it is similar to the magnetic and electrical principles; having probably its negative and its positive, an attracting and a repelling power, which may either balance each other, or over-balance and control one the other." This substance was thought to be "abundant in persons of strongly nervous temperament, and . . . developed so as to overcharge the system of the person who is under great excitement of body or mind." As the more "sensitive" of the sexes, women were believed to have an unstable abundance of such energy, especially as adolescents. As this same author writes in diagnosing the "generally young, . . . inexperienced, and female" mediums of Spiritualism, "They are just that class whom we ordinarily speak of as persons of high nervous temperament, of an acute mental organism. It is the very class of persons in whom the nervous principle is active, from whom we seem to see the nervous energy thus flowing off" (24–25, 39).

As the two entities most closely associated with the mysteries of the life force, women and electricity were deeply imprecated in Victorian questions of spirituality. Building on a larger Victorian ideology of the ineffable moral purity and higher spirituality of women, the Spiritualists would go on to produce a theory linking electromagnetism and femininity in a divine alliance. If communication with the dead were possible, reasoned most, then women, having brought life into the world through their "receptive reproductive economy," would be the most likely candidates for bringing the living spirits back onto the mortal plain through their "exquisite sensitivity." Yet, even though the "nervous energy" of women may have been more abundant and unstable, it was still ultimately subordinate to a more powerful masculine force. Pondering the ineffable mysteries of sexual, spiritual, and electrical attraction, one theorist proposed, "Since one class of persons (healthy males) are known to be positively electric, and another class (delicate females) are known to be negatively electric, and since in their nervous energies there may be the same difference, when by the naturally exciting manipulations each is charged like a Leyden jar, why should there not be between the two a mutual attraction, in which the stronger will control the movements of the weaker?"[60] Despite the efforts of such dominating powers, however, these peculiar convergences of sexual and electrical discourse at midcentury suggest that the fundamental "nature" of both these unruly forces remained at the center of scientific controversy and cultural speculation.

Catalyzing much of this electrical, spiritual, and sexual speculation, telegraphy provided a conceptual model for grounding such abstract theories in the seemingly more concrete examples of applied technology. As the preferred operators of celestial telegraphy, the successful feminine medium integrated domestic, spiritual, and even electrical expertise into an unprecedented form of social authority.[61] Spiritualism's electronic rearticulation of femininity's intrinsic "passivity" and nervous instability presented an important opportunity for empowering women, whose physical disenfranchisement from nearly all aspects of public life and knowledge severely limited their sphere of social activity. Not surprisingly, Spiritualism's development was closely aligned with the emerging cause of women's rights, a social movement that, like Spiritualism, had its roots in upper New York State in the 1840s. Braude argues that the Spiritualists distinguished themselves from other progressive movements of the period "by lifting women's rights out of the reform platform as preeminent. . . . As investigation of the manifestations swept the nation, Spiritualism became a major — if not *the* major — vehicle for the spread of woman's rights ideas in mid-century America."[62] Most certainly, many Spiritualists, male and female, were in some sense disenchanted with the prevailing social and political climate at the middle of the century, and viewed women's rights issues as key to social reform.

Appropriately, then, while Morse's telegraph carried news of banking, commerce, and other concerns of the masculine sphere, the spiritual telegraph addressed issues of vital concern to women. Mediums frequently strayed into such political territory during "trance" sessions, public events where the medium would enter a trance state and channel the words of a departed soul eager to comment on the mortal world's political landscape.

Channeling such a spirit for an audience in New York, for example, Emma Hardinge challenged the audience to improve the fate of the city's six thousand prostitutes. "The six thousand women are *'outcasts.'* Where are the six thousand men? In your saloons, and halls of legislature, your offices of trust, and places of honor, chanting the hymn of model America's 'FRATERNITY,' whilst gibing demons cry 'Amen.' "[63] Communicating at séances through the circuit of telegraph and medium, the spirits of a higher and more refined plane of existence repeatedly argued that women needed to be liberated from the "limited education that restricted the development of their intellects, from unjust laws that denied them access to their property and custody of their children, from unequal marriages that subjugated them to men, and from economic restrictions that forced them into dependence."[64]

Such advocacy, however, did not necessarily brand these women (and men) as extremists. Within the context of Spiritualism's model of electronic presence, women "mediums" and "trance speakers" were able to raise feminist issues and debate them freely without necessarily challenging directly the overall social order.[65] In a complex and somewhat ironic process of ideological negotiation, Spiritualism empowered women to speak out in public, often about very controversial issues facing the nation, but only because all understood that the women were not the ones actually speaking, at least not women who were still alive. "Mediums presented not their own views but those of the spirits who spoke through them," notes Braude. Both in drawing rooms and large auditoriums, "The essential passivity of women was asserted in a public arena, displayed before thousands of witnesses."[66] Women could thus only assume such an "active" role in Spiritualist thought and practice through their fundamentally "passive" natures, a constitution electrically inscribed in their enhanced sensitivity.

Existing at the fringes of Victorian science's understanding of electricity, femininity, and spirituality, the medium occupied a strategic political and intellectual space that allowed her to intervene in the public sphere through a combination of supernatural and technological discourses, a model legitimated by the equally incredible yet incontrovertible evidence of the telegraph. While the technology of the telegraph transformed America into a wired nation, the *concept* of telegraphy enabled endless displacements of agency, projecting utopian possibilities onto a disembodied, invisible community and recasting an often radical political agenda as an act of supernatural possession. The telegraph, spiritual or otherwise, not only made one interlocutor physically absent; it also placed the ultimate source of transmission in irresolvable ambiguity. Spiritualism as a movement exploited this intrinsic mystery of electronic telecommunications to make possible both new means and new forms of political discourse. Mediums exploited the indeterminacy of telegraphy's electronic presence to "throw their voice" both physically and politically in a most complex form of ventriloquism. Arguably, such a masquerade would have been impossible without the provocative example of Morse's telegraph and its powers of disembodiment. For a brief moment at least, Spiritualism presented a unique and even subversive articulation of femininity, electricity, and technology, recasting women's physical and mental "inferiority" into a form of technological authority — an expertise frequently invoked in support of women's rights, abolitionism, and other "radical" causes.

Hysterical Telegraphy

Considering the highly gendered social formation in which it flourished and the often explicitly political ends to which it was employed, "spiritual telegraphy" clearly involved more than a simple-minded belief in the occult. The Spiritualists would appear to have had a more instrumental investment in the reality of this phantom apparatus. In fact, even many commentators of the period considered the entire movement to be based on a politically motivated hoax. "The connection of spirit-rapping, or the spirit manifestations, with modern philanthropy, visionary reforms, socialism, and revolutionism, is not an imagination of my own," grumbled one critic. "It is historical and asserted by the Spiritists, or Spiritualists themselves."[67] Another skeptic proposed that Spiritualist women took advantage of their protected social position, as propriety dictated that they were less likely to be questioned as frauds. "Whether the 'spirits' think of it or not, we mortals know that their *sex* and *costume* is a fine security against detection. And may this not be the reason why most of the raps are through lady mediums?"[68] Such suspicions and resentment grew as the movement matured, and in the second half of the nineteenth century, the delicate instrument of the medium came under increasing attack. Although they had been at odds from the earliest days of the movement, Spiritualism and medical science became increasingly antagonistic rivals after the Civil War as each sought to legitimate its own models of "nervous" physiological and psychological phenomena. Walkowitz writes that physicians, "alarmed by the growing popularity of spiritualism among the educated classes," mounted an all-out attack on the movement. "They caricatured spiritualists as crazy women and feminized men engaged in superstitious, popular, and fraudulent practices. Spiritualists responded by elaborating an iconography of male medical evil, portraying the doctor as a fraud and as a sexually dangerous man, a divided personality whose science made him cruel, blood-thirsty, and hypermasculine because it suppressed his feminine, spiritual part."[69] In this debate, no less an authority than J. M. Charcot, France's foremost theoretician of hysteria, warned of Spiritualism's effects on the mind. "Of all causes productive of these traumatisms of the cerebral functions," mused Charcot, "there is perhaps none more efficacious, and whose influence has been oftener acknowledged, than inordinate belief in the marvelous, in the supernatural."[70]

The importance of telegraphy as a conceptual construct is especially apparent when one considers that telegraphic metaphors not only gave structure to Spiritualist belief, but also presided over the movement's eventual delegitimation and extinction. Ironically, the empowering model of telegraphic technology would eventually be turned against the Spiritualists, leading to a new articulation of femininity and electronic disassociation that would serve to restrict drastically the autonomy of women (often quite literally). In opposition to the liberating fantasy of corporeal transcendence harbored by the Spiritualists, emerging (and often competing) sciences such as neurology and psychiatry employed "telegraphic" knowledge to articulate their own theories of feminine physiology and psychology. As the century unfolded, critics of Spiritualism increasingly aimed these "rationalist" sciences at mediumistic women in an attempt to place their bodies back under medical and thus political control. As Walkowitz observes, "Special female powers also rendered female mediums vulnerable to special forms of female punishment: to medical labeling as hysterics and to lunacy confinement."[71]

Sharing the premise that women possessed a unique sensitivity, the emerging science of neurology sought its own explanations as to the electrical relationship of consciousness and the body. Spiritualism and its medical antagonists developed rival theories to address what both paradigms saw as a very specialized and highly telegraphic relationship between gender, consciousness, and electricity.[72] The Spiritualists believed a woman's surplus (or imbalance) of "nervous energy" made her a more receptive candidate for receiving the higher electromagnetic transmissions of the spirits. Medical science believed this surplus led instead to dysfunctions of the body, where the nervous system, as a great telegraphic network, was overtaxed by the variable intensity of this flow. Whereas mediums viewed themselves as channeling invisible streams of "spiritual electricity," a capacity enabled by the more "plastic" and "religious" feminine mind, many physicians of the period saw women as extraordinarily prone to electrical "dysfunctions" of the nervous system. This was no idle debate. For its advocates, celestial telegraphy led to revelation, enlightenment, and the elevation of feminine voices in a resoundingly patriarchal society. The collapses of "nervous telegraphy," on the other hand, led to the seemingly ubiquitous nineteenth-century maladies of hysteria and neurasthenia. What the Spiritualists saw as "mediumistic phenomena," medical science labeled "mania" and "insanity." This telegraphic breakdown of the nervous system brought with it stigmatization, institutionalization, and even death.

Physicians increasingly favored electrical etiologies in the late nineteenth century, and were often just as quick as the Spiritualists to adapt electromagnetic and telegraphic metaphors in their discussions of neurasthenia, hysteria, and nervous energy. As John and Robin Haller write in their history of Victorian medicine:

> It was not without reason then, with all the talk about neurenergen and nervous expenditure, that physicians discussed the nervous activity of the human body in terms of "current," "electricity," "nerve molecules," "conductibility of the neuron," "transmission of impulses," and "fluid theory." In describing the brain and nervous system, physicians frequently compared them to a galvanic battery "whose duty is to provide a certain and continuous supply of its special fluid for consumption within a given time."
>
> Nineteenth-century physicians pointed out that, like electricity, the nervous energy in the human body was a compound fluid, one negative and the other positive. The natural balance in quantity of these fluids in a particular substance was known as "natural electricity," while the liberation of fluids produced a phenomenon of "active electricity."[73]

Just as the female medium's powers to "speak" were based on a paradox, so too were a woman's proclivities for neurasthenic and hysterical dysfunctions. "In one sense," write Haller and Haller, "the medical profession interpreted woman's symptoms of nervous exhaustion as a product of the role she played in society." The routine existence of domestic confinement provided little opportunity to discharge nervous energy, a condition thought to be exacerbated by the rapid social, cultural, and technological changes taking place outside the home. The solution, however, was not to better integrate women in the public sphere, for this too held dangers. Once outside the home, women "saw their nerve centers lose control and go astray, traveling along 'forbidden channels.' " Physicians, in turn, used this logic to explain woman's "natural inferiority . . . and her susceptibility to nervous disease when she took on too many duties, moved out of the home, or just presumed too much in a man's world."[74] Mediums, of course, were particularly vulnerable to such attacks in that they had dared to emerge from domestic life to take a place on the public stage.

When confronted with an overtaxed nervous system, mediumistic or otherwise, the physician's task was to restore this economy through the precise application of electrical flow.[75] As one theorist wrote, "If there is an induced current so acting as to diminish the normal current, then effects, such as paralysis, or anesthesia are produced; if it acts so as to increase the nerve force, then such phenomenon [*sic*] as excessive motor activity or hyperaesthesia is the result."[76] Haller and Haller describe the logic behind such "electro-therapeutics."[77] "The use of electricity on the neuron, it was believed, restored 'conductibility' which, due to prostration, had become resistant to the nerve current. By exciting the nerve tissue, a condition of 'electrotonos,' or a change in nerve excitability, occurred, in which the neuron found newer paths of transmission for its nervous impulses."[78] As physicians adopted electricity as a popular treatment for a variety of physical complaints in the second half of the century, it became especially important in treating mental and nervous disorders. " 'We like it," wrote one asylum director, "find it beneficial in most cases, valuable in a majority, and indispensable in certain forms of hysterical insanity, in primary dementia, and neurasthenia.' "[79] For many physicians, belief in mediumistic abilities was both cause and symptom of a disordered nervous economy, a condition that would eventually lead to full hysteria. Charcot compared Spiritualists to children, writing that the movement "indicates clearly the danger there is, especially to persons nervously predisposed, in superstitious practices, which unfortunately have for them so great an attraction, and in that constant tension of mind and imagination to which those are brought who apply themselves to spiritistic performances and the search of the marvelous, an occupation in which children take so much delight."[80]

Spiritualism's struggle against "nonbelievers," medical or otherwise, suggests that as a popular fantasy quickly capturing the public imagination, telegraphic disembodiment made possible new avenues of social liberation even while extending old and more familiar relations of gendered power. Within an already dynamic field of social struggle, the electrical animation of telegraphic presence significantly informed increasingly antagonistic regimes of knowledge, producing theoretical spaces (and technological models) that could generate either calls for social change and political reform or criteria of insanity and institutionalization. Mediums became complex and contested "devices," linking for some the living and the dead, science and religion, masculine technology and feminine spirituality, but signifying for others the fundamental fragility of women and their inability to adjust to the modern world and its many wonders. Operating at the provocative fringes of religion and rationalism, spirit and science, mediums presented themselves as a "technology" constructed from and yet in conflict with the more colonizing embodiments of traditional religion and rationalist science. In doing so, they walked a fine line between empowerment and institutionalization. One might say, whereas the Spiritualists imagined telegraphic technology as a means of transcending material existence in an "out-of-body" experience, medical science employed telegraphic metaphors to reground consciousness within the bodies of women who were thought to be "out-of-their-minds."

In the end, however, what made Spiritualism both particularly effective and yet potentially dangerous for women was the absolute indeterminacy bound to this earliest form of electronic presence. Given the state of nineteenth-century knowledge, who really could prove, ultimately, whether spiritual telegraphy was fact or fiction? Moreover, how could one be sure if a "medium" was or was not actually hysterical or insane? Such an enigma presented a significant legal question of the age, with one physician admitting, "The difficulty would be to determine what individuals actually believed and what ones only assumed and claimed to believe, for the purpose of deception, gain, or self-glorification."[81] This writer concluded that those who believed spirits in general could communicate with the living were not insane, but those who believed that they were in *actual* communications with the spirits were insane. The problem proved even more vexing for directors of asylums, who were put in the difficult medical/ideological position of determining whether a Spiritualist medium was insane, merely deluded, or just affecting the phenomena. The case history of an institutionalized young medium in 1859 indicates the ambiguities involved in such diagnosis:

> During the next several successive days, she would appear constantly pos-
> sessed and controlled by spirits. Sometimes they spoke through her, com-
> manding her in the third person, at one moment to go to a distant part of the
> town with a message to a certain one, and in the next breath directing her to
> go to another room of the house, where it would be told her what she should
> do. . . . In the effort to obey these commands, many of which were trivial,
> contradictory, and impossible, she would be greatly perplexed, and at times
> in utter despair. Generally, however, her state was one of exaltation. Her
> voice was loud, her manner imperious, and she resisted with much strength,
> though not passionately, when interrupted in carrying into effect the direc-
> tions of the spirits, and would appear to her friends perfectly natural in
> manner and speech.[82]

Although today such symptoms might seem to indicate the onset of a schizophrenic episode, the doctor in the case observed that "her fellow Spiritualists assured her that nothing was wrong with her, and that she was only passing through a special and extraordinary experience, in her devel-opment as a medium" (324). After much consideration as to the ultimate status of what might be seen either as this woman's hysterical "symptoms" or paranormal "communications," the doctor finally asked his colleagues,

> For, granting the theory that the belief in the agency of spirits was the pri-
> mary underlying delusion of the patient, what part of the entirety of the
> mental disease . . . does this statement of fact express? How much of the in-
> sanity does this delusion represent? If a dozen years ago, and previously to
> the first development of the Spiritual phenomena, an hypothesis of the
> relations of disembodied spirits to men, like that which has come to dis-
> tinguish a numerous sect, had belonged to a single individual, that man
> would have been, without doubt, mad. There can be just as little doubt that
> at present thousands of persons, of nearly, at least, an average soundness of
> intellect, hold precisely the same belief, in terms, as did our patient. The
> simple belief, then, in spiritual phenomena, as actual or possible facts in her
> experience, was not previously to her attack of mania, and is not since her
> convalescence, an insane delusion.[83]

Or, as another exasperated doctor noted, "The physician who examines hysterical patients has always to bear in mind that they intend to deceive him, to hide the truth, and feign things that do not exist, as well as to disguise things that do exist."[84] The same might have been said of "mediums," women who by strategically adapting the scientific language of technology and exploiting the electronic mysteries of telegraphic presence, crafted a fantastic language in which to affirm gendered authority and extol progressive social intervention.

The Telegraphic Imagination

In the months after the Rochester knockings, the Fox sisters and their mother traveled extensively to provide public demonstrations of the spirit phenomena. Skeptics examined the girls and their communications repeatedly but could not account definitively for the source of the rappings. Such disbelief did little to dampen enthusiasm for the growing movement. In a letter published in the *New York Herald* in April of 1851, however, a relative of the girls claimed to know the "true" source of the manifestations. Kate Fox, the youngest of the Fox daughters, allegedly explained to this relative that she produced the raps by cracking the joints in her knees and toes, a skill both she and Margeretta had mastered as children by pressing their toes against the footboard in bed. Despite this admission and numerous counterattacks, the movement continued to flourish. In 1888, fully grown and somewhat down on her luck, Margeretta made a public confession of the less than paranormal source of the manifestations (according to some, because she had received money to do so). Interestingly, Margeretta recanted the confession no sooner than she had issued it, placing the matter once again in some degree of ambiguity.[85]

Started as a girlish prank, perhaps, the spirit manifestations rapidly assumed a public life of their own. As the two girls secretly instructed others in how to produce the phenomena (or as others devised their own techniques), this diverting charade expanded its influence in parlors and auditoriums across the country as mediums conveyed messages from departed loved ones, fallen national heroes, and colorful figures across all of human history. The advent of the "planchette" and "Ouija board" allowed families to experiment with spiritual communications in their own home. At some point, this "game" of raps and knocks evolved into a doctrine of religious belief that inspired many devout followers and led to ever more elaborate manifestations of the spirits. By the 1870s, Spiritualism was a vital social, philosophical, and commercial enterprise, generating journals, books, and speaking tours that examined the wonders of the spirit manifestations and sought to either validate or repudiate the veracity of Spiritualist claims. At its height of influence, belief in Spiritualism could be found in freed southern slaves and blue bloods of Boston, in mediumistic teenage girls and members of Congress. During these years, Spiritualism no doubt incorporated a wide variety of participants exhibiting a range of motivations — adolescent girls who enjoyed the attention and power of their "mediumship" while knowing full well it was a hoax; mediums who actually convinced themselves of the reality of their own manifestations; reformers who recognized that the manifestations where fraudulent yet saw in them the opportunity to increase their political influence; religious zealots who exploited Spiritualism as a convenient opportunity to receive messages directly from God; and "average Americans" who, although not obsessed by Spiritualist doctrine, found the manifestations an interesting source of discussion and speculation.

In a period distinguished by the mysteries of electricity, an emerging turbulence in the politics of gender, and an overall utopian enthusiasm for technologies of deliverance, this unlikely juxtaposition of toe joint and telegraph helped articulate what would eventually become a fully developed fantasy of electronic transmutability. Through images of discorporation, anthropomorphization, and even cybernetics, Spiritualism produced the media age's first "electronic elsewhere," an invisible utopian realm generated and accessed through the wonders of electronic media. The conceptual appropriation of telegraphy by Spiritualism (and medical science) suggests that as telegraph lines stretched across the nation to connect city and town, town and country, they also stretched across the nation's imagination to interconnect a variety of social and cultural spheres. For the Spiritualists, the bodiless communication of telegraphy heralded the existence of a land without material substance, an always unseen origin point of transmission for disembodied souls in an electromagnetic utopia. Each time a medium manifested occult telepresence, be it through rappings or spirit voices, planchette readings or automatic writing, she provided indexical evidence of a social stage continually displaced and deferred that held the promise of a final paradise. Such unbridled enthusiasm for the wonders of an "electronic elsewhere" would have no real equal until the recent emergence of transcendental cyberspace mythologies in our own cultural moment.

By the end of the nineteenth century, Spiritualism as a "science" was for the most part discredited, but Spiritualist belief survived to inform cultural fantasies surrounding the next century's new telecommunications marvels. The "electronic elsewheres" imagined in connection with wireless, radio, and television, however, would be much more sinister and disturbing than the Spiritualist fantasies of electronic utopia. As telegraphy gave way to wireless, and as the nineteenth century gave way to modernity, new articulations of telepresence were to be more anxious than beatific, suggesting a realignment in the social imagination as to the powers and possibilities of electronic telecommunications.

By the end of the nineteenth century, the spiritual telegraph survived only
as a metaphor. Besieged by the attacks of scientific rationalism, few Spiritualists were willing to defend the idea that Benjamin Franklin still toiled
in the phantom laboratories of a spiritualist technocracy, fashioning imaginative electronic technologies to uplift the mortal world. Mediumistic
women across the country still performed séances for the benefit of skeptical critics and grieving relatives, and a few even achieved some degree of
fame, but they were no longer conceived as a negatively charged "terminal" in the cosmic schematic of some interdimensional telecommunications device. Speculative interest in Morse's terrestrial telegraphy, meanwhile, yielded to the wonders of telephony and the promises of wireless.
But waning excitement over the novelty of telegraphy did not mean psychic researchers had abandoned their search for a link between electronic
presence and the paranormal. For many, interest in occult media inten-
sified in the late nineteenth and early twentieth centuries as research into
psychic phenomena became more empirical and systematic. At first discredited but then increasingly informed by the doctrines of scientific rationalism, Spiritualism's fanciful portraits of a benevolent spirit world
gave way in the age of modernity to a program of pragmatic experimentation focused squarely on verifying the act of communication itself. During
this period of transition, organizations such as the Society for Psychical
Research emerged in England and the United States to assess the validity
of paranormal communications through the protocols of the "scientific
method." Intriguingly, many of the researchers who would have an important role in developing electronic telecommunications in the new century
were also acutely interested in paranormal phenomena and the scientific
possibilities of spiritual contact. Perhaps no longer willing to believe that
spirits assembled technologies in the afterlife, many citizens of the modern age did believe that a mortal genius in this world might one day
develop a working system to verify contact with the realm of the dead. At
the very least, many of the most celebrated scientific minds of the period
believed that as yet undiscovered forces governed mediumistic phenom-

ena, and that applied research and experimentation in the new century might very well solve the apparent enigmas of Spiritualism.

Sir William Crookes, for example, was a noted physicist and chemist who also served as president of London's Society for Psychical Research from 1896 to 1899. Crookes was most known in the study of parapsychology for his work with mediums Florence Cooke and D. D. Home. He attended many sessions with both mediums and devised a variety of scientific tests to investigate the reality of their manifestations, publishing his observations in books such as *Psychic Force and Modern Spiritualism* (1871) and *Researches into the Phenomena of Modern Spiritualism* (1905). A firm believer in contact with the dead, Crookes also discovered the element thallium, invented the radiometer, and most important in terms of telecommunications history, pioneered the technology of the cathode-ray tube, a crucial component in the subsequent development of electronic television technology.[1] Sir Oliver Lodge followed Crookes as president of the Society. A researcher in electricity and thermodynamics, Lodge also had a lifelong interest in "thought transference" and contact with the spirit world. Lodge's contributions to modern telecommunications included inventing a new coherer used in early wireless research, while in the field of psychic science, he published titles such as *Man and the Universe* (1908) and *Ether and Reality* (1925). As a fitting culmination of his life as a scientist *and* spiritualist, Lodge made arrangements for a posthumous test of the spirit world through which he hoped to contact members of the SPR after his death.[2]

Nearing the end of America's most celebrated public career in research and design, Thomas Alva Edison announced a project that, if realized, would have produced the ultimate mechanical marvel in modernity's seemingly inexhaustible procession of scientific and technological wonders. "I am building an apparatus," revealed Edison in 1920, "to see if it is possible for personalities which have left this earth to communicate with us."[3] Perhaps encouraged by the news that America's foremost professional genius was attacking this problem, a delegation of psychic researchers meeting in Paris in 1925 announced their own plans for such a device. These forward-thinking delegates sought a machine that would do no less than "eliminate mediums," those once-revered spiritual guides whom the twentieth century increasingly deemed too unreliable for effective contact with the other world.[4] Working in an era of continuing popular fascination with mind, machinery, and the supernatural, many inventors and scientists imagined psychic technologies that they predicted would one day gather spectral messages from the open air.[5] Such a device seemed both plausible and even inevitable in the wake of modernity's most startlingly supernatural invention — wireless communication.

The arrival of Marconi's astounding wireless system at the dawn of the new century promised to unlock the mystical enigmas of the ether, that mysterious substance once believed to be the invisible medium through which all light, electricity, and magnetism moved. Appropriately, Marconi had originally been inspired in his own research by the comments of Lodge and Heinrich Hertz on the "fantastic" presence of "ethereal vibrations" in the atmosphere. Near the end of his own life, Marconi also pursued the possibility of electronic contact with the dead. In what seemed to be a natural and intuitive extension of radio science, Marconi worked to create a device that would receive living voices from all human history, hoping even to someday hear the last words of Jesus on the cross.[6]

A number of historians have discussed the supernatural discourses evoked by the unique qualities of electronic telecommunications, noting as well the similarities between the popular reception of wireless and that of telegraphy and telephony in the previous century. "The feeling that the wireless had somehow put men on the threshold of the innermost secrets of nature paralleled that elicited by wire telegraphy," notes Daniel Czitrom. "The relationship between the wireless and ether stirred anew the old dream of 'universal communication,' a dream expressed in religious terms by early commentators on the telegraph."[7] Susan Douglas, meanwhile, also notes the parallels in utopian discourses surrounding the two media. "Like its predecessor the telegraph, wireless was cast as a moral force that would bring the world closer to peace. *Popular Science Monthly* observed that, through wireless, 'the nerves of the whole world [were], so to speak, being bound together, so that a touch in one country [was] transmitted instantly to a far-distant one.' "[8]

It is true that many similarities existed in the popular reception of telegraphy, telephony, and wireless, both in terms of the breathless wonder and utopian potential evoked by the new media. But there was also a significant and telling difference in the cultural visions of paranormality accompanying wireless that clearly distinguished it from telegraphy and telephony. Although no less awestruck than the speculative narratives and supernatural theories that greeted telegraphy, fantastic accounts of wireless technology were decidedly more anxious, pessimistic, and melancholy. In the first three decades of the new century, a variety of paranormal theories, technologies, and fictions challenged the otherwise wholly enthusiastic celebration of the emerging medium by suggesting an eerie and even sinister undercurrent to the new electronic worlds forged by wireless. This chapter examines a variety of such speculative fictions and scientific debates inspired by the strange qualities of wireless and shaped by the more alienating aspects of modernity's social and technological transformations. Appearing between 1902 and 1935, these diverse (and frequently displaced) accounts of wireless — from Edison's bold predictions in *American Magazine* to the pulpish oddities of *Weird Tales*— presented a new and often disturbing model of consciousness and communication, one that replaced the fascination for telegraphy's now mundane "lightning lines" with the more abstract wonder of electronic communication through the open air.

Whereas the "live" qualities of electronic transmission in telegraphy and telephony had put the listener in immediate, fairly intimate, and ultimately physical contact via a wire with another interlocutor across time and space, wireless offered the potentially more unsettling phenomenon of distant yet instantaneous communication through the open air. Abstract electricity in the "ether" made for messages and audiences that were at once vast and communal yet diffuse, isolated, and atomized. "Radio presented a new reality," notes Catherine Covert, "the immediate experience of a remote person or event, an experience in company with millions of others, yet strangely separate. Here were the ambiguities: the sense that one was participating, yet alone; in command, yet swept blindly along on the wave of sound."[9] Wireless thus presented a paradox: alone at their crystal sets and radios, listeners felt an electronic kinship with an invisible, scattered audience, and yet they were also acutely aware of the incredible distances involved in this form of communication that ultimately reaffirmed the individual listener's anonymity and isolation. Amid the utopian enthusiasm for the new medium, continues Covert, "came reports of individual alienation from social and personal involvement, an alienation which appeared to be encouraged by peculiar aspects of the process, content, and form of the new technology."[10]

Inhabiting a modern world where nameless hundreds could now die suddenly through technological failure or, even worse, where nameless thousands could die through technological success, there is little wonder that citizens of the early century were astonished by wireless and yet remained apprehensive about the often terrifying world it seemed to bring into the home. As a popular fantasy of disembodiment, wireless suggested that one's consciousness might someday be free to encircle the earth in a form of electronic omniscience, the radio set only hinting of powers yet to be. Through news of distant wars and disasters, on the other hand, wireless collapsed the previously unambiguous and safe boundaries that divided individuals from a larger world of trouble. As wireless put more people into contact around the world, then, it did so with a sense of melancholy. Boundaries of time, space, nation, and body no longer seemed to apply, and although this provided a giddy sense of liberation for some, it also threatened the security and stability of an older social order in which body and mind had been for the most part coterminus.

In refiguring the concept of transmission from the wired connection to the more mysterious wandering signal, accounts of wireless and radio returned consistently to the structuring metaphor of the "etheric ocean." Bound at first, perhaps, to the medium's origins in maritime applications, this most fluid of communication metaphors became a powerful conceptual tool for engaging not only the new electronic environment of the early century, but the emerging social world as well. Oceanic metaphors proved versatile in capturing the seeming omnipresence, unfathomable depths, and invisible mysteries of both radio's ether and its audience — mammoth, fluid bodies that, like the sea, were ultimately boundless and unknowable. Following the logic of this metaphor, the electronic message, once set loose from the swift currents of the insulated wire to fare upon the open sea of the electromagnetic spectrum, became a small boat tossed about on the waves of this etheric ocean, just as many citizens found themselves adrift on the new century's social currents.

Although a number of media historians have noted the importance of the "ether" as a popular model for the comprehension of wireless in the early century, there has been little discussion of the symbolic import and cultural resonance of the etheric ocean as both a communications and social metaphor. How did tales of the etheric ocean, interlaced with motifs of estrangement and death, come to encapsulate in a popular language the atomizing and frequently sinister forces of modernity? In a time when philosophers, scientists, and artists alike were redefining concepts of space, time, identity, and consciousness, these "fantastic" accounts of oceanic wireless presented an increasingly uncertain world, one populated by citizens cut loose from previous social ties and now suffused with electromagnetic waves set free from tributaries of cable and wire. Although most accounts of wireless celebrated communities increasingly interconnected by the technology, these other tales brooded instead over lives and souls transmuted and dispersed into the enveloping ether. In a world now super-naturally blanketed by human consciousness afloat in the air, stories of paranormal radio as the "voice from the void" pondered the fate of the still corporeal yet increasingly isolated individuals who found themselves bathing, often reluctantly, in the waves of the wireless sea.

The DX Dead

The often mystical dialogue over the emerging wonders of wireless took place during a period of unprecedented cultural transformation in the United States and Europe. Profound changes in the economic and social order between 1880 and 1920 created a new form of national identity and new varieties of individual experience. Stephen Kern has documented modernity's experiential change in space and time and its impact on the aesthetically revolutionary practices of modernism at the level of high culture.[11] But the cultural manifestations of modernity went beyond philo-sophical and aesthetic debates within the world's salons and galleries. New urban realities presented less esoteric restructurings of space and time for the nation's growing industrial workforce, whose mass migration to the city came to be the chief engine of modernity's sweeping social and cultural transformations. This migration also created the core of the mass audience for the arrival of cinema, radio, and television.

The more dehumanizing demands of industrial life, coupled with in-creasing separation and estrangement from previous ties of family and community, produced a new urban environment marked by accelerating tension and increasing isolation. This period of anxious transition saw the erosion of many of the previous century's social certainties. T. Jackson Lears notes that one of the most profound changes in American culture in this period was its increasing secularization.[12] Lears invokes Nietzsche's diagnosis of modernity as an era of "weightlessness," the dawning of an age when the Western world was to lose a previously unquestioned moral and cultural grounding, leading to an increasing sense of isolation and alienation. Nor was there any longer a consensus about "America" itself as a national community. The turn of the century saw another massive wave of immigration to the United States, bringing with it spirited and often vicious public debate about the nation's "true" constituency. Many wanted immigration halted immediately to preserve an Anglo ideal of the American social fabric, and also called for those non-Anglo Americans who had already immigrated to the country to renounce their previous ethnic and national identities. Seemingly inclusive debates about the United States as "the melting pot" thus carried their own subtexts of exile, isolation, and atomization. Many citizens seeking to conserve an ideal of homogeneity thought the influx of immigrants endangered both the nation's social order and its cultural purity. For immigrants themselves, meanwhile, life in America often meant denying older cultural traditions and possibly losing one's identity.[13]

In a great paradox of modernity, the very cities that led to larger public communities held the potential for increasing individual alienation. And in what became a central paradox of wireless, the very technology that expanded the possibilities of public communication carried with it reminders of individual isolation. Through its early association with shipping, the sea, and distant lands, wireless evoked both the wonders of distant communication and a slight apprehension over the depthless and inescapable void the technology had revealed to the world. The ether was its own ocean, at once vast and diffuse, that beckoned explorers to navigate its unfathomable depths. This involved drifting through the spectrum in search of transmissions from the most distant points around the nation and globe, a journey traversed primarily across mysterious expanses of silence and static. Such exploration was described in these earliest years as the decidedly nautical practice of "DX fishing."

For the medium's vanguard users, DX fishing was radio's primary attraction, presenting a new form of telepresence so intriguing that, in the early days of the technology, wireless *contact* was of more interest than wireless *content*. Writing some forty years before Marshall McLuhan, a commentator for *Collier's Weekly* said of radio that "it is not the *substance* of communication without wires, but the *fact* of it that enthralls."[14] Beginning in the era of wireless and continuing into the early days of radio broadcasting, reception itself was the main attraction of the medium rather than the monotonous time codes, ship-to-shore relays, and other early, routine radio transmissions. Dedicated listeners often kept logs of what stations they had received, and a magazine like *Scientific American* could be sure to snare radio enthusiasts with as simple and self-evident a headline as, "Man Who Heard Washington in Hawaii."[15] The *Collier's* columnist discussed DX fishing as an addiction, describing himself as a "wandering Jew of the ether" and quipping that his first contact with radio represented "a compact with the Lord of Darkness, known in Dr. Faust's day as the devil, and now called DX. . . . You may be able to flirt successfully with morphine, but with DX — otherwise known as the Distant Stations — you toy at your exceeding peril."[16] The appeal of DX was so great that it even allowed American francophobes to tolerate the continental excesses of the Eiffel Tower, which as one writer noted, "for some time was regarded as a useless mass of iron, [but] is now proving itself of great service in the extension of wireless telegraphy."[17]

In what has become a predictable theme in the introduction of telecommunications technologies, most accounts of DX fishing lauded radio's miraculous ability to bring the vast expanses of the world into the cozy domestic space of the home. A passage from *Scribner's Magazine* typifies the many jubilant accounts of this merging of distant worlds with the privacy of home and hearth:

> Here we have sat in the little back bedroom in a home in Indiana, and, with not even a wire extending beyond the lot, have gone to Detroit and Pittsburgh for a musical treat, heard the boys talking all over America, caught some of the chatter between sea and shore, set our watches by Naval Observatory time, taken a lesson in French direct from the Eiffel tower, heard Panama and Hawaii, and a great chorus of others we did not stop to identify. The meaning of it all fairly staggers the mind. It is a great step out of the every-day into the sublime.[18]

Early accounts of wireless frequently celebrated this "sublime" paradox of distance, marveling at how the humble crystal set in the home could serve as a portal to the vast etheric ocean that enveloped the earth. Truly a mystical pleasure, DX fishing left the operator to ponder his or her own place in the face of this larger realm of invisible consciousness. "We have been toying with the intangible, the eerie something out of which Northern Lights are made, the ripples in the boundless vastness of space," offered the *Scribner's* columnist. "Who knows where it will lead us as we bend the mysterious forces to our call and read the thoughts flying on the wings of the ether?"[19]

From the medium's inception, however, these "mysterious forces" evoked lingering fears as well as fascination. "Toying with the intangible" may have provided operators with the unprecedented experience of eavesdropping on messages from thousands of miles away, but at the same time this paradox of presence that brought distant signals into the family garage could make for more unsettling forms of contact. Covert argues that the growth of wireless was "tinged by an uneasy impression that radio was . . . ominous and somehow foreboding"[20] and that it often led to a "strange new sense . . . of being one of an atomized mass."[21] Even the most enthusiastic accounts of radio's future often contained a subtext of potential despair and loneliness, an alienation rising from the medium's ability to separate and isolate even as it enabled contact and communication. In an otherwise enthusiastic prediction of wireless telegraphy's future as a medium of interpersonal communication, P. T. McGrath imagined an aural and social "ghostland" to be brought about by radio:

> If a person wanted to call a friend he knew not where, he would call in a very loud electromagnetic voice, heard by him who had the electromagnetic ear, silent to him who had it not. "Where are you?" he would ask. A small reply would come "I am in the bottom of a coal mine, or crossing the Andes, or in the middle of the Atlantic." Or, perhaps, in spite of all the calling, no reply would come, and the person would then know that his friend was dead. . . . It would be almost like dreamland and ghostland.[22]

There is a sadness in this vision of the coming radio "ghostland," an aural landscape where the fragile "small reply" of a distant friend struggles to be heard through the ether, and where the cessation of transmission indicates the death of a friend or loved one. Gathering voices from the sky through a filament no thicker than a "cat's whisker," radio could only remind listeners of how tiny and fragile the sparks of life and consciousness were in a social world that seemed to be shrinking even as the etheric ocean around it continued to expand beyond imagination. In the new sound world of wireless, the electromagnetic signal stood as a precarious conduit of consciousness and an indexical mark of existence — "I transmit; therefore I am."

Press coverage of wireless encouraged such somatic and even existential associations by focusing on the "uncanny" behavior and ambiguous status of radio, portraying the medium's oceanic presence as an omnipresent and inescapable force that could bathe and even occupy the body. Some believed the human body itself could function as an aerial or even a transmitter for these strange signals. "Some time ago an eminent physicist thought that he had discovered the emission of a special form of radiation

HUMAN CHAIN ACTING AS A RADIO ANTENNA

Illustrations in *Literary Digest* (1928) instructed readers in techniques they might use to "interact" with their new radio receivers.

by the human body; but the 'N' rays are still an unproved hypothesis,"[23] noted one reporter. Undeterred, the magazine went on to instruct readers on how to make a human chain serve as a radio antenna and how to electrify human hands (when clad in kid gloves) to serve as headset speakers. Even more uncanny were stories of wireless reception via everyday household objects, incidents that often appeared decidedly supernatural by imbuing inanimate items with the "living" voice of radio. In an item tagged "Electric Radio Ghosts," one magazine told of an elevator in Des Moines that would mysteriously play radio music and of a "singing" coal shovel in Sweden that aroused, we are told, much superstitious fear.[24] As late as 1935 an article on "weird electrical freaks" in *Popular Science,* meanwhile, pondered strange activities in Mason, Ohio, after the opening of a new five-hundred-thousand-watt transmitter for station WLW. "An ordinary waterspout at the corner of a farmhouse hums the strains of a symphony, or declaims a dramatic bit from a play. A tin roof, next door, makes political speeches, or bursts into song. Inquire among the farmers, and nearly all will tell you of hearing these mysterious, ghostly voices issuing from inanimate things."[25] Other items tell of a house perpetually "haunted" by radio signals and of a woman who fainted one morning in the bathroom after her mirror greeted her by saying hello (apparently the lead and glass in the bathroom had served as an antenna for a nearby station).[26] As popular knowledge of radio principles grew, Americans began to realize that they were all continually negotiating an invisible world of radio waves, whether they wanted to be or not, and that anything from a coal shovel to shoddy dental work could serve as a potential gateway into the mysterious realm of ether.

Fantastic accounts of wireless suggested hazards of disembodiment and dissipation lurking in these mysterious atmospheric oceans. Not only did the metaphor of the "etheric ocean" encourage the idea that one could become "lost at sea," but it also implied that, as with the oceans of the earth, unknown creatures might stalk this electronic sea's invisible depths. Published in 1902, the same year as McGrath's portrait of the coming radio "ghostland," Rudyard Kipling's short story "Wireless" was perhaps the first tale to explore this territory of isolation and despair in paranormal radio.[27] A man who accepts an invitation to see a demonstration of the century's new technology narrates Kipling's story. The wireless operator, Mr. Cashell Jr., attempts to send a radio signal from his uncle's store to a distant receiver across the English countryside. The true focus of the story, however, is on a young shopkeeper at the store named John Shaynor. Listening to Shaynor's hacking cough and rattling lungs, the narrator quickly surmises that the young man is dying of tuberculosis, although Shaynor will not admit this fate to himself. The narrator also observes that Shaynor is infatuated with a young girl named Fanny Brand. Watching them at a distance, the narrator sadly muses that Fanny will outlive Shaynor and will probably soon forget him. Later, after drinking a hot toddy in the room next door to Cashell's wireless, Shaynor slips into a trance. He begins to speak and then later write fragments of poetry by Keats. When recovered from his mysterious state, Shaynor claims to have never heard of Keats, much less know his poetry well enough to recite or transcribe it. The ambiguous tale ends with the mystery of this ghostly "transmission" placed in explicit parallel with the groundbreaking experiments of the nearby wireless operator. From where does this transmission emanate? Kipling provides no definitive explanation.

Kipling's tale was in many ways paradigmatic of the haunted wireless stories to follow, introducing the conventions that would typify the genre over the next thirty years. At the conclusion of this supernatural tale, for example, Kipling includes an interesting yet seemingly mundane passage describing two warships at sea unable to make wireless contact. Appearing just as Marconi succeeded in sending the first transatlantic signal, Kipling's story confirms that wireless, in its earliest days, was most often thought of as a nautical technology, providing radio's most explicit connection to the ocean. But Kipling's use of the sea goes beyond simple historical detail. In this tale, as in many to follow, the sea stands as both a medium and symbol of separation — a vast body that overwhelms the pathetic efforts of the would-be interlocutors aboard their tiny ships on the Atlantic. Through the associative power of the oceanic metaphor of presence, the story imbues the etheric ocean with a similar ability to engulf and disperse consciousness. The boundless ether allows radio signals to stray and wander, passing one another like "ships in the night." Interestingly, in this fantastic story about the wonders of wireless communication, the men in Cashell's shop spend most of their time engaged in failure, engrossed finally by the futile saga of ships and signals lost on their respective seas. This maritime exchange ends with a singularly bizarre sentiment as one ship signals, in closing, "disheartening, most disheartening," a communication made even more strange by the fact that the sender realizes his messages have failed to reach their target, much as Shaynor's attempts to connect with Fanny Brand remain fruitless and futile. The final communications between the boats and between Shaynor and Keats are less messages than lonely soliloquies offered to the very ocean that defeats and absorbs all attempts at interpersonal exchange. In the end only the mysterious transmission from the dead poet comes through loud and clear, emanating from a void Shaynor will soon be joining. Their communication links the medium to the final separation of death and the ultimate isolation of those on the earth below. "Our open casements facing desolate seas / Forlorn — forlorn —," writes Shaynor as Keats, and then later, "Our magic windows fronting on the sea / The dangerous foam of desolate seas . . . For aye."[28]

Although wireless applications quickly moved to shore in the first decade of the century, fantastic tales of wireless retained this fascination with the symbolic affinities between the forbidding oceans of water and ether. In John Wilson's story "Sparks," published in 1911, a woman urgently signals by wireless to her lover at sea with whom she has quarreled.[29] But in anger and pride the man at sea refuses to respond, not aware that his lover has discovered she is terminally ill. Unable to hail her love, the woman dies without the man ever knowing what is wrong. Years pass, and a witness to that woman's sad night, who serves as the tale's narrator, encounters the man again at sea. Tortured by his refusal to answer his lover in her time of need, the man has become a desperate figure. Later that

"Sparks": A dying woman attempts wireless
contact with her estranged lover. She later makes
contact from the "beyond." (*McClure's Magazine,*
1911)

night, as the two men talk in their cabin about a strange and powerful static
hovering over the Pacific, an eerie message comes through on the wireless. "I've been calling you, Harry, so long, so long, to tell you that I didn't
mean what I said, and for you to come back to me. . . . It killed me. . . . I
need you, Harry." Realizing it is a message from his dead lover, the
overwrought man taps out his own message on the wireless key, "O.K.
I'm coming." The tale ends with the narrator going to the ship's bridge to
inform the captain that "his wireless operator was dead."[30]

As in "Wireless," this tale employs the oceanic metaphor to full effect,
portraying ether and ocean as "moats" dividing the young lovers. But the
tale does more than simply equate the two oceans. Like many wireless
tales, "Sparks" generates its suspense by foregrounding the extreme discontinuity of experience in traveling each ocean's distinctive waves; that

is, the story's dramatic effect hinges on the ironic relationship between the two seas as equally vast bodies subject to quite different modes of navigation. Traversing significant distances on the watery ocean still took days at a time in 1911, slow progress that was becoming increasingly maddening in the age of the railroad and automobile. Traversing the etheric ocean, on the other hand, was instantaneous. Fantastic accounts of wireless frequently contrasted this disparity of time, using the sea as a narrative device to create a sense of panic, urgency, and frustration as the operator attempted, but often failed, to make successful instantaneous contact across the etheric ocean. Separated by thousands of miles, Harry could have instantly known about his lover's illness — and yet in the end both oceans prove equally daunting.

In his discussion of D. W. Griffith's 1908 film *The Lonely Villa,* Tom Gunning demonstrates how such themes were already in circulation around the telephone.[31] Stage and screen at the beginning of the century saw a number of productions that featured distraught husbands listening helplessly on the phone as intruders in the home attacked their families. Tales such as Wilson's "Sparks" translated these themes into the more mystical oceanic metaphors of wireless, exploiting the medium's historical connection to the sea to cultivate even more alienating themes of frustration, futility, and death. These oceanic themes of separation and simultaneity, however, found their most powerful and pervasive expression, not in a work of fiction, but on the front pages of the world's newspapers. The sinking of the *Titanic* concretized the potentially agonizing paradoxes of wireless like no other event, a disaster that seemed to confirm the most sinister suspicions of the new worlds created and accessed by radio. As is well known, the *Titanic* struck an iceberg on the night of 15 April 1912, taking more than fifteen hundred people to their death at the bottom of the Atlantic. Few disasters attained as immediate a symbolic weight as did the sinking of the *Titanic.* In the days following the catastrophe, the sad ironies of the *Titanic*'s fate demanded reflection, commentary, and interpretation to accompany the grim lists of victims and survivors. Promoted as the fastest, sturdiest, and most technologically advanced of all the world's ocean vessels, the *Titanic* was quickly laid low by a simple iceberg, a supreme human achievement utterly destroyed by the elemental forces of nature. As such, the vessel became a potent symbol of technological hubris and human vulnerability, a reminder that humanity's most impressive achievements were still subject to a higher law and judgment.

It also became a symbol of the accelerating hazards to be found in the otherwise exhilarating modern age. As Kern notes, "This generation had a strong, confident sense of the future, tempered by the concern that things were rushing much too fast. The *Titanic* symbolized both."[32]

Interestingly, accounts of the *Titanic* concentrated on the role of wireless in the aftermath of the catastrophe as much as on the disaster itself. As Douglas notes, the *Titanic*'s wireless operator, Harold Bride, became a national hero in the days following the disaster, the *New York Times* publishing Bride's personal account of the incident and his attempts to call for help.[33] At the same time, the amateur operators who filled the air in the wake of the ship's initial distress call were uniformly attacked by the press for cluttering the airwaves and making it difficult to receive accurate information concerning the ship and its fate. Through such mass coverage the concept of wireless found its largest audience ever, as a technology that had existed primarily in the abstract suddenly became inextricably and vividly bound to the public's imagination of a tangible disaster. In this context wireless forged an even stronger relationship with separation, death, and absence. As Douglas writes, "Although the ship had been drastically underequipped with lifeboats, and the captain had taken the ship too quickly through an ice field, wireless emerged as the invention that had both permitted many to survive and caused many more to die."[34]

Interest in the *Titanic* frequently centered, as did tales such as "Wireless" and "Sparks," on the fragility, futility, and frustration of radio communication. For example, in addition to the ship that responded to the *Titanic*'s SOS call, the *Carpathia,* two other ships that evening were in range to save passengers. But the *California* had shut down its wireless system for the night and did not learn of the disaster until the next morning, while another ship, the *Lena,* had no wireless system at all. Even the *Carpathia* responded only because its wireless operator had returned, by some twist of fate, well after his final shift to conduct a "time rush," a comparison of times on two ships to calibrate the clock. As the *Carpathia* returned with survivors, having signaled to shore of the disaster, it temporarily fell out of radio contact and was unable to transmit further details, providing the papers with another anecdote of wireless frustration. Much of the subsequent fascination with the *Titanic* tragedy centered on this series of missed or near-missed opportunities, as commentators alternately championed radio as the night's saving technology or bemoaned the sad accidents that allowed so many more passengers to die. The most tangible legacy of this fascination was the Radio Act of 1912, which provided stricter guidelines concerning maritime wireless designed to prevent such tragedies of missed communication in the future. But the *Titanic* left another legacy as well, forever imprinting on the mind's eye the image of unfortunate souls spread across the icy void of the Atlantic, struggling to stay above the surface. Above this tragic scene, in turn, hovered the eerie ocean of wireless, which had provided the agonizingly immediate account of the catastrophe even as it powerfully reiterated the gulf separating sender and receiver, victim and savior.

The nation's experience of World War I reinforced such oceanic associations between wireless, separation, and death. For many Americans, World War I represented the first time members of the family were compelled to be separated by vast distances for an indeterminate period of time. Families that had never sent children to Europe suddenly found their sons and daughters going overseas, possibly never to return. Crossing the Atlantic was for many soldiers, no doubt, like crossing the river Styx. The only contact families had with their children during this traumatic period was through a precarious relay of wireless and telegraphy. Such close contact to distant danger did little to reassure the home front, however. It only meant that bad news could now be instantaneous. Most dreaded was the black-bordered radiogram, the sign that a relative had died in the war, perhaps on that very day.

Not surprisingly, the war's electronically mediated paradoxes of immediacy and separation sparked a temporary resurgence of interest in Spiritualism and séances. The trauma of war, both on the battlefield and on the home front, inspired many tales of clairvoyance, ghostly combat, and soldiers speaking from beyond the grave.[35] When the son of the famous physicist Oliver Lodge died in battle, his father (a leading theorist in matters of ether and electricity) began to collect spiritualist communications that were eventually published in the widely read volume, *Raymond*.[36] Even more fascinating was the anonymously authored *Thy Son Liveth: Messages from a Soldier to His Mother*, published in 1918.[37] In this brief drama, a young American wireless enthusiast sent to France dies in battle, but then communicates with his mother through the wireless set left idle in his room at home. As with most spiritual messages from soldiers killed in the war, the son's message is one of peace and hope. He assures his grieving mother that he is still "alive"; only he now resides in the beautiful spirit land that awaits us all.

But the relationship between death and radio in World War I was not always so comforting. Kern observes that wireless made possible new and more impersonal relationships between soldiers and their commanders that led to unprecedented atrocities. "The distance between the fighting and the decision-making created an experiential and emotional gap between the generals and the men at the front that enabled commanders to continue to spin table-top plans for offensives and be shielded from direct contact with the disastrous results."[38] Orchestrated and reported by wireless, the appalling spectacle of trench warfare implicated the medium in another void of modernity, the barren expanses of what came to be called "No-Man's Land." Perhaps no single spectacle encapsulated the horrors of the new century and its new technologies better than the devastation of trench warfare. And, as with the *Titanic,* radio seemed to watch over this scene of death impassively. By decade's end wireless had thus brought the American public modernity's two most macabre ascensions, suggesting that souls rising from their watery grave in the Atlantic or from the trenches along the Siegfried line had evaporated into the flowing ether, perhaps to be retrieved by wireless or perhaps to wander forever. So strong were these associations between wireless and discorporated death, stories of the DX dead continued to circulate after the war's end and well past radio's boom year of 1922, surviving even in wireless's conversion to broadcasting. At one point in the mid-twenties, for example, the decidedly eerie DX practice of "ghost broadcasting" came into vogue. An incredulous reporter explains, "The method used in broadcasting the shades is to turn on the microphone and, with the studio doors locked and no one in the room, to listen for mysterious sounds on the station carrier, which is assumed to be quiet."[39] It is difficult to say how popular this form of "dead air" was with the listening public.

Mental Radio

Complementing these tales of the etheric ocean as a place of the dead were accounts of wireless as a medium of telepathy. In this case DX fishing meant tuning in the mental telecasts of friends and lovers who were far away. Although believing in contact with the dead may have been patently incredible, radio's demonstrable ability to transmute consciousness into electrical signals and back again seemed to provide an empirical foundation for telepathic possibilities. As one commentator on radio observed,

"There seemed something uncanny, something savoring of telepathy, something which did not obey the recognized rules that have been derived in other fields, in these long-distance communications."[40] When respected journalist and writer Upton Sinclair published accounts of telepathy experiments with his wife, he chose a succinct title that would have made intuitive sense to his contemporary audience — "Mental Radio." In perhaps the ultimate scientific validation of this research, Sinclair's book featured a laudatory preface by Albert Einstein, who noted that the book deserved "the most earnest consideration."[41]

The relationship hypothesized between wireless and telepathy inspired a flurry of scientific theorization and experimentation in the first years of the century. Many believed the age-old human mysteries of disembodied consciousness — telepathy, clairvoyance, intuition — were to be resolved in a careful study of the ether and its various natural and supernatural wave forms. Just such a project was undertaken by Sir William Crookes, who proposed that telepathic thought existed as high-frequency vibrations, not unlike radio and light waves. "It may be," wrote Crookes, "that [x-rays] and the radium waves are only the threshold of the wonders of the unseen universe. . . . If communications of spirits are through vibrations of ether or in some still more subtle substance, we should have in this a possible explanation of telepathy."[42] Articles such as "Analogy between Wireless Telegraphy and Waves from Brain to Brain" continued to explore this possible "scientific" relationship between telepathy and radio into the next decade.[43] In 1921 Frank Podmore, another prominent commentator on Spiritualism, proposed a theory that ghosts were not spirits of the dead, but the product of "telepathic hallucinations" between sympathetic minds. "We know . . . that there are gaps in the scale of ethereal vibrations," wrote Podmore, citing Crookes. Imagining telepathy and ghosts as a mysterious form of radio transmission, Podmore conjectured that "there is nothing to forbid the supposition that one or the other of these gaps may hereafter be found to be filled by undulations competent to convey intelligence from one brain to another."[44]

In September of 1929, famed psychic and paranormal researcher Joseph Dunninger sat behind a microphone at NBC studios in New York as the host of the "Ghost Hour," an experiment in mental telepathy using the now nationwide audience of radio broadcasting. Over the course of the hour, Dunninger sat in silence, projecting three thoughts across the airwaves: the name "Lincoln"; the number "379"; and the image of a small house

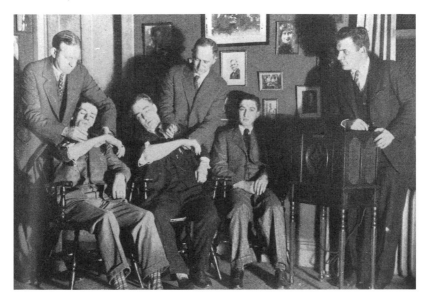

Hypnotism by radio: A photo from the June 1927 issue of *Popular Radio* provided more evidence of the medium's fundamentally uncanny powers.

consisting of four windows, one door, a triangular roof, and chimney. In the weeks following the experiment, NBC received over two thousand letters from all areas of the country and reported that over 55 percent had some part of the thoughts correct.[45] Whether or not one chooses to believe NBC's admittedly self-serving promotion of the event, the "Ghost Hour" testifies that as radio entered the age of network broadcasting, the idea that radio waves were in some way analogous to "thought waves" still had great purchase in the American imagination.

As with the premise of the DX dead, speculative writers of the period produced many tales of wireless telepathy and mental control, ranging from the farcical to the sublime. In "The Celebrated Pilkey Radio Case," for example, a young couple is rehearsing their marriage ceremony when suddenly the groom begins barking like a dog. Convinced he is a "rathound," the groom proceeds to dig holes in the garden, fight dogs, and chase rats, all to the horror of the wedding party. In the end they discover that the groom has been accidentally mesmerized by a radio hypnotist, who in turn finally de-hypnotizes the young man.[46] In "The Voice of the People" a movie idol lapses into a coma. After several conventional attempts to revive him fail, the star's girlfriend devises a more innovative plan. She asks the star's fans to all assemble at movie theaters at a specified time and, via a radio cue, project their collective thoughts urging the idol to awaken. This too fails, but in the process an engineer detects a strange signal. He traces an ultrasonic wave to the idol's screen rival, who has devised a method of broadcasting a "sleep signal." The star soon recovers.[47] Other telepathy stories, however, returned readers to the depthless metaphysical mysteries of the etheric ocean. In "Out of the Air," for example, the narrator walks along an island beach at night, where he sees a "sensitive" girl, Eileen, standing in the distance:

> Some riddle seemed to beset her, filled the air about her — some inarticulate cry, you might say, elusive, impalpable, afloat in the ether. And with her arms flung wide, it was as if she were resolved to tear that riddle from the air by some occult process . . . her sensitive fingers spread out, attuned to things beyond mortal comprehension. Like antennae — was my odd thought at that moment, suggested doubtless by the stricken wireless tower just beyond her — stark against the leaden sky like her own palpitant, expectant figure.[48]

Once again utilizing the familiar motifs of the sea and separation to cultivate suspense, "Out of the Air" imagined an invisible realm saturated with stray thought waves wandering through the atmosphere to be captured by a human aerial. "Yes, she was like that — just that . . . energized by some mysterious power outside of herself, attuned to harmonies of the ether that we mortals never hear."[49]

Many tales of wireless and telepathy centered on separated lovers. The romantic couple, of course, is a convention of much popular fiction, and stories such as "Wooed by Wireless" (1908) and "Wireless Elopement" (1907) had already linked the emerging technology to new modes of courtship in the century's earliest years. This technology seemed a logical mode of interaction for modern lovers, men and women who now had more choice in selecting potential mates than previous generations. But haunted tales of wireless telegraphy employed the romantic couple strategically, exploiting them as the most productive site to engage the isolating properties of the medium as a whole. Although many stories played on the novelty of radio as a facilitator of romance, in other words, these tales employed wireless as a device of tragic, or at least bittersweet, separation. These tales frequently attached misfortune and loss to radio's binaries of

The "sensitive Eileen" stands before the "stricken
wireless tower . . . attuned to harmonies of the ether that
we mortals never hear." (*Harper's,* September 1922)

presence and absence, intimacy and distance, rendering the most intimate
of all interpersonal contact into the most remote of transactions.

Even the most crudely plotted of these stories appearing in otherwise
adolescent and decidedly "unromantic" pulps such as *Weird Tales* often
cast the romantic couple as a narrative focus. In "The Experiment of Erich
Weigert," for example, a story billed as "a startling tale of thought transmission by radio," an evil scientist connects his wife and her suitor to
radio sets in different rooms to test for telepathic communications. In a
gruesome final experiment, the jealous scientist kills his wife so that her

aspiring lover may experience the agony of "reading" her dying thoughts of love. Afterward, as he shows the man his now dead wife, still connected to the radio set by a series of electrodes in the skull, the evil genius remarks, "The sending must be done, at least with the crude apparatus I have, direct from the emanating source. And that, of course, is — *the brain!*"[50] The central irony in this story is that the lover's union can take place only at a distance and that its telepathic consummation results in the woman's death. Radio thus stands once more as a device promoting profound separation over intimate communication, putting into terms of pulp dramaturgy the potentially alienating nature of all radio communication.

A more involved tale of radio, telepathy, death, and romance is Clinton Dangerfield's "The Message."[51] This story is narrated by a priest who sits with a condemned man, George McMorrow, on the night of his execution. As they await the final hour, the radio in the jail cell mysteriously turns itself on. A voice fades in and out, saying, "a hard time . . . a hard time fighting for wave control . . . don't turn it off . . . very difficult to get wave control." The voice on the radio is that of the prisoner's lover, Alma Fielding. She tells him that he must make a choice. She has knowledge that the governor has found evidence of George's innocence and plans to pardon him. A messenger is on his way to the prison with a pardon in hand.[52] If George wants to, Alma says, he can live the rest of his life as a free man. But there is a catch. He will be without his beloved Alma. She tells him that she can speak to him on the radio because she is now dead, having been killed in a railroad accident earlier in the evening. She then presents a second choice. Alma says that she can telepathically distract the messenger with the pardon so that he is too late, and George would be executed as planned. He would then be able to be reunited for eternity with Alma that very evening. The priest thinks to himself that Alma is still alive and has dreamed up this elaborate and technically complex scheme to provide hope to her lover in his last moments on earth. After deliberating, George chooses to be executed. He dies serenely. A few moments later the pardon does arrive from the governor, as well as the news of Alma's death in the train wreck, proving to the astonished priest (and reader) that her story was indeed true.

One can only wonder what readers were supposed to feel at the end of these tales. Was it the sadness brought about by a tragedy of separation or the joy of lovers reunited? Many of these tales ended in ambivalence —

romantic unions are made, but only after the lovers suffer the pain of distant and decisive separation. Even when radio does bring the lovers together, however, it ultimately underscores the distance between them, suggesting a terrifying gulf that separates all social beings. This is perhaps the core of the terrifying fascination underlying the nation's obsessions with DX fishing and the etheric ocean. Long-distance radio communication may have created new and expansive electronic communities, linking amateur operators, fledgling stations, and casual listeners; but it also served as a reminder of the individual listener's separation and even alienation from this larger social world. These tales of ghosts, telepathy, and tragic love portray a world where radio promises a tantalizing sense of inclusion and belonging, and yet also present a phantom realm that casts the solitary listener adrift on the lonely etheric ocean.

Edison's Ghosts

For a few worried souls, radio's uncanny liberation of the body in time and space seemed not only alienating, but also absolutely blasphemous. As one commentator protested, "When John Jones is in the middle of the ocean, John Jones is in the middle of the ocean, and it is not for you and not for me to talk to him. Why annihilate time and space impertinently?"[53] It was in the midst of such swirling electronic, social, and moral uncertainties that Thomas Edison conceived the theoretical foundations for his device to contact the dead. Confronting the accelerating tensions and social disintegration of the modern era, Edison's project rested on the comforting premise that the unique individual, despite living amid modernity's often annihilating forces, would survive intact in the afterlife. "I am working on the theory that our personality exists after what we call life leaves our present material bodies," said Edison in a 1920 interview. "If our personality dies, what's the use of a hereafter? What would it amount to? It wouldn't mean anything to us as individuals. If there is a hereafter which is to do us any good, we want our personality to survive, don't we?"[54] Building on this premise that our thought structures remain the same even after the body has wasted away, Edison imagined an entire physics of discorporated consciousness that eerily attempted to reconcile fears of discorporative anonymity with a reassuring survival of the autonomous individual. As Edison writes,

Take our own bodies. I believe they are composed of myriads and myriads of infinitesimally small individuals, each in itself a unit of life, and that these units work in squads — or swarms, as I prefer to call them — and that these infinitesimally small units live forever. . . . These life units are, of course, so infinitely small that probably a thousand of them aggregated together would not become visible under even the ultra-microscope, the most powerful magnifying instrument yet invented and constructed by man. These units, if they are as tiny as I believe them to be, would pass through a wall of stone or concrete almost as easily as they would pass through the air. (11)

Edison believed these discorporated and quite literally atomized "swarms" would retain social relations established on earth. "The probability is that among units of life there are certain swarms which do most of the thinking and directing of the other swarms," Edison argued. "In other words, there are probably bosses, or leaders, among them, just as among humans" (11). For those who felt lost in the new century, Edison's dream of cohesion, order, and hierarchy no doubt provided a comforting alternative to the prevailing supernatural discourses of dispersal and dissipation.

Although Edison would probably have discounted the influence of Marconi's invention on his own thought, it is difficult to imagine such a theory of the afterlife before the invention of wireless. Evoking radio's fundamentally unsettling paradoxes of presence within absence, isolation within community, and intimacy within separation, Edison's device, like tales of the DX dead and wireless telepathy, cast an oceanic void around the globe as an indeterminate body where electrified consciousness could ebb and flow. But Edison's theory spoke to a dream of retaining one's individuality (and even social status) in a world that was increasingly a realm of anonymity and dissipation. When perfected, his apparatus was to offer a guarantee that at the moment of death, our electromagnetic consciousness would not simply evaporate and drift away, but would remain decidedly material, unified, and coherent, even in the face of the etheric ocean's infinitude. Like many other occult stories inspired by wireless phenomena, Edison's vision of the soul attempted to come to terms with the unnerving empirical evidence of radio, a technology that provided an almost daily reminder of the tenuous link between bodies and consciousness. In a world still separated by vast oceans of water and yet only recently joined through an ocean of electromagnetic waves, Edison's apparatus was a fitting response to these troubling uncertainties of modernity and a testament to the uncanny convergence of consciousness and technology seemingly intrinsic to all forms of electronic media.

Rather than bringing an end to this paranormal speculation, Edison's peculiar machine served as the conceptual and technological catalyst for a shadow history of telecommunications that continues to this day. Born in the wake of radio's discarnate voices and in the full hubris of modernity, Edison's project survives in each new generation of electronic telecommunications technology that sounds an echo of this original voice from the void, defying once again corporeal common sense and encouraging speculation that the technology's power to transmute and transmit might be more than a metaphor. Each new communications technology seems to evoke as well the nervous ambivalence of wireless, a simultaneous desire and dread of actually making such extraordinary forms of contact.

Much as Samuel Morse's death led to his frequent manifestations in the communications of spiritual telegraphy in the nineteenth century, the spirit of Edison is alleged to have advised many mortal inventors of this century in the continuing quest to perfect an electronic device to contact the dead. In 1941, for example, the spirit of Edison (as channeled through the medium of Mary Olson) is said to have contacted J. Gilbert Wright, who, conveniently enough, already worked as a researcher at General Electric. Wright and his partner, Harry Gardner, claimed that Edison told them about the machine he had been working on at the time of his own death, and informed the two men where they could find the long-lost blueprints for the unrealized device. Gardner and Wright eventually found the missing plans and built the Edison apparatus. They could not make it work. Later, however, they went on to devise a machine of their own design utilizing a small "sound box," a microphone, and loudspeaker.[55] Still at the cutting edge of such technology, Edison is said to have offered helpful suggestions along the way.

In the 1960s, British electrical researcher Mark Dyne constructed a system using a Morse buzzer and lamp. Echoing Crookes's theories at the turn of the century, Dyne argued, "Just as ordinary radio and TV signals are unseen vibrations through the air, so I believe there are disturbances in the ether caused by the spirit world." Like so many before him, Dyne proposed a commonsense solution that was simple and straightforward. "All we have to do is to find the wave length and frequency and we shall be able to pick them up."[56] Dyne's comments demonstrate that the question guiding such research, even at the dawn of the computer age, was not *if* electronics could be used to contact the dead, but rather *how* they would be used. The affinity of spirits and electricity remained unquestioned, as did the search for a technological bridge between the two worlds.

Moving beyond attempts at merely contacting the dead, artist Attila von Szalay claimed to be the first researcher to actually record the discarnate voices of the spirit world. Von Szalay's quest began in 1936, while he worked in his darkroom. He claimed to hear in this darkened chamber the voice of his deceased brother calling his name. A subsequent interest in Yoga, mediation, and Eastern philosophy made him better able to hear such voices, and in 1941 he attempted for the first time to record the spirits on a 78 rpm record (with disappointing results). It wasn't until 1956 that von Szalay "successfully" recorded such phenomena, this time using a reel-to-reel tape recorder. Perhaps unaware of their importance in the history of telecommunications, the first recorded spirit voices offered such banal messages as "This is G!," "Hot dog, Art!," and "Merry Christmas and Happy New Year to you all."[57] These pioneering sessions were reported by noted psychic researcher Raymond Baylass in a letter to the *Journal of the American Society for Psychical Research* in 1959.

Also in the late 1950s, Friedrich Jürgenson, a Swedish painter and documentary filmmaker, put a microphone and tape recorder at his open window to record birds singing in his garden. Playing the tape later, Jürgenson claimed to have heard his dead father's voice and then the spirit of his deceased wife calling his name. After four years of experiments taping what he believed to be the voices of the dead, Jürgenson held an international press conference and announced his startling discovery to the world. His 1967 book *Radio Contact with the Dead* detailed Jürgenson's work in using a standard radio receiver to make spiritual contact, confirming once again the world's intuitive investment in the uncanny qualities of the electromagnetic spectrum. Susy Smith describes Jürgenson's work with radio in more detail:

> Almost from the very beginning, one voice on Jürgenson's tapes kept saying, "Make contact through radio." This was a woman, and she was most insistent, so after about a year he tried radio and succeeded. Jürgenson now uses a technique that he calls the "interfrequency method," based on radio reception. Using a standard broadcast AM receiver, Jürgenson sets the tuning to receive an unmodulated carrier signal. Such a signal is equivalent to

a radio frequency transmission with no audio signal impressed upon it. Through the radio receiver, an unmodulated carrier signal sounds like white noise contrasting slightly with the normal static background found between stations. . . . Except when his voices are manifesting, there is only quiet hissing — no music, talking, or other broadcast frequencies. With this technique he has a clear form of communication, a dialogue, questions and answers.[58]

Through his role as a documentary filmmaker, Jürgenson later worked on a film about Pope Paul VI. During his time at the Vatican, Jürgenson claimed to have discussed the paranormal radio phenomena with the pope, as well as many cardinals and archbishops, all of whom were said to be quite interested and sympathetic to Jürgenson's work.[59]

Von Szalay and Jürgenson may have been the first to stumble on this method of supernatural contact, but the greatest popularizer of the recorded spirit voices was to be Dr. Konstantin Raudive, a Latvian philosopher, psychologist, and university professor who had studied at Oxford University and with Carl Jung in Switzerland. Raudive had read Jürgenson's book, and after attending recording sessions with Jürgenson to see the phenomenon firsthand, he began his own series of experiments in the late 1960s. His results were eventually published in the German volume *Unhoerbares Wird Hoerbar* (The inaudible made audible), which was translated and published in the United States in 1971 as *Break Through: Electronic Communication with the Dead May Be Possible.*[60] Raudive's widely read book would inspire psychic researchers around the world, both amateur and professional, to investigate what became known popularly as "electronic voice phenomena" or, as it is most frequently referred to in psychic circles today, "EVP."[61]

Like Jürgenson's, Raudive's initial method involved using a microphone and tape recorder to record the ambient sound in an apparently empty room. The experimenter then replayed the ten-to-fifteen-minute section of tape several times, listening very closely for voices that emerged only with intense scrutiny and concentration. Again following Jürgenson, Raudive eventually moved to radio as a way of intensifying the phenomenon and even engaging the spirit voices in dialogue. In a nod to their Spiritualist heritage, both men claimed the presence of a "mediating voice" on the other side was necessary to instruct the experimenter on exactly how to proceed via radio. As Raudive notes, "I was able to hear

Jürgenson's mysterious 'mediator' on one of his tapes. She asked him to wait for the recording till 9 p.m.; hints about people and events also came through in her strangely hissing voice."[62] Raudive had to wait six months before such a mediator emerged in his own tapes, allowing him to make the transition from microphone to radio recordings. Under the guidance of an entity named "Spidola," Raudive would tune slowly "from one end of the wavelength-scale to the other," listening carefully "for a voice that [would] hiss 'Now,' or 'Make recording!', or some such hint" (23). In other experiments, Raudive used Jürgenson's interfrequency method, tuning to and recording an empty wavelength for later playback.

Over the course of his research, Raudive found the medium of radio to be a favored form of contact.[63] Writing of the radio voices, Raudive observed, "They differ from microphone-voices in that their pronunciation is clearer and their messages are longer and have more meaning."[64] Even more incredibly, Raudive claimed that "the voices themselves have expressed right from the start a preference for radio-recordings." *Break Through* provides a transcript of recording sessions in which various spirit voices make their format preferences known.

"Please radio!"
"Bit by bit only through radio."
"Just let the radio loose!"
"Better through radio!"
"Speak through the radio! Kosti, you are the gate!"
"Through the radio."
"What a rascal, switch on the radio!" (171)

Harkening back once again to the early days of Spiritualism, Raudive even claimed to have evidence that spirits in the afterlife had their own technologies and broadcasting techniques for contacting our world. "The astonishing conception that 'other-worldly' transmitting-stations exist," notes Raudive, "emerges quite clearly from many of the voices' statements. Information received indicates that there are various groups of voice-entities who operate their own stations" (174). In particular, Raudive made frequent contact with two such stations, which he designated "Studio Kelpe" and "Radio Peter."

In his recordings, Raudive distinguished A-, B-, and C-quality voices, depending on their volume and intelligibility, and kept elaborate transcripts of what the spirits had to say. Interpreting the voices was not an

Konstantin Raudive demonstrates a modified
radio device used to hear the voices of the dead.
(Leif Geiges, Staufen, Germany)

easy task. In addition to their faintness against the background noise of the
recording, the voices also had several strange characteristics that made
their interpretation difficult. Raudive summarizes these challenges:

1. The voice-entities speak very rapidly, in a mixture of languages,
   sometimes as many as five or six in one sentence.
2. They speak in a definite rhythm, which seems to be forced upon them
   by the means of communication they employ.
3. The rhythmic mode of speech imposes a shortened, telegram-style
   phrase or sentence.
4. Presumably arising from these restrictions, grammatical rules are
   frequently abandoned and neologisms abound. (31–32)

Such difficulties testify either to the genuinely mysterious complexity of
spiritual communications or to the number of allowances Raudive was
willing to make to convince himself of the reality of such communica-

tions. As a consequence of these conditions, hearing the spirit voices required a trained, patient, multilingual, and, perhaps most important, willing ear. Raudive worked alone and with collaborators and is said to have made many converts of skeptical theologians, physicists, and electrical engineers, all of whom have vouched for the genuinely supernatural (or at least preternatural) source of these transmissions. So convincing was the technical evidence, apparently, that Raudive made converts even though the telegraphic and polyglot speech of the voices frequently generated statements that bordered on the surreal. "Jetzt-jetzt vilka! Ich will gaisa," says a spirit in a mix of German and Latvian, translating in English to "Now, now she-wolf! I want air" (220). "Pistole musu cilveks" (Pistol is our man), offers another (153). Finally, a spirit advises inexplicably, "Atnes Heilbuti!" (Bring a halibut!) (155).

Beyond such fleeting non sequiturs, what do these broadcasters of the afterlife have to tell us? Have they found eternal peace and happiness? Sadly, the answer would seem to be no. Indicative, again, of the increasingly chaotic world that must be negotiated by the century's living citizens, the Raudive voices tell of entities that often seem lost and confused. Heard as hissing channeled through radio or as whispers caught on tape, these entities remain somehow attached to earthly life and yet forever in exile as interstitial beings that are neither body nor spirit. When Raudive remarks that "the soul is free of the body after death," a forlorn spirit replies, "Ta nav, Kosti" (It is not so, Kosti) (137). In these often troubling fragments, electronic voice phenomena describe an afterlife that continues to serve as an anxious mirror to the modern world and its uncertainties. Raudive's voices hint that there is no peace, no resolution, no wisdom in death. There is only continuing strife and the terrifying phenomenon of interstitial uncertainty, a disassociation of mind, body, and spirit that seems impossible to reintegrate. Indeed, it is difficult to read the transcripts of Raudive's radio conversations with the dead without thinking of the formless narrator of Samuel Beckett's *The Unnamable,* who begins his own story of dissipation by asking, "Where now? Who now? When now? I, say I. Unbelieving."[65] A now nameless entity lost in time, lost in space, lost in identity, and no longer certain of the line dividing life and death, Beckett's narrator concludes his tale: "It will be I, it will be the silence, where I am, I don't know, I'll never know, in the silence you don't know, you must go on, I can't go on, I'll go on."[66] With similar despair, a spirit voice calls out to Raudive, "Here is night brothers, here the birds burn.

Kostja, you are far away."[67] "We suffer," says a forlorn spirit, while another adds ominously, "Ah, there are penalties here" (156).

There are, of course, any number of rational explanations one might offer for these allegedly paranormal phenomena, and any number of motivations to which one could attribute the interpretations of the radio voices made by Raudive and others. Interference, circuitry problems, and scrambled reception were among the theories offered by sound engineers. The most persistent attacks on Raudive's work, however, came not from the science of electronics but from the fields of psychology and psychoanalysis. Those psychologists who did comment on the phenomenon attributed EVP to the unconscious mind of the experimenter. These skeptics believed the psychic researchers who listened so deliberately to these tapes over and over again were merely projecting their own fears and desires onto the hissing static, fashioning "spirit voices" from the debris of their own psyche and, in the end, hearing what they wanted to hear.

Confronted with this Freudian assault, Raudive defended himself through a most audacious strategy. Raudive defiantly answered his critics by dismissing the "unconscious" itself as a "scientific fiction," likening its role in psychology to that of the ether in premodern physics (6–7). Confronted with the monumental cultural authority of Freud, Raudive proclaimed his own position with equal conviction, writing that "the apparently acceptable supposition of an 'unconscious' fails immediately when we are faced with a new reality, namely *post-mortal life*" (8). Although Raudive never really explained why the unconscious and the afterlife are mutually exclusive concepts, his comments do invite an interesting comparison between his own necromantic science and Freud's science of the mind, one that reveals a certain shared project and many provocative parallels. Both Freud and Raudive, for example, were in their own way interested in contacting "voices from the void." Raudive's kingdom of the dead revealed itself through the analysis of multilingual neologisms, Freud's unconscious through the interpretation of the abstract and often baffling logic of dreams. In each case, however, the analyst's task was to combat resistance (electrical or interpersonal) in order to access complex, condensed, and frequently distorted language, all in an effort to better understand the life of a secreted, phantom realm. In probing their respective occult silences, each was interested as well in language as a key for liberating hidden entities, be they the personal "ghosts" of a lone subject's mind or the despairing spirits of a shared afterlife.

Although there was no direct intellectual contact between the two men, of course, these parallels suggest a strange reciprocity between the two "analysts" in terms of their mutual interest in the rather occult mysteries of human subjectivity. Their respective "sciences" for confronting these mysteries, however, place them at opposite ends of the newfound technologies and attendant anxieties of the modern age. As is well known, Freud began his career as a devout mechanist, believing that all mental life depended in some way on the mechanical circuitry of the brain. His work on hysteria and his ever-developing theory of the unconscious eventually led him away from this position, arguing instead that bodily symptoms could have purely psychological causes. Freud's eventual formulation of the divided subject, an entity haunted by a mysterious realm in the psyche that forever denies the subject a unity of self-presence, is perhaps the foundational and most terrifying of all modernity's many voids. Charles Darwin, as many have noted, dethroned humankind's sense of itself as a unique and separate species. Freud went one traumatic step further by destroying the comforting illusion of a sovereign consciousness. Fleeing the mechanist belief that mental dysfunction could be eradicated through wholly physical intervention, Freud proposed a more mysterious and often disconcerting model of what seemed at times a willfully unfathomable psyche.

The spiritual hope (and mortal trepidation) raised by Raudive's voices, on the other hand, can be seen as one of many responses to modernity's increasingly unsettling model of the subject. Even if their messages were often bleak, the Raudive voices did speak of an immortal essence that transcends the alienating models of Darwin, Freud, Sartre, and all other demystifying assaults on the transcendental dimension of the human psyche. The irony, of course, is that Raudive remystified the soul through the validating authority of an electronic technology. Freud himself, no doubt, would have dismissed Raudive's search for immortal life in much the same way he condemned the traditional religions.[68] Possessed by the powerful cultural mythology of electronic presence, however, Raudive and his followers argued that radio contact with the dead was much more plausible than breaching hidden walls of the mind. In this respect, Freud's project — not Raudive's — seemed the one hopelessly mired in metaphysics and the occult. In the search for a successful "break through," radio and tape technology at least offered some form of tangible evidence, however suspect, that was available for putatively "objective" material analysis.

At their core, both of these "interpretive" sciences shared the hope that their practices could overcome the trauma of a profound loss. They sought to repair a decisive moment of separation — either in the founding moment of psychic repression or the final moment of bodily death — that left "conscious" subjects abandoned and alone. This mutual though antagonistic interest in the occluded mysteries of human subjectivity suggests that "electronic voice phenomena" and the "talking cure" might be closer conceptual cousins than either analyst would care to admit, in goal at least if not in actual model and method. I would argue the very possibility of EVP (and psychoanalysis to some degree) remains fascinating because it evokes this general estrangement of consciousness, be it through theory or technology, even as it promises the individual subject's eventual reconstitution. EVP remains an intuitively reasonable possibility in the popular imagination — even one hundred years after Marconi's first experiments in wireless — because the disassociative powers of electronic telecommunications technology remain so uncanny and the abysses of the modern age remain so palpable. There is a distinct lineage in the electronic metaphysics of technological disembodiment that links the tradition of the Spiritualists, Crookes, Lodge, and Edison with the more "modern" practices of EVP. But there is also an underlying anxiety, cultivated in the age of wireless, that profoundly divides these visions of electronic presence. In contrast to the almost always comforting messages channeled through Spiritualist technology in the nineteenth century, EVP as a "therapeutic" discourse, like psychoanalysis, promises healing revelation and reintegration only after opening the terrifying void that surrounds the modern psyche. One might say in this respect that although the technophilic dream of electronically contacting the dead has not died, the hopes of finding a unified and coherent spirit body have been for the most part shattered.[69] Or, as one of Raudive's voices comments from the more troubling afterlife of modernity, "Secret reports. . . . It is bad here."[70]

3 Alien Ether

Wherever streams of consciousness and electrons converge in the cultural imagination, there lies a potential conduit to an electronic elsewhere that, even as it evokes the specter of the void, also holds the promise of a higher form of consciousness, one that promises to evade the often annihilating powers of our technologies and transcend the now materially demystified machine that is the human body. Ghosts, however, are not the only entities to haunt the history of electronic telecommunications. Over the course of the century, American popular culture has demonstrated a similar fascination for another form of "unearthly" communications. A. G. Birch's serialized novella of 1922, *The Moon Terror,* begins with a wireless mystery:

> At twelve minutes past 3 o'clock a.m. during a lull in the night's aerial telegraph business, several of the larger wireless stations of the Western Hemisphere simultaneously began picking up strange signals out of the ether. They were faint and ghostly, as if coming from a vast distance — equally far removed from New York and San Francisco, Juneau and Panama.
>
> Exactly two minutes apart the calls were repeated, with clocklike regularity. But the code used — if it *were* a code — was indecipherable.[1]

Scientists are concerned because no one can trace the origin of these transmissions, nor can they decode them. When they speculate the signals are from outer space, a growing sense of dread and panic grips the nation. Who (or what) is transmitting these signals, and for what purpose? Exploiting once again the mysterious presence associated with early wireless technology, Birch uses the now familiar device of the unexplained alien transmission to imply a potentially sinister force enveloping and maybe even threatening the world. In this particular tale of "strange signals out of the ether," however, the indecipherable code signifies the existence of a material intelligence — a creature of superscience rather than of the supernatural. The beacon radiates as the signature of a civilization freely traveling the farthest reaches of the etheric ocean and beyond. This alien signal that permeates the atmosphere, from "New York and San Francisco" to "Juneau and Panama," makes *The Moon Terror* an anxious story, not only of radio, but also of the then emerging practice of broadcasting.[2]

The Moon Terror's tale of alien transmission appeared at a time when the institution of radio was in the midst of a major transformation. Most media historians designate 1922 as the year radio exploded into a national sensation. During the early 1920s, as radio's transmission of music and voice finally replaced the invisible dots and dashes of wireless telegraphy, this tinkerer's technology moved from the garage and attic into the family living room. Military and amateur applications gave way to commercial exploitation as the institution of broadcasting displaced a medium previously confined to point-to-point communication. It was in this pivotal decade of the twenties that radio became, in Bertolt Brecht's words, "primarily a system of distribution" and no longer a means of true "communication."[3] A decade that began in confusion over jurisdiction, application, and implementation of the new medium ended with the orderly ascension of "chain broadcasting" and network control.

The transition from amateur wireless to corporate broadcasting represented more than a change in ownership and spectrum allocation. The move from point-to-point radio communication to a system of mass broadcasting represented as well a fundamental *experiential* change in the institution of radio. And as the institution, apparatus, and experience of radio changed with the advent of network broadcasting, so too did its qualities of electronic "presence." The early fantasy of contacting ghostly consciousness via wireless had played on the initial fascination with radio as a form of electronically disembodied consciousness, calling to earth across the void of space or through the void of eternity. Such forms of paranormal radio presence suggested access to an unseen and fleeting order of consciousness lost in the ether. With the growth of broadcasting, however, the once spectral presence of radio no longer appeared as a mysterious "voice from the void," becoming instead the familiar "live" and "living" voices of the national networks. Domesticated through the broadcast schedule, the radio signal was no longer an elusive and uncanny presence as it saturated the entire atmosphere and blanketed the social body. And yet, although the technology and phenomenon of radio broadcasting were no longer sources of amazement in and of themselves, they did provide access to a newly realized, often amazing, and potentially threatening public sphere. In this new listening environment, engaging the presence of radio no longer meant searching for stray voices in the ether, but implied joining a nation of listeners in the simultaneous consumption of broadcast culture. As the fleeting transmissions of wireless — stray messages traversing the depths of the etheric ocean — were driven out by the routine and virtually omnipresent signals of broadcasting, the ether became less a free-flowing ocean and more like a net or blanket.

Although Americans may have offered little in the way of organized resistance to the encroachment of the network system, signs of dismay, disenchantment, and apprehension over the institution of broadcasting nevertheless pervaded popular culture. Magazines aimed at early radio enthusiasts, for example, such as Hugo Gernsback's *Radio News,* provided a pessimistic commentary on broadcasting's gradual entrenchment as it continued to champion the increasingly lost cause of amateur radio. Educational and religious organizations, meanwhile, issued challenges to commercial broadcasting and met with limited success in raising debates over the philosophical foundations of broadcasting and its national mandate. Such concerns even took legislative form — albeit in a highly compromised fashion — in federal regulations of the 1920s and 1930s that defined the airwaves as a "public resource" and required broadcasters to be "licensed" by the government.

Some of the most forceful responses to the advent and domination of broadcasting came from the realm of speculative fiction. Novels such as Birch's *Moon Terror* and George Winsor's *Station X,* as well as many short stories appearing in pulp science fiction and adventure magazines, began to express in this period a more horrific aspect of broadcasting that was inextricably linked to the emerging "presence" associated with the changing medium's new applications. Although utopian treatments of radio communications continued (especially in accounts of radio's bringing "high" culture to the great unwashed masses), such enthusiasm was increasingly offset by apocalyptic accounts of "alien radio" as a medium of catastrophe and control. Stories of a more totalitarian radio tempered and even displaced romantic accounts of the oceanic mysteries of DX. In these new tales, radio became a marker of an unknown alien presence, extraterrestrial or otherwise, and a harbinger of potential subjugation. With the growth of broadcasting, authors skeptical of the new medium's social implications reimagined wireless as invisible puppet strings with the potential to manipulate the earth's docile population.

This chapter examines this transformation in the popular perception of electronic presence from one of melancholy mystery to one of escalating alienation (and quite often aliens). As a technology, conceptual category, and auditory experience, radio meant something quite different in 1922 than it had in 1912, and different again in 1932 than in 1922. As a result, the medium's electronic properties of simultaneity and instantaneousness — its quality of live and living presence — also underwent an imaginative transformation. In the transition from amateur wireless to network radio, tales of alienated and alien contact came to express this experiential transformation in the institution of radio evoking as well the social struggle over determining radio's purpose and future. The fascination with "alien ether," then, provides a fertile cultural terrain in which to track the listening public's changing relationship with the institution of earthly radio and its changing paradigms of presence. Like radio's future, the prospects for extraterrestrial communication had not always been so bleak. Nowhere was this transformation in attitude toward both aliens and radio more apparent than in speculation over contact with earth's nearby planetary neighbor, Mars.

Martian Wireless

Dreams of contacting Mars began well before scientists chose radio as the most likely medium of communication. "The idea in itself is not at all absurd, and it is, perhaps, less bold than those of the telephone, or the phonograph, or the photophone, or the kinetograph," argued M. Camille Flammarion in 1890.[4] Flammarion was an astronomer who devoted much attention to the question of extraterrestrial life and the possibilities of contacting "men in the moon" and inhabitants of Mars. Linking the nascent twentieth-century fascination with the outer space of the universe and a still strong nineteenth-century fascination with the inner space of the soul, Flammarion hypothesized, "May there not exist between the planetary humanities psychic lives that we do not know of yet? We stand but at the vestibule of knowledge of the universe."[5]

Standing before this "vestibule of knowledge" at the end of the nineteenth century, many astronomers, scientists, and speculative writers felt that the age-old question of life on other worlds was close to being answered.[6] Mars, the Moon, Venus, and even the Sun were thought to be likely candidates for carrying life forms of one kind or another. The simplest way to solve this enigma, many reasoned, was to contact the various planets directly, a logistically and semantically difficult project occupying many minds at the turn of the century. Researchers realized that for such communication to be even possible, much less meaningful, "signals have to be devised that are *intrinsically* intelligible, so that the messages may be deciphered by any intelligent man, or other creature, who has made nearly as much advance in pure and applied science as ourselves."[7] This particular author proposed a system using a flashing light to send modified Morse code across space. By devising a code centered on mathematical equations, he was confident that within three and a half hours earthlings and Martians would share a vocabulary of twenty-nine terms, including such concepts as "area, brackets, circle, dodecagon, earth, etceteras, minus, picture-formula, rhumb, polygon and Venus."[8]

In 1891 a donor bequeathed a hundred thousand francs to the French Academy of the Sciences to be awarded to the first person to devise a means of verifiable communication with another planet, a project that continued well into the next century.[9] One rather imperialistic engineer suggested taking advantage of the "useless" Sahara Desert in North Africa. "Why not . . . construct a figure on the desert by means of canals? The now useless land would be irrigated and Europe's overcrowded population would find an outlet."[10] The engineer proposed constructing canals that formed a right triangle in the desert, thus communicating to whomever might be interested that the people of earth were fluent in mathematics and geometry. He further proposed illuminating the twenty-four-hundred-mile canal system with electric lights. "Conceive, if you can, this gigantic figure ablaze with light! . . . The people of Mars could not fail to see it almost without the aid of telescopes."[11] Other plans included signaling with a series of cloth reflectors at least ten by two hundred miles in area, and through a ten-million-dollar set of mirrors.[12] "What Shall We Say to Mars?" asked one article pragmatically, proposing finally a system that matched coded images with words in the hopes of reaching Martians well versed in the theories of structural linguistics. "Followed consistently," argued this advocate, "this practice will compel the Martians to the conclusion that these marks are arbitrary symbols for the various objects pictured."[13]

Amid these grandiose and unrealized projects for interplanetary communication lurked another and perhaps more unsettling question concerning the red planet. What if the Martians were already trying to contact us? The advent of wireless made this a distinct possibility. In 1899, working alone one winter night at his laboratory in Colorado Springs, Edison's chief rival, Nikola Tesla, picked up a series of inexplicable signals on his wireless set. Like the befuddled scientists in Birch's *Moon Terror,* Tesla believed the signals emanated from a great distance and that they were almost certainly ordered in a way that suggested a deliberate, intelligent agency in their transmission. Finding no terrestrial explanation for the phenomenon, Tesla suggested the signals might be from outer space, perhaps from the planet Mars. Tesla, already reputed to be somewhat of a crackpot for his belief in mental telepathy and the reincarnation of pigeons, was not taken all that seriously in this hypothesis. Mars was too far away, argued most scientists and wireless experts, for any radio signal to travel and remain detectable. The incident did provoke public discussion and speculation in the press, however, and helped to associate the idea of wireless with distant, interplanetary communications. Two years later Marconi succeeded in the much more humble task of sending the first wireless signal across the Atlantic.

Anticipating NASA's SETI (Search for Extraterrestrial Intelligence) program, Amherst professor David Todd suggested in 1909 sending men to a position ten miles above the earth's atmosphere in balloons equipped to receive whatever Hertzian waves might be aimed at the earth from other planets.[14] Speculation about Martian radio signals peaked again in the early twenties when no less a wireless authority than Marconi himself claimed to have received mysterious transmissions, possibly from space.[15] Researchers, scientists, and science fiction writers began to speculate on the ramifications of trading radio signals with Mars. Tesla, apparently buoyed by Marconi's corroboration of his earlier claim of extraterrestrial contact, proposed that Earth might eventually communicate with the Martians through a form of interplanetary television, thus solving the language barrier. "Pictures have been transmitted by telegraph," observed Tesla. "Why not by wireless? Granted always that on some of the neighboring planets there exist intelligent beings, as far advanced in civilization as we, or farther, who understand wireless telegraphy, we should be able to flash pictures — say of a human face — by wireless and receive in return pictures by wireless. When that step is taken the whole riddle of interplanetary communication is solved."[16] Others suggested mobilizing the entirety of the country's electric power to spark a single, powerful message to Mars in the hopes that the Martians would return the earth's signal with one of their own.[17] The new interest in Martian radio in the twenties even inspired Professor Todd to propose once again sending a receiver aloft into the upper atmosphere, this time in a radio-controlled dirigible.[18]

The figure of the wireless experimenter tuning his apparatus to contact

Professor David Todd (*top*) and his assistant monitor a device designed to detect radio signals from Mars. (*Wireless Age,* 1926)

Mars was in such common circulation by the early twenties that it was already a ripe target for parody. In a story from 1923, "The Great Radio Message from Mars," an operator formerly interested in wireless contact with the dead turns his attention to the red planet. Using a special crystal taken from a meteorite, the experimenter makes a weak connection with the Martians, who tell him in a garbled message that the "negative animal magnetism" of his family is interfering with their transmissions. The experimenter's hasty solution is to kill his entire family with an ax! Visiting the operator in jail, the story's narrator asks what else the Martians had to communicate. Their message? "Yes, we have no bananas."[19] That same year, Hollywood's first attempt at a "3-D" feature, *Radio Mania* (also released as *M.A.R.S., Mars Calling,* and *The Man from Mars*), told the story of a starry-eyed inventor who believes he has made a two-way radio connection with Mars only to discover in the end that it was all a dream.

What all of these theories shared, of course, was the premise that Mars is indeed inhabited by intelligent beings. Speculation as to what this life might be like took many forms, from the sword-wielding gladiators of the Edgar Rice Burroughs novels to lithe, wispy creatures surviving in a barren desert landscape. The main advocate of life on Mars was astronomer Percival Lowell. His books, *Mars and Its Canals* (1906) and *Mars: The Abode of Life* (1908), marshaled all known scientific data on Mars to argue that life did indeed exist on the red planet, a civilization advanced enough to build what seemed to be an intricate series of canals across the planet's surface. Although many thought life on Mars was unlikely, few scientists in the teens and twenties were willing to rule it out entirely. Science fiction writers, meanwhile, produced elaborate portraits of Martian anatomy and civilization. Based on Lowell's work, H. G. Wells speculated on the appearance of the Martians:

> They will probably have heads and eyes and backboned bodies, and since they must have big brains, because of their high intelligence, and since almost all creatures with big brains tend to have them forward in their heads near their eyes, these Martians will probably have big shapely skulls. But they will in all likelihood be larger in size than humanity, two and two-thirds times the mass of a man, perhaps. That does not mean, however, that they will be two and two-thirds times as tall, but, allowing for the laxer texture of things on Mars, it may be that they will be half as tall again when standing up. And as likely as not they will be covered with feathers or fur. . . . I can find . . . no necessary reason to make me believe the Martians are bare-skinned.[20]

Describing creatures adapted to a world with little water or gravity, Wells concluded, "It would be quite natural to imagine the Martians as big-headed, deep-chested bi-peds, grotesquely caricaturing humanity with arms and hands."[21]

Many of the authors on Martian life assumed that the planet's civilization was more ancient than our own and was therefore more advanced in its science and technology. Some speculated that Mars had long been sending wireless signals to Earth, waiting for its slower sister planet to develop the necessary technology to enable interplanetary communication. This familiar association of advanced electronic communications with futuristic civilizations indicates the importance our own culture has placed on electronic media in visions of technological progress. Alien radio (or television, or virtual reality, for that matter) thus hints at our own society's better and more advanced future, an aspiration attached to almost all emerging electronic media in their day. As James Carey and others have noted, new modes of communication always seem to hold the promise of more cooperative and constructive dialogue, as if the very existence of the new technology will somehow erase rather than embody the social conflicts of the society that developed it in the first place.[22] It should not be surprising, then, that early enthusiasts of Martian wireless invested great imagination in describing an entire other world of superior civilization and technology. Just as Spiritualists had done in the previous century, advocates of Martian life constructed yet another "electronic elsewhere" to rival the previous century's invisible spirit world. And, as with the Spiritualists, these promoters of extraterrestrial life saw this other world as embodying Earth culture in a more perfected form. Those who speculated on communications with Mars, for example, frequently projected earthbound ideas of utopian technology and social structure onto the red planet. The Martian canals, it was thought, gave evidence that the Martians were not only highly advanced, but an utterly peaceful species as well. "All the beings on that planet must combine in a far more effective way for existence than conditions on earth necessitate," offered one commentator on why Martians did not make war with Earth or with each other.[23] The difficulty of life in the harsh Martian climate demanded cooperation. "Irrigation on Mars is existence."[24] Like twentieth-century Americans, meanwhile, Martians were also thought to be essentially benevolent beings with a high curiosity in science and exploration. In the mind's eye of the early century, Martians sat at their own equivalents of wireless receivers, scanning the Martian ether for evidence of life on Earth. With both species working toward this goal, interplanetary communication seemed imminent.

This "pioneering" aspect of radio made extraterrestrial contact a major component in the "boy's culture" of wireless during this period. As many have discussed, wireless was an obsessive hobby of many boys and young men before and after the First World War. Assembling receiving sets out of household odds and ends, these early radio operators concentrated on receiving the most distant signals possible, eavesdropping on the navy, commercial vessels, and fledgling stations in the middle of the night. As Susan Douglas writes, "A young man's life was indeed made more exciting by involvement in radio. The amateurs came to feel that their lives were intertwined with truly significant events as they overheard messages about shipwrecks or political developments and transmitted these messages to others."[25] As radio became increasingly central to the then highly masculine genre of science fiction, "scientific" publications such as *Radio News* and *Popular Science* began publishing adventure stories based on the principles of science and frequently incorporating radio technology.

Stories of wireless written for young boys
emphasized adventure and exploration. Here,
young experimenter Tom Swift watches as his
wireless tower is destroyed by an earthquake in
Tom Swift and His Wireless Message. (Grosset
and Dunlap, 1911)

Meanwhile, in books like *The Radio Boys* series and *Tom Swift and His Wireless Message* (1911), red-blooded American boys solved mysteries and punished misdeeds through their clever application of wireless. The association of radio and boys was so strong, in fact, that the story of two girls building a wireless set by themselves ("refusing all help from father and brother") warranted an entire feature article.[26]

Whereas stories of radio and girls focused almost exclusively on romance or supernatural themes of paranormal reception, boy's radio fiction centered on invention, exploration, and investigation. As Jack Binns encouraged in his first book for boys on wireless, "Radio is still a young science, and some of the most remarkable advances in it have been contributed by amateurs — that is, by boy experimenters. It is never too late to start in the fascinating game, and the reward for the successful experimenter is rich both in honor and recompense."[27] After relating the inspiring story of E. H. Armstrong's boyhood experiences with radio, Binns concluded his prefatory remarks with Herbert Hoover's bracing statement, "I am for the American boy."[28] As a medium marked by unbridled enthusiasm, endless possibilities, and growing prestige, radio allowed young boys to imagine themselves as experimental pioneers in the ether, exploring new and invisible frontiers. As Douglas observes, before radio's mass entrance into the American public, the medium "was portrayed as an invention that provided entree into an invisible realm unfamiliar to the less technically adventurous. This hint of exclusivity further romanticized the amateur's activities while implying that they were helping to shape and bring about the future."[29] The quest for Martian radio represented the apex of the oceanic model of presence associated with early wireless, evoking images of countless boys and young men casting their lines into the ether and beyond. Without doubt, contacting Mars would be the high point of the new radio future and the ultimate "catch" of DX fishing.

Martian mania was not caused by radio alone, certainly, but wireless technology was central to this enthusiasm as the most likely means of contacting our neighboring planet. Such communication seemed the logical ultimation of a technology that gave almost daily evidence that the world (and universe) was shrinking. If an amateur operator in Chicago could routinely pick up Los Angeles and New York, and on a good night receive Tokyo and London, why shouldn't experts equipped with the latest in wireless equipment and knowledge be able to hail the planets? It is difficult now to imagine just how fantastic the shape of the universe must have seemed in the teens and early 1920s to everyday readers of such magazines as *Popular Science* and *Popular Mechanics, Radio Broadcast* and *Scientific American,* and even *Harper's* and *Cosmopolitan.* Readers would have encountered numerous articles side by side on the ever-increasing powers of radio and the ever-nebulous secrets of Mars. Although such readers might scoff at the idea of using radio to contact the dead or read minds, it seemed eminently reasonable, indeed almost inevitable, that radio would one day be used to contact the inhabitants of Mars, an "alien" civilization enough like Earth's to possess similar communications technology. As of the early 1920s, then, the radio wave stood as the world's most intrepid explorer, ready to rise through the ether and across the void of space to contact our telecasting brethren.[30] The red planet, in turn, was a major body in the constellation of these wireless possibilities.

The Chains of Broadcasting

But even in these giddy days of radio's expansion after the First World War, as young men across the country saw themselves in the radio vanguard proudly ushering in a new era of communications, radio as an institution was beginning a rapid transition, one that would greatly transform speculative accounts of the new medium, as well as temper enthusiasm for the prospects of interplanetary contact. Although radio to this point had been primarily a means of sending and receiving messages in Morse code, by 1920 amateurs and fledgling stations increasingly began broadcasting music and speech, "beginning in the Northeast and moving south and west, reaching unprecedented levels of intensity by the spring of 1922."[31] That same year, the previously exclusive boys' club of radio became a truly national phenomenon. Popular national magazines began to cover the radio craze, providing articles on novel applications of wireless and tips on acquiring a home receiving set. Such coverage accelerated interest in the medium, which in turn led to the increased production of preassembled radio sets and laid the groundwork for the growing dominance of commercial broadcast stations. The amateur "radio bugs" who had been experimenting in the medium for the previous decades watched with satisfaction, but also with regret no doubt, as their once exclusive playground became both public and corporate property. As one wireless veteran observed:

> But what a change has come. Really, it does an old-time radio-bug's soul good nowadays to be stopped on the street, or cornered at the club, by one of these erst-while doubting friends, who pulls out an envelope with some scribbled figures and diagrams on the back, and, with great seriousness of manner and cordiality of approach, proceeds to ask a lot of questions about "this wireless business." "Putting in an outfit?" we venture. "Oh! Just thinking some about it, that's all." Then on the way home that evening we spot a couple of wires strung from his house to a pole on the garage.[32]

Suddenly, the entire country was fishing at the DX pool, and this once exclusive and prestigious activity became a common national obsession.

Thousands of Americans were now "dial-twisters," restlessly scanning the spectrum for distant and exotic signals, Martian or otherwise.

Ironically, this new demand for receiving sets and the growing influence of broadcast stations threatened to destroy the core pleasures of DX fishing that had provoked this initial fascination with wireless in the first place. A headline from *Literary Digest* put it best: "Is the Radio Amateur Doomed?" The article went on to describe the amateur as dispossessed:

> To-day, the percentage of "radio amateurs" as compared with other radio users has nearly or quite lost its two ciphers, dividing it by 100. The amateur, once alone in his fascinating field, finds himself jostled and trampled upon by a horde of common folks who want to hear a concert or something — that's all. He is in about the same predicament as an aristocratic old family when a real estate operator surrounds the ancestral estate with a development full of $4,000 houses. He is just as heroically trying to maintain the old traditions and live the old life, and with about the same chance for success.[33]

As the ether grew more crowded over the course of the decade, the airwaves became increasingly partitioned and regulated. The ether was no longer a boundless ocean buoying mysterious and surprising messages; instead, it quickly became a saturating deluge of announcements, advertisements, and regularly scheduled entertainment. No longer was indiscriminate and random reception, DX or otherwise, the feature attraction of the new medium. The emerging broadcast industry encouraged a more stable form of radio consumption.

In an attempt to sell domestic receivers (so that listeners could in turn be sold to advertisers), radio ads of the period often depicted this transition from old to new radio habits in terms of modern progress. One ad, for example, pictured a circa 1919 listener struggling to hear a signal through awkward headsets while in an adjacent panel a family of 1929 sits comfortably in their living room with a radio on the mantelpiece. Another ad contrasted the happy radio family of 1926 with a bewildered caveman attempting to tune in an antique crystal set. Such revisionist portraits of early radio rewrote the initial romance for the medium in terms of the drudgery of primitive, bygone days.[34] Not only was old technology being ridiculed, so too were the early, non-network pleasures of wireless. The pleasures of DX exploration were rewritten as the frustrations of inconve-

An advertisement admonishes readers to abandon radio's "prehistoric" era of DX fishing and join the modern age of domestic broadcast consumption. (*Radio Broadcast Advertizer,* April 1926)

nience, a problem easily remedied by acquiring the now commercially manufactured receiver. Bound to this image of the modern domestic receiver, at least implicitly, was the message that radio was no longer a fantastic technology, a magic box in the garage that captured the stray voices of the ether. The medium was now an increasingly familiar, convenient, and wholly unremarkable presence in the home, less a bridge to the "unknown" than a machine echoing (or, more ominously, orchestrating) the structure of daily life.

For many radio enthusiasts, especially the amateur operators who had done so much to propagate the cause and technology of the medium, radio's gradual colonization by the network oligopoly represented a certain betrayal. As Douglas argues, "It was not at all clear in 1899 how, or even if, corporations could own or manage 'the air.' In other words, wireless would overcome some of the very side effects of industrialism and corporate control that previous technologies had engendered. Many of these visions suggest that, with the advent of wireless, Americans would be free from reliance on other, more entrenched networks controlled by either corporations or the government."[35] The influx of commercial broadcasters, of course, soon led to the legal codification of radio as a one-way medium, and what had been a veritable "free-for-all" of the airwaves became, through the various radio acts and conferences, a fully functional oligopoly dominated by NBC, CBS, and eventually ABC. This, of course, was the pivotal moment in the creation of the American commercial broadcasting system, the period when the political economy of the industry was set in stone for the next fifty years. When television followed the same corporate and governmental path some twenty years later, it reaffirmed that broadcasting would remain a centralized and commercially controlled operation.

For many radio bugs, the increasing mass production of previously home-built radio sets, the spreading commercialization of unilateral broadcasting, and the exiling of amateur transmitters to the hinterlands of the spectrum must have suggested that the unlimited wonders of wireless did seem, at last, to have limits. For those who had participated in radio's early boom years, there must have been something slightly oppressive about the increasing order the networks brought to the airwaves. Some attempted to resist this colonization, at least temporarily. During the mid-twenties, for example, many large cities scheduled a "silent night" once a week when all local broadcasters would shut down to allow the indulgences of the DX community. Some electronics magazines, meanwhile, even advertised a device designed to block out *local* radio signals, thus thwarting local broadcasters and their advertisers while keeping the fleeting pleasures of DX fishing alive. A coalition of interest groups, finally, formed to battle corporate domination of the airwaves. As Robert McChesney writes, "This opposition insisted that network, for-profit, commercial broadcasting was inimical to the communication requirements of a democratic society and attempted to generate popular support for a variety of measures that would substantively recast U.S. broadcasting."[36] Some believed that centralized control of radio could only lead to blatant propagandizing and public manipulation, and demanded that radio retain a space for nonprofit educational and religious broadcasting. Despite this opposition, the networks were able to elude the potentially damaging connotations of a "radio trust" and successfully pushed their agenda through Congress.

Although there was little substantial legislative opposition, nor an organized popular revolt against the networks, the new system of radio broadcasting was not uniformly championed even by the vast new listening audience that had displaced the amateur experimenters. Particularly contentious was the issue of advertising. A study by Paul Lazarfeld estimated that by 1945 at least a third of the radio audience was "anti-advertising."[37] Many thought the interruptions and hard sells presented by advertising were too intrusive for a medium that enjoyed such a prominent position in the American home. Earlier research by Lazarfeld and others indicates that by the mid-thirties, as radio ceased to be a novelty and truly became a mainstay in the American home, listeners had devised effective strategies for repelling the domestic intrusions of advertisers. The chief defense was a new mode of selective listening. Describing what would become a classic struggle between audiences and advertisers throughout commercial broadcasting, one study claimed that listeners expressed their discontent by paying increasingly less attention to radio, even though they still left the radio set on for many hours a day. "In other words," proposed the study, "instead of millions of families rushing about the sitting room tuning the radio, on and off, as conventionally pictured in the broadcast studio, the great American audience has learned to let the radio run — and turn *itself* on and off. Collectively. And individually."[38] Whether such selective attention was a calculated resistance to the commercialization of the medium or a simple distraction from unimportant and uninteresting radio fare, this new mode of attending to radio testifies to how vastly different audience practices were from those seen just ten years earlier.

As these struggles suggest, the twenties presented a pivotal reversal in the metaphors of electronic presence informing telecommunications. Radio was no longer a technology that required the undivided attention of a single listener isolated in headsets. The experience of radio now came to be characterized by an increase in programming, a predictability of scheduling, and a new and larger collectivity of the listening public. As the networks gained in audience and power, DX fishers ceased trolling for distant stations, while stations, in turn, began trolling for listeners (as potential consumers). In effect, the radio audience was now at the bottom of the etheric ocean, under the weight of synchronized, centralized, and standardized transmissions. The new state of "presence" was inherent in the very name of the institution that came to dominate radio — the network. Designating a chain of interconnected stations, the network was also quite literally a net covering and ensnaring its audience. This model of presence as a net, chain, or blanket would inform radio and television for the next half century, usurping the free-flowing sense of a boundless etheric ocean with the managed distribution of corporate broadcasting's sweeping net.

If radio bugs, reformers, and social scientists had little luck in attacking the emerging paradigm of radio, spirited symbolic challenges to the new order of broadcasting did find voice in the popular entertainment of the era. As the transformation in radio from two-way wireless to one-way broadcasting accelerated in the twenties and thirties, new subgenres of radio fiction began appearing in movies, magazines, and pulp novels. Increasingly sinister and apocalyptic, these tales suggested that the new practice of domestic "broadcasting" held horrors quite different from the wondrous tales of haunted ether that attended earlier applications of radio. As evidenced in Birch's *Moon Terror* and many other books of the period, this new form of speculative fiction often portrayed the medium as intimately connected to the potential for social control and mass catastrophe.

In addition to *The Moon Terror's* now familiar enigma of the "unexplained signal," two other tales of radio anxiety from the early broadcasting period are worth examining for their use of narrative devices that would become prevalent in the network era. "Symphony of the Damned," a *Weird Tales* story of 1934, tells of a maniacal genius who plans to broadcast a cursed piece of music that will drive its nation of listeners to mass suicide.[39] In a theme that has become ubiquitous in critiques of mass media, "Symphony of the Damned" suggested that radio's newfound access to the domestic sanctity of the entire American public presented the potential for sinister abuse. The radio "net" could now ensnare, subjugate, and even kill listeners in their very own homes. The 1950 film *The Next Voice You Hear* conceptualized this authoritarian relationship in metaphysical terms, with God using radio to communicate His word, a premise rehashed in sci-fi form in *The Red Planet Mars* (1952), where Martian transmissions are discovered in the end to actually be from the Lord. With such real and imagined fears in mind, the National Association of Broadcasters for many years maintained a prohibition against the live broadcasting of hypnotists on radio and television (no attempt was made, of course, to distinguish what separated hypnotists from advertisers).

If tales like "Symphony of the Damned" captured broadcasting's power to invade domestic space and control the home, another tale from the period exploited fears over radio's ability to drive listeners out of their homes through forced patriation in a menacing public sphere. In "The Night Wire," published in 1926, a radio operator receives sporadic transmissions telling of a deadly fog smothering a small Mexican city. Periodically updated amid the chaos, the broken transmissions report that the lethal fog is spreading, and before long the seemingly safe operator (and reader) realizes that the cloud of death will soon engulf the entire world.[40] Tales in this tradition demonstrated that, for better or worse, the entire world was now interconnected through communications media. At any moment radio might bring catastrophe into the living room or, even more ominously, warn of an impending apocalypse that the listener would be powerless to prevent. Such associations dated back as far as the *Titanic,* of course, but what made these tales different in the network age was their sense of impending doom. Stories such as "The Night Wire" were horrifying, not simply because they described the distant deaths of strangers via radio, but because radio itself could provide a simultaneous account of the future death of the listener. "The Night Wire" generated its suspense through the now familiar plot device of the "sporadic transmission," a narrative structure simulating disruptions in the electronic blanket of mass communications in a tale of global chaos and catastrophe. In the age of mass media, audiences learned very early that the seamless net of corporate broadcasting would be torn for only a few extraordinary events — perhaps nothing less than the end of the world.

As these two tales suggest, the institution of broadcasting came with a price: the invasion and even dissolution of the private sphere of the home and forced participation in a vast and possibly terrifying public sphere. Under broadcasting, American listeners were now both potential targets of manipulation and potential witnesses/subjects to traumatic disaster. Founded on the new metaphor of a blanketing and inescapable sense of electronic presence, these tales were less a meditation on extraordinary, paranormal forms of communications than a lesson in the implicit horrors of the "network" as a system for binding together a national audience, even against its own will. The plausibility and effect of such tales, in turn, depended on the public's growing awareness of the network as a type of "web" covering the nation. Such tales exploited the audience's mounting experience with daily news reports of disasters and misfortunes, traumatic incidents of varying magnitudes that continually suggested an intimate connection between radio and catastrophe. Indeed, the relationship between radio and disaster was so close that it must have seemed at times as if the very existence of radio was itself responsible for such catastrophes. The instantaneous experience of mass public tragedy by radio was a genuinely new human experience, as was the mass participation in the private tragedies of individual citizens. Events such as the explosion of the *Hindenberg* and the kidnapping of the Lindbergh baby hailed a nation of new electronic witnesses, foregrounding radio's ability to link the nation and in the process forever tying its sense of simultaneity to the potential for sudden disaster. Live disasters by radio dramatically foregrounded this sense of blanketing network presence and anxious public culture already implicit in the broadcasting institution. Science fiction and horror tales such as "Symphony of the Damned" and "The Night Wire" only embellished this property of the medium by pushing the anxiety over network presence to its logical conclusion: radio as the ultimate live witness to both its own destruction and the complete annihilation of its audience. It is within this network context of electronic presence that the red planet Mars once again captured the public imagination. On the night of 30 October 1938, the more sinister implications of broadcast "coverage," both in terms of radio's surveillance power over public disaster and its ability to blanket a national audience, found their most forceful expression in what remains radio's most legendary hour.

The "Panic" Broadcast

The Mercury Theatre production of *War of the Worlds,* directed by Orson Welles, remains a major benchmark in media history. As is well known, this infamous radio play presented a tale of Martian invasion in the form of an emergency radio broadcast. The first moments of the play featured programmatic music interrupted by an announcer telling of mysterious explosions on Mars, and then of a seeming meteorite crash in the New Jersey countryside. The story went on to use various announcers, scientists, government officials, and other experts as candid narrators relaying a live account of an invincible Martian force conquering the world. As is also well known, newspapers reported that thousands of listeners had taken the performance as fact and that a nationwide "panic" had ensued. Everything from heart attacks to car wrecks to suicide attempts were blamed on the broadcast. As a result, the Welles production of *War of the Worlds* became a familiar chapter in the popular memory of American media and stands even today as a common reference point for critics who wish to invoke a parable of the media's awesome power over its audiences.[41]

In the weeks following the broadcast, critics immediately seized on the program's implications for the media's powers of social control, frequently discussing the broadcast as a lesson in the potentially fascistic use of radio. Commentary on the "panic" centered on the power of radio as a propaganda tool, an anxiety that seemed especially salient in the age of the Nazis. "Those who argue that radio is the strongest arm of dictators, since it reduces an entire country to the size of one room," argued *Time* in the broadcast aftermath, "gasped at this graphic example of its power over susceptible multitudes. Never had radio's ability to control people been so vividly proved, nor provoked so much widespread indignation."[42] Or, as a commentator for *The Nation* observed, "The disembodied voice has a far greater force than the printed word, as Hitler has discovered. If the Martian incident serves as even a slight inoculation against our next demagogue's appeal for a red hunt or an anti-Semitic drive it will have had its constructive effect."[43]

Other writers, meanwhile, lay the blame for the panic at the doorstep of the American public, which was seen as lacking a certain fundamental skepticism that should have protected it from such a hoax. Commenting on those who believed in the veracity of broadcast, for example, a columnist for the *Christian Century* wrote, "The credulous people . . . , believing everything, believe nothing; believe nothing with their entire being, with their hearts. They have tied their hearts to nothing, to stand or fall with it; therefore they fall. They are in a sense, an evil sense, free: free as the foam on the wave, driven away by every wind that blows, dissipated into air, into thin air."[44] In this strand of commentary, the "panic" broadcast stood as a damning indictment of a rootless mass culture. For these critics, the American radio audience, lacking in "authentic" values and "informed" judgment, faced the danger of repeated victimization at the hands of broadcasters.

Few commentators, however, examined the panic in terms of the audience's relationship to the institution of radio itself. Although some attributed the panic to anxieties over international tensions percolating in the late thirties, there was little discussion of anxieties over the public's newly forged relationship with the centralized authority of network radio. And yet, whatever power *War of the Worlds* had to "panic" its audience clearly resided in its status as an imaginary emergency newscast that invoked such an authority. "It didn't sound like a play the way it interrupted the music when it started," related a participant in Hadley Cantril's study of the panic.[45] Cantril observed that "this unusual realism of the performance may be attributed to the fact that the early parts of the broadcast fell within the existing standards of judgment of the listeners" (68). The "panic broadcast," in other words, exploited a certain social knowledge in the audience to create its realistic effect by skillfully mimicking the already conventionalized features of the emergency news broadcast. The play thus successfully orchestrated the medium's qualities of "simultaneity" and "presence" as experienced through the relatively newfound control of the networks, playing on the public's new familiarity with radio as an extensive net and on the new social phenomenon of disaster as an instantaneous, mass experience. Indeed, the *War of the Worlds* broadcast demonstrates just how successfully the listening public had internalized a working model of the American broadcasting system by 1938; that is, the panic hinged on an intuitive understanding of the technical practices, routine operation, and social authority of the networks. The program's shock effect depended on the audience's having naturalized a new set of listening protocols attendant to network radio, a listening pattern of social control based on the routine rhythms of schedule, flow, and segmentation. The terror could be realized only if the listener understood how electronic news gathering and dissemination operated, realized the social significance of disrupted network transmissions, and, above all else, invested in the radio's new sense of presence as both a national authority and a means of social surveillance. In short, one had to "believe" in radio, or as another participant in the Cantril study stated, "We have so much faith in broadcasting. In a crisis it has to reach all people. That's what radio is here for" (70).

But what does it mean to have "faith" in broadcasting? This isolated comment testifies to the extent of the changes in public attitude and social knowledge about radio by 1938. *Faith* implies a social investment in radio as a system of belief. Unwavering faith in "what radio is here for" suggests that much of the public by this time had ceased to imagine other possible communicative cosmologies. By concentrating on one pole of the listener-broadcaster axis and citing the broadcast as evidence of either the potential power of aspiring fascistic demagogues or the increasing stupidity of the listening public, commentators ignored (or perhaps repressed) the implications of the radio institution's recent transformation into a "system of distribution." The medium of network radio was seen as an essentially neutral apparatus that, in the "wrong" hands, might convey potentially irresponsible messages. In taking this line of argument, commentators missed the more important realization that broadcaster, audience, apparatus, and institution were all equally implicated within a regime of power. By concentrating on radio as an instrument rather than an effect of such political power, these early critics ignored as well the often reluctant social bond of radio's newfound "presence," its sense of massing an invisible audience in a simultaneous electronic community.

The cultivation of "faith" in the listening audience (then and now) must be seen as a process every bit as political as the actual information carried by radio and television. Such faith is a form of social control linked, not to the actual messages of the media, but to the very intractability of the apparatus itself. In his "Requiem for the Media," written some thirty years after the famous Welles broadcast, Jean Baudrillard argues what has become a standard yet still compelling critique of electronic media: "The mass media are anti-mediatory and intransitive. They fabricate non-communication — that is what characterizes them, if one agrees to define communication as an exchange, as a reciprocal space of a speech and a response, and thus of a responsibility. . . . *They are what always prevents response,* making all processes of exchange impossible. . . . This is the real abstraction of the media. And the system of social control and power is rooted in it."[46] The "panic" broadcast presents the first and still most famous example of a national public trauma and subsequent mass social paralysis mediated (or perhaps one should say "nonmediated") by the centralized institution of mass telecommunications. Such events have occurred many times since the 1938 broadcast (Pearl Harbor, the Kennedy assassination, the *Challenger* explosion, to name a few), moments when the listening public is reminded of its larger social bond while also experiencing most profoundly the effects of atomization and isolation. *War of the Worlds* was thus, paradoxically, an extraordinary moment in the history of *noncommunication,* a cogent reminder of the American public's inability to intervene in anything through the mass media. It foregrounds in dramatic terms the usually invisible operation of all broadcasting (and the social order it embodies) as a function of unilateral power. As Baudrillard continues, incorporating Mauss's work on exchange, "Power belongs to the one who can give and cannot be repaid. . . . The same goes for the media: they speak, or something is spoken there, but in such a way as to exclude *any response anywhere*" (170).

What made the *War of the Worlds* broadcast particularly compelling to its original audience was the manner in which it portrayed three levels of catastrophe, centering on the destruction of military technology, the media, and the social body. Writing about television's fascination with disaster, Mary Anne Doane observes, "Catastrophe does . . . always seem to have something to do with technology and its potential collapse. And it is also always tainted by a fascination with death — so that catastrophe might finally be defined as the conjuncture of the failure of technology and the resulting confrontation with death."[47] The catastrophes of the panic broadcast included the collapse of the American military machine at the hands of the attacking Martians, and the collapse of the media that vainly tried to normalize the disaster in its simulated reporting. As the earliest and perhaps most famous public fiction of communications technology in crisis, *War of the Worlds* presented a story of Martian invasion, but perhaps even more significant, it presented the sounds of the radio institution itself in collapse. With its staged interruptions, recurring confusion, and mounting desperation, *War of the Worlds* was (and is) as much about the destruction of the media as about the destruction of humanity. Or, as Orson Welles stated in the play's closing announcement about this elaborate Halloween prank, "we couldn't soap all your windows or steal all your garden gates . . . so we did the next best thing. We annihilated the world before your very ears, and utterly destroyed the Columbia Broadcasting System."[48] After announcing the destruction of the world and CBS, Welles continued: "You will be relieved, I hope, to learn that we didn't mean it, and that both institutions are still open for business."[49]

Catastrophe continues to fascinate. Nick Browne has argued that the broadcast schedule serves to naturalize the logic of the social order by establishing a routine that mirrors the rhythm of the workweek.[50] Catastrophes presented "live" are perhaps the only remaining challenge to this entrenched apparatus and routine. As Doane writes, "If Nick Browne is correct in suggesting that, through its alignment of its own schedule with the work day and the work week, [broadcasting] 'helps produce and render "natural" the logic and rhythm of the social order,' then catastrophe would represent that which cannot be contained within such an ordering of temporality."[51] Doane argues that death is the subject most capable of disrupting this routine of media and social life. "Catastrophe is at some level always about the body, about the encounter with death" (233). Patricia Mellencamp makes a similar observation when she writes of television, "TV time of regularity and repetition, continuity and 'normalcy,' contains the potential of interruption, the thrill of live coverage of death events. It is here, in the potential and promise of disruption — a shift between the safe assurance of successive time and story and the break-in of the discontinuity of the real in which the future hangs in the balance, the intrusion of shock, trauma, disaster, crisis — that TV's spectatorial mechanism of disavowal, which is retroactive, operates most palpably."[52]

As Doane suggests, this is why the intersection of media and catastrophe, whether simulated, as in *War of the Worlds,* or actual, as in the Kennedy assassination or the *Challenger* explosion, is at once frightening and yet extremely fascinating. Such crisis moments defy the normalizing mechanisms of the media, disrupting the usual flow of the broadcast schedule and the social flow of the audience (the 1992 uprisings in Los Angeles, the Los Angeles earthquake, the O. J. Simpson "chase," and the deaths of Princess Diana and John F. Kennedy Jr. are the more recent and perhaps most explicit examples of this dual disruption). At these moments the audience experiences most acutely the entrenched "presence" of the network media as a net or blanket. The special bulletin and emergency broadcast, whether of an impending hurricane or a political assassination, always signal an explosive threat to the social order. Such intrusions by catastrophe also draw attention to the otherwise naturalized and unexamined cycle of the broadcast day and its virtually silent colonization of our lives.

One might even say that violent disasters and catastrophes evoke a certain exhilaration in that they promise momentary liberation from the mass-mediated social order. This dark possibility would certainly help explain the lasting fascination with the *War of the Worlds* broadcast, which seems to have attained a symbolic status in popular culture far greater in importance than its actual significance in the history of telecommunications. This mythologizing of the incident began almost immediately in its aftermath. Although there were many editorials and commentaries about *War of the Worlds* in the weeks following the broadcast, very little direct coverage of the so-called panic appeared in the nation's major newspapers in the days immediately following the incident. In fact, most papers simply ran an Associated Press piece detailing the stories of a New York woman who broke her arm running out into traffic and a New Jersey man who died of a heart attack, each purportedly because of the broadcast. Listening to the broadcast today, moreover, it is clear that although some may have been fooled by the opening few minutes of the program, most no doubt quickly determined through common sense that the story was in fact just a story. Indeed, civilization is completely destroyed by the half-hour break in *War of the Worlds*—even the most gullible listeners could have ended their fright simply by looking out the window. Direct evidence that thousands of Americans were in an actual panic over the broadcast is thus limited at best, and even Cantril's detailed document of the "panic" does little to distinguish people who genuinely experienced panic from those who simply claimed retroactively of having been scared so as to participate vicariously in what was already a rather notorious pop culture phenomenon.

And yet the legend of a paralyzing "mass" panic lives on. Clearly there has been a desire, experienced both individually and collectively, that this panic be seen as "true." The story of thousands of Americans pushed to the brink of pandemonium by a mere radio play is an alluring narrative, not just to the media effects researchers whose expertise is validated by such a panic, but by Americans themselves who seem to have an investment in the credibility of the panic. Contrasting the episode's incredibly prominent status in histories of mass media with the lack of credible evidence of a genuinely widespread panic suggests that the "panic broadcast" may be as much a function of fantasy as fact. The use of the term *fantasy* here is not meant to dismiss entirely accounts of a panic (a few unfortunate listeners were probably genuinely fooled). Rather, as a "fantasy" narrative, the panic broadcast, like many other myths and legends, might best be seen as a story with a basis in fact that has over time been elaborated and exaggerated to serve a more important symbolic function for the culture at large. The *War of the Worlds* incident has thus become the most famous parable of the oppressive presence associated with network broadcasting, a horror story in which the monster ultimately is not the invading Martians but the invasive broadcaster.

By simulating the simultaneous collapse of the social body and the radio institution, *War of the Worlds* exposed and then exploited the media's usually faceless gaze as it fell under siege. In the process, the institution of network radio came dangerously close to betraying itself; that is, the *War of the Worlds* broadcast almost provoked the radio audience into a "crisis of faith" and a potentially unsettling examination of its own investment in the medium. This is where *War of the Worlds* serves most palpably as a mass fantasy, a famous media moment that allows us to ponder the entrenchment of chain broadcasting and entertain a darkly liberating vision of its absolute destruction. The broadcast's power as a source of panic and as an enduring parable of media studies resides in its ability to evoke a usually disavowed connection between the order of media networks and the ordering of the social body. More than a cautionary tale about irresponsible broadcasting or gullible audiences, *War of the Worlds* continues to fascinate by reminding us of the repressed potential for panic and disorder that lies just behind the normalizing functions of media technology, a terror that is at once terrifying and yet suggestively enticing. In this way, the *War of the Worlds* broadcast might be thought of as a form of media "death wish," expressing a desire for chaos as a return of the repressed for the mechanisms of order imposed by broadcasting that had so recently transformed radio's "presence." As it stands, the play remains the most famous public lesson in an uncomfortable political reality: the collapse of the media is by definition a collapse of the social.

In labeling *War of the Worlds* a fantasy of technological and social destruction, I do not mean to say that listeners of Welles's broadcast actually wanted Martians to kill them and thus deliver them from capitalist media enslavement. The resiliency of this panic fantasy suggests a more utopian longing at work in the experience and memory of the *War of the Worlds* broadcast, one that must have been especially salient to an audience of 1938 that could remember the less complicated and less threatening world that existed before broadcasting. As a witness to the panic reported, "Being in a troublesome world, anything is liable to happen. We hear so much news every day. So many things we hear are unbelievable. Like all of a sudden six hundred children burned to death in a school fire. Or a lot of people thrown out of work. Everything seems to be a shock to me."[53] The incursion of the broadcast signal as a smothering presence inextricably interwoven into the very fabric of the social order was perhaps too unsettling a political reality to be confronted directly in 1938 (or even today for that matter). Perhaps engaging in the fantasy of the *War of the Worlds* panic indulges no more than a desire to escape the faceless gaze of the media, to flee not only the saturation of the broadcast signal but also the troubling public sphere it seems to have created.

By the time of the *War of the Worlds* broadcast, then, radio no longer offered a tantalizing means of escaping the mundane perimeters of the social order (by reaching the dead and alien others beyond it), but was instead permanently implicated in that social order's routine functioning. America's initial contact with Mars was thus much different under the new institution of network radio than it had been imagined in the early days of wireless. The "presence" of radio, in turn, figured much differently as well. Gone were the wonders of DX fishing and the hopes of contacting benevolent and strangely familiar Martians across the mysterious void of space. This utopian wish had been replaced by a vision of an interplanetary apocalypse in which the "presence" of radio was no longer a link to the mysterious, a means of eavesdropping on the universe. Instead, this presence as mediated by the newly entrenched institution of broadcast radio created a powerful yet ultimately paralyzing social bond shared by an audience listening to its own destruction. "I didn't do anything. I just kept listening. I thought if this is the real thing you only die once — why get excited?" offered one witness to the panic.[54] Or, as a particularly misanthropic observer stated, "I was looking forward with some pleasure to the destruction of the entire human race and the end of the world. If we have Fascist domination of the world, there is no purpose in living anyway."[55]

Take Me to Your Leader

In the legendarily awful science fiction film of 1953, *Robot Monster,* another alien arrives on Earth to eradicate humanity and colonize the planet. The film tells the story of a small band of humans determined to survive and defeat the alien occupation. What makes *Robot Monster* so infamous in film lore is not its rather predictable plot, but the incredible low-budget surrealism of the movie's "alien creature." To signify an alien from another world, the filmmakers borrowed a gorilla suit from one of the Hollywood studios, replacing the head with a deep-sea-diving helmet rented at the Santa Monica pier. As a finishing touch, they crowned their creation with a pair of "rabbit ears" — two antennae sprouting from the alien's head. Alien antennae are such a familiar convention in science fiction that their presence now seems wholly naturalized. We generally accept that little green men and women are in some way wired to receive radio transmissions, either naturally (antennae that emerge from the skull) or prosthetically (the radio helmet). Here too is a marker of "alien radio" and in many ways a distant echo of the cultural logic bound to the *War of*

The "Robot Monster": Ape and aerials. (© 1953 Astor Pictures Corp.)

the Worlds broadcast and legend. The symbolic power of alien antennae is even more pronounced when presented in conjunction with another convention for signifying "alien ether," one dating back to the earliest days of network radio.

At a standing-room-only performance in January of 1927, only a few months after NBC officially began service as the nation's first network entity, patrons of the New York Metropolitan Opera embarked on an "otherworldly" musical voyage. Onstage that night Professor Leon Theremin presented the American debut of a most unusual musical instrument. A small wooden cabinet containing two oscillating generators, the thereminvox (or theremin as this device came to be known popularly) was the world's first electronic musical apparatus. A two-foot-high antenna serving as a pitch control rod extended from the top of the cabinet. A looped antenna for controlling volume protruded from the cabinet's side. By moving his hands in proximity to these two antennae, yet without ever actually touching them, Professor Theremin could control the pitch and volume of a continuous electronic tone, producing what a reporter from *Radio Broadcast* described as "violin-like" notes marked by strong vibrato and tremolo. At this particular engagement Professor Theremin played such favorites as "Song of India" and "Ave Maria" in a program, appropriately titled, "Music from the Ether."[56] For its debut audience that evening, the strange apparatus no doubt evoked the mysterious call of that other electronic device designed to materialize music from the open air.[57] With its protruding antennae and warbling glissandos giving voice to electricity itself, the theremin was most obviously a cousin to radio.

Despite an enthusiastic initial reception, few composers ever worked to develop a repertoire for this bizarre yet ultimately limited instrument. As a result, the theremin never became a feature attraction of the concert hall. But the theremin did find a lasting home in Hollywood. In the ensuing years, the wavering tones of the theremin came to be one of Hollywood's most familiar "voices," used both as a sound effect and as lead instrument in numerous musical scores. Through its consistent use in horror and science fiction soundtracks, the theremin's eerie, soprano-like warblings made it Hollywood's signature instrument of the "otherworldly," cue-ing movie audiences to the looming presence of a menagerie of "alien" beings, whether they be monsters emerging from a swamp, ghosts prowl-ing a graveyard, or as was most often the case, invaders landing from another planet. Although the theremin serenaded a variety of extraordi-nary creatures in its Hollywood career, the instrument was especially prominent in science fiction films of the forties and fifties. In productions as diverse as the prestigious *Forbidden Planet* (1956) to the 3-D schlock of *It Came from Outer Space* (1953), the theremin's distinctive tones con-tinued to evoke the long-standing radiophonic association between elec-tronic presence and the presence of the paranormal.

The conventional alliance of alien antennae and otherworldly theremin was so common in the 1950s that, by the 1960s, it was available for more comic applications. The irascible Uncle Martin of CBS television's *My Fa-vorite Martian* is probably the most famous such figure, followed closely by the "Great Gazoo" on *The Flintstones*. A Martian traveler stranded on earth, Uncle Martin had many extraordinary powers, including the ability to extend or retract his Martian antennae at will (a maneuver invariably ac-companied by the sound of a theremin). Such comic use of this convention in the 1960s testifies to its ubiquity in the previous two decades, standing as a parodic example of what had earlier been a far more sinister relation-ship. In more sober-minded science fiction of the forties and fifties, the cultural alliance of alien, antennae, and theremin most often expressed relations of authoritarian obedience and imperializing power. Martians

Uncle Martin of *My Favorite Martian.* Martin could produce and retract his antennae at will, accompanied by the unearthly sound of the theremin. (© 1963 CBS Television)

were typically portrayed during this period as a remote-controlled race, plugged in through their antennae to a central command post, and serving as little more than stooges of totalitarianism. What antennae ultimately came to stand for in postwar science fiction was the absence of "humanity." In contrast to the rugged individualism of the human protagonists, antennaed Martians were cold, aloof, logical, and, above all else, corporate, wired to a central social authority that they obeyed without question. Their mission on earth, often executed to the eerie tones of the theremin, was to wholly permeate, slowly occupy, and eventually conquer all of humanity. On meeting earthlings, these hard-wired alien subjects frequently made a demand logical to such a totalitarian species: "Take me to your leader."

Through a highly condensed cultural logic, then, this alliance of alien, antennae, and theremin compressed an entire history of anxious speculation over Mars, radio, and global totalitarianism, the very elements so pivotal in the panicked accounts of *War of the Worlds*. Indeed, it may well be that in addition to providing media history with its most infamous "prank," the legacy of the *War of the Worlds* broadcast has been to forever intertwine concepts of aliens, radio, and fascism in the popular imagination. In a bizarre and stunning act of cultural disavowal and displacement, however, it has been the Martians, not the Americans, who came to be seen as a "wired" species. Even though Americans were suffocating beneath the new blanket of corporate radio, the antennaed Martian developed as an icon in postwar America on which to project anxieties over the forms of social control endemic to broadcasting.

Postwar science fiction often rehearsed these barely displaced anxieties over media control by incorporating a crisis of alien subjectivity into their plots, the "antennaed" antagonists of the stories forced to come to terms with their own colonized consciousness after meeting freedom-loving humans. The aforementioned "Robot Monster" is in frequent radio contact with his superior on the home planet. When commanded to kill the few remaining humans left on earth, he struggles with the demands of his "wired" culture pitted against the "hu-man" love and emotion he has experienced on Earth. "I must, but I cannot," he agonizes. "Where on the graph do 'must' and 'cannot' meet?" In *Santa Claus Conquers the Martians* (1964), meanwhile, Martians kidnap Santa Claus to entertain their children, who have grown listless and bored from watching too much Martian television! When not watching TV, the Martian children remain wired through radio helmets to their parents, government, and other forms of social authority. "Why are the Martian children so sad all the time?" asks an Earth child who accompanies Santa Claus to the red planet. The antennaed subjugation of the Martian youth speaks for itself. Novelist Kurt Vonnegut, finally, presents a most explicit portrait of these "antenna politics" in his popular science fiction tale *The Sirens of Titan*. As a human enlistee in the Martian army, Vonnegut's protagonist, Unk, learns disturbing information. "At the hospital they . . . had to explain to Unk that there was a radio antenna under the crown of his skull, and that it would hurt him whenever he did something a good soldier wouldn't do. The antenna also would give him orders and furnish drum music to march to. They said that not just Unk but everybody had an antenna like that—

doctors and nurses and four-star generals included. It was a very demo-cratic army, they said."[58]

The egalitarian enslavement of a mass society by mass electronic media remains a familiar premise in dystopic science fiction. Of course, in con-temporary parables of electronic mass mediation, the low-tech antenna has been replaced by the mind control possibilities imagined in micro-chips and the programmed mirages of virtual subjectivity. The cyborg slaves and deluded virtual subjects that populate contemporary science fiction have their paranoid roots in these earlier mass-society critiques of media and the body politic. George Orwell's *1984* would become the most famous and influential of such tales in the age of television, but this alien history of radio also encapsulates, in a more displaced form perhaps, the emerging horrors perceived at the heart of centralized broadcasting. As we have seen, early radio brought with it a sense of simulated consciousness adrift in the ether, a fleeting stream of thought to be accessed through the proper receiving technology. The first stories of the radio dead and contact with benevolent aliens emphasized the marvelous aspects of such com-munication, suggesting that whole other worlds existed invisibly along-side our own material realm or at the edges of a new frontier in space. Yet this wonder was often tinged with a sense of despair over the distance and desolation evoked by radio, a form of personal "alienation" that sug-gested the radio listener was but an atomized entity isolated from the larger social world. With the advent of commercial broadcasting, how-ever, the "mysterious" presence of radio transformed into a more "im-perious" presence. Once the medium's qualities of "liveness" and "si-multaneity" came to be managed by centralized network control, radio's "presence" further emphasized the listener's participation, whether will-ing or unwilling, in both an anonymous mass audience and a vast and often terrifying public sphere. In the network age, presence became omni-presence. Such anxieties became even more profound as they encountered another uncanny dimension of media presence — electronic vision.

4 Static and Stasis

"Getting a TV ghost?" asks a television repair ad of 1962. "There's a house on our block that everyone thought was haunted. . . . As it turned out, the only thing that was haunted about this house was the TV picture." Above the ad copy looms the silhouette of a suburban home, a large white ghost hovering over the house's rooftop antenna.[1] Such "television ghosts" are probably the most familiar creatures in the uncanny imagination of electronic media. In this particular incarnation, "ghosts" refers to the eerie double-images that appear on a TV set experiencing signal interference. The derivation of the term is obvious. This form of interference creates faint, wispy doubles of the "real" figures on the screen, specters who mimic their living counterparts, not so much as shadows, but as disembodied echoes seemingly from another plane or dimension.

At times these metaphorical ghosts of television can become more tangible. "Ghosts on a TV screen can be a problem," wrote a reporter for *Television Digest* in 1954, "but it's a rare occasion when one drives a housewife 'crazy' and ends up in the police station." As with the Travers family of Long Island, who had to turn their haunted set to the wall to avoid its scaring the children, the Mackeys of Indianapolis also received a cathode-ray visitor who refused to leave the screen. In this case, however, the apparition was not a famous entertainer, but the image of Mrs. Mackey's dead grandfather. As evidence, Mrs. Mackey claimed the ghost was wearing the very same suit in which her grandfather had been buried only a few months before. The set was moved to the police station two days after the initial appearance when Mrs. Mackey said she was "going crazy" because of the apparition. More than five hundred people visited the police station to view the ghost before it finally disappeared.[2]

Building on what was already a familiar premise by the mid-1950s, J. B. Priestley's humorous short story "Uncle Phil on TV" features a British family that uses insurance money collected after the death of an uncle to buy a new television set. While watching the new set, Mrs. Grigson spots someone in the background who she thinks looks like the dead Uncle Phil. Each time she watches the set, this figure invades the diegesis of the program, making his presence increasingly distinct with each appearance.

Clip-art for television repairmen
warning potential customers of the
"TV ghost." (McGraw-Hill, 1962)

Convinced finally that it is the ghost of Uncle Phil, she tries to tell the rest of the family about the bizarre phenomenon, but no one will believe her. Gradually, however, each member of the family has a video confrontation with Uncle Phil, who becomes increasingly belligerent with each screening and begins insulting the family directly. Appearing on a game show about buried treasure, Uncle Phil rants, "Talk about treasure! You Grigsons haven't done so bad with that hundred and fifty quid of mine." Finally, with the entire family assembled in front of the set, Uncle Phil accuses them of hiding his heart medicine and causing his death, which prompts one family member to throw a stool at the screen, destroying the set and its cantankerous apparition.[3]

Whether paranoid or parodic in their emphasis, such tales from the early days of television demonstrate the continuity between this new technology and the "occult" powers of radio, wireless, and telegraphy. Like these other media, television presented another means of electrical disembodiment and disassociation, so it should not be surprising that the new medium would foster similar fantasies of paranormal contact. A hundred years after the Fox sisters and the first Spiritualist séances, here was another technology for conjuring the dead, the alien, the interdimensional, the uncanny. Linked to these earlier media, certainly, television was of course a technology of a wholly different order. Going beyond voices gathered from the ether, television offered the added dimension of "distant vision." As one would expect, the addition of this extraordinarily vivid quality to telecommunications had a significant impact on the popular conceptions of "liveness" and electronic presence associated with the new medium. The introduction of electronic vision brought with it intriguing new ambiguities of space, time, and substance: the paradox of visible, seemingly material worlds trapped in a box in the living room and yet conjured out of nothing more than electricity and air. Whereas radio and telegraphy had always provided indexical evidence of distant places and invisible interlocutors (occult or otherwise), television appeared at once visibly and materially "real" even as viewers realized it was wholly electrical and absent. Unnervingly immediate and decidedly more tangible, the "electronic elsewhere" generated by television was thus more palpable and yet every bit as phantasmic as the occult empires of previous media. Its ghosts were truly ghosts — entities with visible form but without material substance.

Although the television ghosts we encounter today may be less than frightening or even fantastic (especially as cable facilitates their extinction), these early video phantoms remain significant emblems of an important transition in the cultural conceptualization of electronic presence brought about by the advent of television. This shift marked a transformation of the previous century's interest with paranormal communications into a fascination with paranormal media. Whereas earlier audio technologies served primarily as a fantastic yet essentially "neutral" conduit for channeling occult forms of communications (be they ghosts or aliens), "sighted" media such as television often appeared as haunted technologies in and of themselves, standing as either uncannily sentient electronic entities or as crucibles for forging wholly sovereign electronic universes.

Static and Stasis

The first "ghosts" of television, in other words, did not speak *through* the technology (as did the "spirits" of telegraphy and radio), but seemed to actually reside *within* the technology itself. Radio "broke through" to the land of spirits. Television (and the other visual media to follow) seemed capable of generating their own autonomous spirit worlds. Over the past half century, diverse accounts of television have frequently targeted the medium's paradoxes of visual presence, playing on the indeterminacy of the animate and inanimate, the real and the unreal, the "there" and the "not-there" to produce a new folklore of electronic media that continues to thrive in contemporary accounts of cyberspace and virtual reality. I would argue the dreams (and terrors) of virtual subjectivity that have so captured the imagination of both contemporary entertainment audiences and media critics have their foundations in these earlier, more humble tales of Grandfather Mackey, Uncle Phil, and their ghostly video brethren — the first beings to populate the strange, ambiguous electrical space of these visual media, manifestly present yet strangely absent, apparently "living" and yet something less than "alive." The following pages look at the early historical development of such mysteries around television, exploring the changing articulations of "presence" brought about by the medium's powers of electronic sight and its invocation of electronic worlds and beings.

The Eyes of Tomorrow

The occult powers ascribed to television developed as a dark underside to what many predicted, even at the turn of the century, would be the medium's most astonishing power: the illusion of live and instantaneous virtual teleportation to another time and place through sound *and* vision. As the development of television accelerated in the 1930s and the experimental technology became more widely known to the public, both scientifically "factual" predictions and wildly "fictional" prognostications of a future with television emphasized the new medium's astonishing qualities of visual presence in terms of electronic transportation. Television was to alternately transport viewers into another world and transport other worlds into the home. During this period of growing enthusiasm, commentators anticipated the medium's illusion of visual presence would far surpass even that of the cinema because television would provide a "living" link to distant vistas rather than a mere photographic record.

Even those earliest representations of the medium that successfully predicted television would one day become a form of electronic theater still emphasized above all else the medium's fantastic ability to teleport the viewer to distant realities. Published in 1932, for example, mystery writer Harry Stephen Keeler's incomprehensibly odd tale of television, *The Box from Japan,* features a long lecture on the various technological principles (real and imagined) of the new medium as prelude to a demonstration of the wonder technology. Seated before an experimental television screen in Chicago, Keeler's protagonist witnesses the transmission of a theatrical scene telecast "live" from a London stage:

> With eyes popping out of his head . . . , so real was the illusion to him that he was simply seated in the front row of a big empty theater, Halsey continued to stare upward without word — like a man who dares not speak lest he interrupt a carefully acted-out performance of some sort. The myriad small sounds carried by the fine sound-reproducing apparatus, itself not anywhere in view, however, were so convincing in themselves, let alone in conjunction with the extremely real figures less than fifteen feet from him, apparently, that he reached down with a thumb and forefinger and pinched himself that he was not merely dreaming a dream that he was a spectator of such a super-perfect fantasmagoria as was this, much less that he was not in London itself.[4]

Films of the 1930s such as *Murder by Television* and *International House* also portrayed television as a medium of overwhelming vividness and even uncanny interactive possibilities. The television pioneer of *Murder by Television,* for example, takes a parlor of invited guests on a breathtaking tour of the world through his new invention (only moments before being mysteriously "murdered by television"), and in *International House,* a testy W. C. Fields becomes embroiled in an argument with the televised image of Rudy Vallee. Apparently unimpressed by the new technology, Fields then shoots the image of a navy destroyer on the screen, causing it to sink into the televised ocean. Playing less on the theme of teleportation, meanwhile, other early depictions of television portrayed the medium as a prosthetic extension of human sight. As of 1945, for example, television was to be "the eyes of tomorrow,"[5] a living electronic extension of human vision that would enhance the audience's sphere of subjectivity and "extend our mastery of the world."[6] Such themes would be taken up twenty years later in the writings of Marshall McLuhan, who

Murder by Television and other early representations of the new technology emphasized the medium's capability for miraculous distant vision. (© 1932 Imperial-Cameo Productions)

would also describe the emerging media universe as an extension of humankind's senses.

This sense of spatial (and at times biological) ambiguity in the new medium would remain a key feature in conceptualizing television even as it entered the home in the 1950s. Advertisers, networks, and audiences alike all celebrated television in its first decade as providing the unprecedented experience of being "in two places at one time."[7] Early critics who promoted television as an artistic form emphasized the importance of "liveness" in the TV aesthetic, suggesting that such "liveness" was integral to the dramatic success of the medium.[8] Others deemed television a "window on the world" that would allow viewers to travel the globe in search of new, exciting, and exotic vistas.[9] As Lynn Spigel notes of this period, "Television at its most ideal promised to bring the audience not merely an illusion of reality as in the cinema, but a sense of 'being there,' a kind of *hyperrealism*."[10] Cultivating this indeterminacy of real and electronic space, the television industry itself consistently encouraged its earliest audiences to think in terms of an "ideology of liveness," and to regard the television as a portal into a dynamic, exciting, and perpetual present on the other side of the screen. Early production manuals for television, for example, often advised directors and producers to make use of this ambiguity of space and indeterminacy of time, citing the intersection of the real and the virtual as the medium's strongest feature. Outlining an aesthetic of "liveness," one handbook suggested that the medium, when used to its full potential, could elicit three types of viewer reactions based on its sense of presence:

(1) The effect of "looking in" on the program from the sidelines, without actually taking part in it . . .

(2) The effect of not only "looking in" on the program, wherever it may be, but of actually taking part in it . . .

(3) The person or persons on the program seem to step into your living room and converse with you.[11]

Examining this list, one finds a virtual continuum from (1) a flesh-and-blood human viewer with the access to survey directly some electrical elsewhere, to (2) an ambiguous interactive zone between real and electronic subjects, to (3) electronic subjects entering into the real space of the home (each effect, it should be noted, has served as a durable premise in science fiction). Even today, when most programming appears on film or videotape, television relies on the illusion of "liveness" to maintain audience viewership and program flow. Some would argue this is television's most insidious feature: the ability to provide the compelling illusion of "being there" as if one is participating in a public arena, when of course television actually transports its viewers no farther than the couch. Raymond Williams described this phenomenon as "mobile privatization": the illusion of mobility cloaked within the increasing privatization and thus isolation of the home.[12]

Although the presence of the TV set in the living room is something less than remarkable today, for a public that had long anticipated a device promoted for many years as capable of visually spanning time and space, the television sets that entered American homes in the 1950s no doubt bordered on the wonders of science fiction. Comfortable (or at least more familiar) with the phenomenon of transmitted voice, television's mysteries of form without substance, space without distance, vision without life made the medium a source of wonder and fascination. The ability of this box in the living room to "talk" and "see," moreover, made the medium something more than a merely inanimate technology. Television exuded a powerful presence in the household, serving in the active imagination as a fantastic portal to other worlds or even as a sentient entity brooding in the corner of the living room. Early television owners recognized that this medium had a qualitative "presence" that distinguished it from radio, a presence that made the medium even more fantastic and perhaps more sinister as well. Many reported a certain uneasiness around the new medium. In reporting on interviews conducted with television owners as early as the mid-1950s, for example, researcher Leo Bogart noted the strange phenomenon that "there is a feeling, never stated in so many words, that the set has a power of its own to control the destinies and viewing habits of the audience, and that what it 'does' to parents and children alike is somehow beyond the bounds of any individual set-owner's power of control."[13] The presence of television was such that its demand to be seen could be stronger than the volition of the audience to look away.

Although this early fascination with an uncanny sense of televisual presence is most explicit in science fiction and horror of the period, such anxiety was not limited to the purely speculative fantasies of narrative fiction. Accompanying this growing sense of uneasiness around the medium's incredible powers within the home, there emerges in the late 1950s and early 1960s (only a decade after television's initial invasion of the home) a significant rearticulation of the medium's apparent ability to "transport" viewers around the nation and globe. In these new discussions of television's uncanny "powers," the medium's distinctive "electronic elsewhere" became instead an "electronic nowhere." Rather than portray television as a magic means of teleportation, these more ominous portraits of the medium saw television as a zone of suspended animation, a form of oblivion from which viewers might not ever escape. These accounts of television essentially reversed and even negated its once most heralded powers, the mobile mysteries of electronic presence yielding to a logic that equated electronic static with cultural and even biological stasis.

Far removed from the pages of pulp science fiction, a 1959 conference on the mass media, sponsored by *Daedalus* and the *Journal of the American Academy of Arts and Sciences,* demonstrates the centrality of static metaphors in intellectual debates over the medium. Featuring panelists such as Edward Shils, Hannah Arendt, Daniel Bell, and Arthur Schlesinger Jr., this symposium ruminated on the fate of high culture and refined audiences confronted by the cultural void of television. In critiquing America's televisual life, panelists frequently discussed mass culture and especially television as producing a form of "suspension" for the audience, moving them away from more engaging, "authentic" forms of culture, both high and low, toward the electronic torpor of anonymous mass consumption. What had been an "active" arena of cultural practice became, with television, a "passive" mode of reception that left the audience in a form of cultural stasis transported and exiled away from real culture, real affect, the real world. Harvard Professor Oscar Handlin, for example, noted that the influx of mass electronic media had infused its audience with "a sense of apathy. The intense involvement of the masses with their culture at the turn of the century has given way to passive acquiescence."[14] Ernst Van Den Haag painted a similarly depressing scenario, suggesting that media technologies such as television had isolated individuals through a form of triple alienation. "Excessive communication serves to isolate people from one another, from themselves, and from experience," he argued. "It extends bonds by weakening them. . . . The total effect of mass culture is to distract people from lives which are so boring that they generate obsession with escape."[15] Finally, Irving Kristol lamented an entire generation lost to the media's seductive electronic whirlpool. "Where television and the mass media are corrupting is in dealing with youth, the teenagers. The most obnoxious aspects of all of these mass media are those that disorient youth, those that destroy their values and prevent them from achieving anything themselves. This is part of what seems to me at the moment to be a world-wide phenomenon . . . in which youths tend to secede from society and establish a community of their own."[16] This "lost generation," exiled by television in a sort of "teen-limbo," posed a genuinely perplexing problem for Kristol. "How to reach them, I don't know," he said in closing his remarks to the panel, as if American youth were quite literally removed from the terrain of life and culture.

Informed by such logic, FCC chair Newton Minow's notorious indictment of television as a "vast wasteland" in 1961 can easily be seen as yet another metaphor for this electronic "nowhere," implying that the cultural, intellectual, and even bodily well-being of the nation was adrift, and that an irresponsible industry had doomed a fundamentally passive audience to wander endlessly through an electronically mediated void. Echoing the concerns of the *Daedalus* conference, such rhetoric was commonplace among America's intelligentsia, many of whom believed that television had deteriorated into a medium that betrayed its original promise. The gradual extinction of critically esteemed "golden age" programming and the national uproar over the quiz show scandals, in particular, left television a suspect and bankrupt cultural form, even for those intellectuals who had originally celebrated the medium's possibilities of enlightening electronic contact with the masses. Such intellectual indictments of television provided the theoretical foundation for the more dystopic forms of science fiction that would follow. In the American home for less than a decade, television thus became, for both social science and science fiction, a zone of electronic suspension and at times even annihilation. So prominent and pervasive was this sense of static and stasis in television that by the early 1960s television itself would begin to play on these uncanny anxieties by integrating them into its own programming. New horror and science fiction programs in this era featured tales of the televisual fantastic that often offered quite self-reflexive meditations on the viewer's potentially dangerous relationship to this new technology and the phantom worlds it evoked. Nowhere was this theme more prominent than on two series of the early 1960s: *The Twilight Zone* and *The Outer Limits*.

There Is Nothing Wrong with Your Television Set

In this era of increasing interest in the uncanny powers of television, what is immediately striking about *The Twilight Zone* and *The Outer Limits* is the manner in which each series used its title and credit sequence to partition off an avowedly occult space within television itself. As Rod Serling informed his viewers each week, *The Twilight Zone* was that realm "as vast as space and timeless as infinity . . . the middle ground between light and shadow, between science and superstition . . . between the pit of man's fears and the summit of his knowledge." To be in "the twilight zone" is now, of course, a part of American folklore, describing any place or situation marked by the weird and uncanny. That original "twilight" space, however, was television itself. The exact wording of Serling's opening introduction changed over the course of the series, but never abandoned the attempt to evoke a sense of suspension, a "betwixt and between" liminality that cast the program (and its viewers) as occupying an "elsewhere," or even a "nowhere." The credit sequence's familiar camera tilt through a field of stars simulated a physical movement into this

The Twilight Zone: an occult space within the world of television. (© 1963 CBS Television)

indeterminate "zone" where viewers would be "lost" for a half-hour. Quite deliberately, *The Twilight Zone* served as the often disturbing, at times humorous, but always perverse "unconscious" of television. It was a self-described "zone" within the usually mundane procession of the broadcast schedules where the boundaries of televisual reality were the most ambiguous and where the typically cheerful world of television frequently found its ironic negation.

Writers for *The Twilight Zone* often evoked the uncanny aspects of their medium simply by turning to the past and dramatizing the cultural memory of previous haunted technologies. During its five-year network run, the series frequently turned to the haunted telecommunications story as a stock plot taken from television's occult prehistory. In "Long Distance Call" (1961), an elderly grandmother gives her grandson a toy telephone just before she dies. In the weeks that follow, the young boy claims that his grandmother talks to him on the phone and wants him to come join her. The parents of the boy finally realize he is telling the truth after he tries to kill himself and they hear breathing on the other end of the toy phone. In "Static," aired a week later, an older man disgusted by television retrieves his old radio set from the basement, only to find that it broadcasts transmissions from forty years earlier. "Night Call" (1964) told the story of a woman receiving mysterious phone calls at night, which turn out to originate from a fallen phone line on the grave of her long-dead fiancé. Finally, in "What's in the Box" (1964), a TV repairman, angered by a rude customer, fixes the set to pick up transmissions from the customer's own future, which leads the customer to a fight with his wife that results in her death.

Other episodes of *The Twilight Zone* addressed the interstitial, "twilight" quality of television most directly, dwelling on both comic and horrific accounts of the disintegrating boundaries dividing the real world and television's ambiguous electronic space. In the comic "Showdown with Rance McGrew" (1962), for example, a TV cowboy star finds himself transported to a real saloon of the old West, where cowboys and outlaws of the past protest their representation on his TV show (it is unclear how the cowboys have actually had an opportunity to ever see the show). Before a shoot-out with Jesse James, the actor pleads to be spared at any cost. Transported back to his own world of Hollywood, he finds that the real Jesse James is now his agent. In "A World of Difference" (1960), a man working in his office discovers his phone is dead and then hears someone yell "Cut!" He finds himself on a soundstage where everyone believes he is actually a drunk and declining actor. In this world he cannot find his real wife and children to prove his identity. His identity crisis causes everyone to think that the drunken actor has finally gone insane, so the show is canceled. At the last second the man runs back to the office set just before it is taken down, pleads with a higher force for redemption, and then returns to his real office and his previous "nondiegetic" existence.

As explicit as *The Twilight Zone* was in its attempts to carve an occult space within television, however, the program's efforts were eclipsed by a slightly less famous but entirely more bleak and apocalyptic generic cousin. More than any other series of the era, *The Outer Limits* consistently recast television's "window on the world" as a terrifying window on the "otherworldly." Elaborating on period accounts of television's ghostly presence and incorporating period critiques of television's alienating "nowhere," the series presented the medium's most compelling critique of television's own powers of annihilation, frequently dwelling on an electronic presence that manifested itself as a form of "oblivion" or "electro-limbo." Indeed, "oblivion" was the only recurring monster in this horror anthology, and it took a variety of forms over the forty-eight-episode run of the series. Regardless of its shape or dimension, however, oblivion in *The Outer Limits* was almost always mediated by some form of paranormal electronic technology and centered most immediately on the American family, a scenario that offered repeated parables about the audience's own relationship to the TV set, and the set's relationship, in turn, to a vast electronic nowhere. Whether faced with new beings, mysterious powers, or strange technologies, the characters in these stories (and the viewer at home) had to struggle against uncanny and frequently electronic forces that threatened not just to kill them, but to dissolve them into nothingness.

This assault on the viewer's autonomy began in the opening images of the program, which, like *The Twilight Zone,* used its credit sequence to remove the program from the terrain of "normal" television. In a medium already renowned for its intrusive presence in the American home, few television shows have featured opening credit sequences as calculatedly invasive as that of *The Outer Limits.* A narrational entity known only as the "control voice" opened each week's episode with these unnerving words of assurance:

> *There is nothing wrong with your television set.*

Their attention suddenly focused on the set, viewers became the targets of an increasingly ominous series of commands and assertions:

> *Do not attempt to adjust the picture.*
> *We are controlling transmission.*
> *We will control the horizontal.*
> *We will control the vertical.*
> *We can change the focus to a soft blur, or sharpen it to crystal clarity.*

On-screen, the control voice demonstrated its power by taking command of the picture tube to program a display of warbling sine waves, vertical rolls, and other forms of electronic choreography. Having now completely gained possession of the family console, the control voice issued its final command and warning:

> *For the next hour, sit quietly, and we will control all that you see and hear.*
> *You are about to participate in a great adventure. You are about to*
> *experience the awe and mystery that reaches from the inner mind to* The
> Outer Limits.

At this cue the theme music would swell for the opening credits, after which the control voice relinquished command, at least momentarily, to the "true" masters of the screen — the commercial advertisers. The voice would come back at the end of each week's episode to "return control" of the television to its temporarily dispossessed owner.

Significantly, the original title planned for the series had been *Please Stand By,* the familiar invocation of panicked broadcasters when confronting social or technological disaster. As evident in the "panic" broadcast of 1938, such interruptions in the routine flow of commercial broadcasting always give viewers pause as they consider the possibility of an impending catastrophe. Such alarm was especially pronounced during the cold war years of the early 1960s, when the intrusion of a network "special report" could signify imminent nuclear annihilation. The very design of the show, then, linked television's unnerving presence to a larger social world of crisis and impending destruction. Debuting in the months immediately preceding the assassination of President Kennedy and vanishing at the threshold of the nation's growing civil unrest at mid-decade, *The Outer Limits* presented a signature moment of unmitigated doom on American television, often suggesting that the sciences, technologies, and citizens of the "New Frontier" were on a collision course with oblivion.

Of course, even as vast and seemingly boundless a concept as "oblivion" exists within some degree of historical specificity. Surveying the ubiquity of this motif across the run of the series and across other forms of television discourse in the early 1960s, one is left to question why the invocation of televisual nothingness should have such resonance within this historical period. Answers to such complex representational questions must remain imprecise, of course, but three looming and often interrelated "oblivions" of the "New Frontier" era would seem key in producing these electronically mediated visions of the void — the infinite depths of outer space, the emotional "limbo" of suburban domesticity, and the specter of absolute nuclear annihilation. Both in the social reality of the audience and the science-fictional "unreality" of the series, television figured as the crucial bridge between these three realms, casting the medium as the pivotal technology in the "new frontier's" melding of space, science, and suburbia. The atom, the universe, and the suburbs all portended oblivion in one form or another, and all three realms had a privileged relationship to television.

The Outer Limits can be considered within the same cultural moment described by Lynn Spigel as informing the "fantastic family sit-com," a cycle of programs in the 1960s she identifies as engaging in a critique of the narrative and social conventions of domestic comedy from the 1950s. Spigel argues that the fantastic sitcom, like much of the popular culture of this new frontier era, developed in response to a series of disappointments in American life during this era, chief among these being the homogenizing conformity demanded by suburban living and the seeming vulnerability of American technology in the wake of *Sputnik*. "This historical conjuncture of disappointments provided the impetus for a new utopian future — one based on the rhetoric of Kennedy's New Frontier and fortified with the discourse of science and technology."[17] As with the programs discussed by Spigel *(Bewitched, I Dream of Jeannie, My Favorite Martian), The Outer Limits* also exploited the era's emerging fascination with space and science to interrogate the bland "ideology of domesticity" cultivated during the Eisenhower years. Under attack, or at least under reconsideration, were a set of normative gender roles and stultifying narrative conventions most prominently expressed in family sitcoms such as *Leave It to Beaver* and *Father Knows Best*. As Spigel writes of the fantastic sitcoms, "Their . . . space-age imagery made the familial strange; it made people pause, if only to laugh, at what had once seemed natural and everyday. This unlikely collision of genres gave audiences the chance to reflect on their own expectations — not only about the sitcom's narrative conventions — but also about the social conventions by which they lived their lives" (228). Born of the same disillusionment with suburbia that informed the fantastic sitcom, *The Outer Limits* also recontextualized TV families within paranormal and supernatural scenarios, producing a defamiliarized account of domesticity that accommodated often trenchant social commentary.

Although *The Outer Limits* shared the same cultural project of the fantastic sitcom in reexamining American family life, differences in terms of genre (horror rather than comedy) and format (anthology drama rather than episodic series) often pushed *The Outer Limits* into territory far more disturbing and apocalyptic. Whereas critiques of domesticity in the fantastic sitcom encountered a series of "safety valves" such as "laugh tracks, harmonious resolutions, and other structures of denial,"[18] *The Outer Limits,* unencumbered by the burden of continuing characters and a consistent "situation," had the occasional license to destroy the centerpiece of both postwar life and episodic television — the nuclear family. The program's weekly promise to present "the awe and mystery that reaches from the inner mind to the outer limits" was not so much a validation of the New Frontier's enthusiastic call to explore space as it was a threat to expose, through the fundamentally uncanny medium of television, the terrors awaiting the nation in the profound mysteries of the human mind, the hollow conventions of family life, and the vast emptiness of the universe. From episode to episode, there was the persistent subtext that America's intense investment in space, science, and domesticity masked an immense abyss, an anomic nothingness lurking at the core of the nation's identity. Acknowledging the "awe and mystery" of these new territories of scientific exploration, *The Outer Limits* also suggested that America might find the New Frontier itself to be a terrifying vacuum, an annihilating and discorporative void accessed through television.

Monsters in the Static

Appropriately, the close association of television and oblivion in *The Outer Limits* began with the program's pilot. In "The Galaxy Being," which also served as the series premiere on 16 September 1963, an inventor scans the airwaves with a powerful transceiving device that draws energy from a nearby radio station. He captures strange signals, "three-dimensional static," that transform on a viewscreen into the image of an alien. When the inventor leaves the radio station that evening, an accident teleports the alien to earth via the transmitted signal, where as a three-dimensional electronic being he quickly becomes the prey of local authorities. Cornered by his attackers, the alien destroys the radio tower as a demonstration of his power. He then warns the encroaching mob: "There are powers in the universe beyond anything you know. . . . There is much you have to learn. . . . Go to your homes. Go and give thought to the mysteries of the universe." The crowd disperses while the inventor and the alien return in peace to the radio station. But the alien laments that he cannot return to his home planet because he has broken a law forbidding contact with other worlds. Exiled from home and only an electronic phantom on earth, the alien consigns himself to oblivion. "End of transmission," he says as he reduces the transmitter power that first brought him to earth, turning the dial until at last he completely vanishes.

This poignant tale was a fit debut for a series that would continue to explore the relationship between electronic transmission, physical discorporation, and social alienation. As a tale of an alien entity contacted and then teleported through the "three-dimensional static" of an intergalactic television set, "The Galaxy Being" dramatized the decades of earlier cultural speculation that wireless might be used to contact other planets. Centered squarely in the rhetoric of the New Frontier, however, "The Galaxy Being" developed this familiar premise into a more disturbing tale of electronic existentialism. "You must explore. You must reach out," says the alien, echoing the words of NASA officials and its patron administration. But although advocating interstellar exploration, this episode also nervously equated the unfathomable dimensionality of traveling through outer space with the uncanny spatiotemporal mysteries presented by television transmission. In the era of the televised space race, "The Galaxy Being" played on the suspense and tension all Americans felt while watching on their own TV sets as NASA launched Alan Shepard, John Glenn, and other astronauts into the great void of outer space. By simultaneously maximizing the drama of these launches and mediating the home viewer's own entry into outer space, television became not only the preferred medium for witnessing the space race, but also a seemingly privileged means of anxious access to space itself. With the galaxy being "tuning" himself out of existence, this debut episode cultivated such anxiety by portraying outer space and television's electronic space as a common limbo where one might be "transmitted" into nothingness.

Such themes continued in the second broadcast episode of *The Outer Limits,* "The Borderland." Here experiments with high-powered electrical fields reveal the possibility of an alternate dimension. During an experiment to contact a wealthy man's dead son, a malfunction disrupts the equipment and blows the breakers, trapping a scientist in an eerie electrical netherworld that exists between the dimensions of life and death. Unable to navigate through this limbo realm, the man cries out helplessly to his wife as he describes the terrifying nothingness that engulfs him. The viewer sees him as a figure thrashing behind a wall of static, as if trapped within the viewer's own television set. In the end the scientist escapes, but not before the wealthy patron of the experiment leaps through the wall of

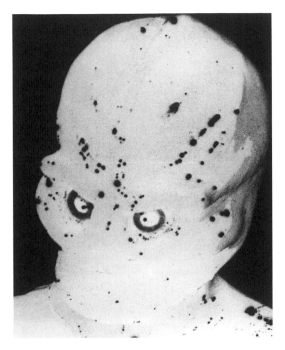

"The Galaxy Being" of *The Outer Limits:*
extraterrestrial, interdimensional, and televisual.
(© 1963 MGM/UA)

static in search of his son, only to be forever lost in the other electrical
dimension.

With their mutual fixation on electronic transmission as a bridge between inner and outer space, both "The Galaxy Being" and "The Borderland" exploited to the fullest *The Outer Limits'* simulation of an intercepted paranormal transmission, suggesting the possibility of alternate
lifeforms and dimensions lurking in the familiar realm of televisual static.
Television transmission in general, even in its more mundane forms, was a
topic of much public interest in the early 1960s, as "ultra high" frequency
TV signals and orbiting space capsules both tested "the outer limits" of
the atmosphere. Beyond the usual articles advising husbands how to take
to the rooftops to improve reception, the popular press also gave wide
coverage to the new decade's emerging forms of signal transmission,
including UHF and color TV.[19] Most influential in associating television
transmission with outer space was the 1962 launch of *Telstar,* the communications satellite that first made possible live television broadcasts

across the ocean. As with a host of other international media that preceded it, *Telstar* inspired a series of utopian predictions concerning telecommunications and world peace that portrayed the space-traveling television signal as a world ambassador.[20] A symbol of the earth united through the heavens, the launching of *Telstar* strengthened an already strong cultural association between television and outer space, and reinvigorated television's status as an extraordinary and fantastic technology.

In the paranormal imagination, however, television transmission presented more a terrifying electronic "nothingness" than an avenue of political utopia, especially when these viewers imagined these signals traveling through the lonely infinitude of outer space. Where does the "galaxy being" go when he turns off the transmitter? What exactly is this strange electromagnetic limbo between life and death encountered in "The Borderlands"? In the paranormal broadcast signal encountered with television, the phenomenon of transmission is not so much a link to other worlds as an uncanny, alternate dimension in and of itself, a limbo realm not unlike the vast expanses of outer space with which television was so frequently identified. This is the horror facing the "galaxy being," the scientists in "The Borderlands," countless other characters on *The Outer Limits,* and even the viewer at home. Television does not threaten to transport them "elsewhere," but succeeds in assimilating them, at least temporarily, into its own "nowhere." Television thus threatened to consume its subjects, if not into the actual vacuum of outer space, then into its own logic and fictions that existed in an ethereal space that, nevertheless, could often feel more real, more "live" than the everyday material environment of the viewer's home.

An interesting antecedent to *The Outer Limits'* fascination with television and oblivion came from the otherwise mundane pages of *TV Guide.* In a piece dubbed "Television's Biggest Mystery," the magazine shared with its readers the enigma of KLEE, a station once based in Houston, Texas:

At 3:30 p.m., British Summer Time, September 14, 1953, Charles W. Brafley of London picked up the call letters KLEE-TV on his television set. Later that month and several times since, they have been seen by engineers at Atlantic Electronics, Ltd., Lancaster, England. . . . The call letters KLEE-TV have not been transmitted since July, 1950, when the Houston station changed its letters to KPRC-TV. . . . A check of the world's television stations confirms the fact that there is not now and never has been another KLEE-TV.[21]

Here again is the mystery of the phantom signal that, as in *The Moon Terror,* provokes an understandable anxiety over the indeterminacy of its source. But what distinguishes the KLEE phenomenon from other phantom transmission stories is its seeming disruption of linear time. In this fantastic scenario, KLEE's signal has somehow become "lost" in what should have been the nanosecond separating transmission and reception, an infinitesimal moment in time transformed into an apparently infinite limbo. Combining anxieties over agency with the mysteries of physics, the KLEE story posited an electrical subject at the center of this riddle, one not unlike the "galaxy being" or the interdimensional scientist of *The Outer Limits.*

Temporarily forgotten, the KLEE enigma returned when the vagabond station was spotted once again, this time on the TV set of Mrs. Rosella Rose of Milwaukee, Wisconsin, sometime in February of 1962, a full twelve years after the Houston station had abandoned the KLEE station card.[22] In this updated version, KLEE's mysterious signal now carried more than just the call letters, allowing a glimpse into an alternate universe on the other side of the TV screen. Mrs. Rose reported briefly seeing the image of an unknown man and woman arguing on a balcony, followed by a particularly strange message. "The picture faded out then and the KLEE flashed on again — and here's the really strange part — superimposed over the KLEE, which was still on, the word 'HELP' flashed on, off, and on again. The screen then went black."[23] This mysterious captive's cry for help suggests that television could serve not only as a realm of oblivion, but also as a seemingly sentient gatekeeper or cruelly malevolent jailer. This installment in the KLEE story thus makes manifest an anxiety common to all other televisual tales of the electronic nowhere. It provokes the fear that viewers too might one day find themselves trapped within the television set, whisked away by this most domestic of technologies into an electronic netherworld.

The KLEE mystery and *The Outer Limits* stories that followed it, be they based on "true" incidents or long-standing legends, are unsettling for the same reasons that the telegraph of 1848 must have seemed so utterly fantastic. The fleeting and inexplicable transmissions of KLEE, the "galaxy being," and the "borderlands" are eerie in that they are symptomatic of a general loss of "self-presence" felt socially in electronic communications as a whole. As readers thumbed through their weekly copies of *TV Guide,* the KLEE mystery reminded them once again that "live" messages

and "living" messengers were no longer coterminus, and that consciousness itself could exist in seeming independence from either a sender or a
receiver. Similarly, these tales alluded to the existence of an invisible and
perhaps imperious empire in the ether. Although the Spiritualists found
this dissolution and reconstitution of consciousness via electronic media
to be a promising mode of spiritual contact, even a utopian key to solving
all of the material world's problems, the wandering consciousness in these
tales suggests that by the time of television, signals once under human
command seemed either out of control or, even worse, under the control of
increasingly sinister forces. Beginning in the age of wireless, the once
wondrous "otherworld" of electronic telecommunications had become by
the 1960s a vast reservoir of cultural anxiety, presenting a localized fear
about TV itself, certainly, but also a more general unease over the increasingly atomized world that electronic media had helped to create. As
radio's electronic elsewhere became TV's great electronic nowhere, the
airwaves no longer represented a gathering of souls, but presented instead
the audience's atomization and dispersal across infinity.[24]

But abduction and assimilation by television's electronic nowhere were
not the only anxieties expressed in these tales. As a story of television's
"distant sight," KLEE also fascinates because it suggests a certain "vision
on the air," positing an electrical omniscience associated with television
broadcasting as an invisible blanket covering the earth. Even if the television cannot actually assimilate us, there remains the disturbing thought
that, just as we can potentially peer into other worlds through the television, these other worlds may be peering into our own living room. Such
anxieties were particularly acute in the early 1960s as both the United
States and Soviet Union raced to launch satellites into the stratosphere for
the explicit purpose of surveying the world below to the smallest detail. In
an age of growing satellite saturation in the sky and absolute set penetra-
tion in the home, the spatiotemporal enigmas of TV transmission provided
a sinister variation on a cultural anxiety dating back to the earliest days of
television. Spigel notes that early discourses on television often expressed
"a larger obsession with privacy, an obsession that was typically expressed through the rhetorical figure of the window, the border between
inside and outside worlds."[25] In its more benevolent form the "window"
of television activated the medium's marvelous "aesthetics of presence,"
showcasing the medium's ability to transport the viewer "live" to lo-
calities around the world. Within this growing complex of surveillance

technologies and political tensions, however, television was also the most plausible agent to serve as a "window on the home." Period accounts of television often pondered the seemingly inevitable reversibility of the watcher and the watched presented by all telecommunications technology. Of *Telstar,* for example, Arthur C. Clarke waxed poetically that "no dictator can build a wall high enough to stop its citizens' listening to the voices from the stars." And yet he also conceded that the launching of such communications satellites would eventually make "absolute privacy impossible."[26] In the mad political and scientific race to colonize, communicate, and survey from the sky, who could know exactly what capacities *Telstar, Comsat,* and their Soviet counterparts actually had or to what uses these secret technologies might eventually be put?

Surveillance technology has long been a fixture of science fiction, of course, and *The Outer Limits* also made frequent use of this device. One episode in particular forged a most explicit relationship between advanced television technology, outer space, and seemingly paranormal forms of surveillance, again playing on public anxieties about television as an electronic eye in the home. "O.B.I.T.," airing on 4 November 1963, told the story of a highly advanced video monitoring system in use at an American military base, a device that allows its operator to monitor secretly the actions of any individual on or near the compound. An investigating senator sets out to learn more about the machine, the Outer Band Individuated Teletracer, or O.B.I.T. as it is known for short. He is told that each person generates his or her own distinct electronic signal and that the O.B.I.T. machine has the ability to tune in these frequencies anywhere within a range of a few hundred miles. In a dramatic courtroom finale, a general appears on the stand to insist that a "monster" lurks on the base and haunts the O.B.I.T. screen. Surveying the courtroom with O.B.I.T. reveals a sinister computer technician to be the monster, an alien from another world whose human disguise can only be uncloaked by this mysterious form of television. The creature boasts that it has brought the O.B.I.T. technology to Earth in order to demoralize, divide, and conquer the planet by instilling fear and suspicion through the entire population. "The machines are everywhere," he says to the stunned humans, "and they'll demoralize you, break your spirit, create such rifts and tensions in your society that no one will be able to repair them!"

A less than subtle reworking of Orwell with a touch of HUAC paranoia added for good measure, "O.B.I.T." nevertheless concretized a suspicion no doubt held by many during this period. If television can be seen anywhere and everywhere at once, this episode proposed, then why could it not potentially "see" anywhere and everywhere as well? The device of the "Individuated Teletracer" expanded the fear of surveillance beyond the actual apparatus of the home television set by appealing to the existence of this larger electromagnetic blanket enveloping the earth, a realm where each person unknowingly sent off electrical signals that could be intercepted and monitored on "alien" TV sets. The story of "O.B.I.T" may have seemed outlandish, but no more so than a *Life* magazine article from 1964 reporting on a device called T.E.S.T., or the "Tanner Electronic Survey Tabulator." *Life* described T.E.S.T. as a "spooky little truck" that patrolled suburban streets, "its innards . . . crammed full of fancy electronic equipment that can and does silently violate the sanctuary of those lighted living rooms to determine 1) whether the occupants are watching their television sets, and if so, 2) on what channel."[27] The inventor of T.E.S.T. predicted his device would revolutionize the imprecise science of "ratings" by covertly monitoring televisions and families in the home, whether they chose to be monitored or not. If a mere panel truck could accomplish such a feat, then it was reasonable to suppose that high-tech satellites could watch over entire nations, cities, and neighborhoods, perhaps even telecasting private images from the home to any number of sinister agencies, be they governmental or extraterrestrial.

The "control voice's" closing narration to the "O.B.I.T." episode reminded viewers that Americans were their own worst enemies in terms of such suspicion. Exploiting the insatiable American desire to know the secrets of both outer space and the family next door, the aliens are confident that this nation of atomized, isolated, and alienated citizens can easily be brought to its knees. A fragmented and distrustful society connected only through the dull glow of its TV screens is no match for this seductive technology of alien surveillance, one that allows these estranged citizens to spy on one another's personal traumas and family secrets. In "O.B.I.T." the central narrational and technological device of the omniscient television set ultimately served a rather tired plot of alien invasion, but it also expressed the more immediate, plausible, and unsettling fear that television would eventually betray the well-guarded secrets of the American household. In these particularly paranoid transmissions from *The Outer Limits,* television threatened to expose another mammoth void structuring American consciousness in the early 1960s — the suffocating emotional oblivion to be found within the American home.

Domestic Asylum

As many social historians have noted, the nuclear family emerged as the primary social unit in American postwar society.[28] In a coordinated effort to encourage commodity consumption, stimulate housing starts, and re-populate the nation, a variety of forces in postwar America coalesced to renew faith in family life and to reinvent its meanings in new mass-produced consumer suburbs. But this reorientation of American social life was not without profound consequences. In flight from the nation's urban centers and severed from a whole nexus of earlier community relations, the nuclear families of white suburbia suddenly stood in self-imposed isolation as their own primary network of personal identity and social support. Within the increasingly isolated family, meanwhile, the middle-class mother became the abandoned keeper of the household. This shift in social identity from the community to the family restructured many Americans' engagement with both the social world and the family circle, providing each member of the family with a new social role to internalize and obey.[29]

Throughout the 1950s and into the 1960s, television developed a highly codified series of narrative conventions to represent this emerging suburban ideal, constructing a middle-class utopia of labor-saving appliances, manicured lawns, and spacious architecture, all designed to showcase the suburban housewife as the ultimate symbol of material success and domestic bliss. Within this ordered space postwar wives traded one form of "freedom" for another: exiled from the workplace and public life they were "liberated" within the home through a series of consumer goods. As Mary Beth Haralovich notes of this arrangement, housewives were "promised psychic and social satisfaction for being contained within the private space of the home; and in exchange for being targeted, measured, and analyzed for the marketing and design of consumer products, [they were] promised leisure and freedom from housework."[30] Even with its newly purchased array of "emancipating" ovens, irons, and washing machines, however, the suburban home and the rigid social order it stood for could be a prison at times, especially for women, but also for men who became caught up in the "rat race" of consuming for status. Yet, as Elaine Tyler May observes in her study of postwar families, there was little incentive to change the decade's often oppressive domestic regime. "Forging an independent life outside of marriage carried enormous risks of emotional and economic bankruptcy, along with social ostracism," observes May. "As these couples sealed the psychological boundaries around the family, they also sealed their fates within it."[31]

At times, however, this sealing of "psychological boundaries" around the family could produce, not only a general sense of disaffection, but clinical diagnoses of psychosis and possible institutionalization. A study of schizophrenia in the early 1950s, for example, revealed that married women were far more likely than married men to suffer schizophrenic episodes and noted that a common stage in the "break-down" of schizophrenic housewives was "the increasing isolation of the wife from family and social relationships, her more-or-less progressive detachment from participation in social reality."[32] Discussing this study some twenty-five years later, Carol Warren notes that "the problems in everyday living experienced by these women — loneliness, isolation, and the stress of the housewife role — were reflections of the conventional structure of marriage and the family in the 1950s. But they were also psychiatric symptoms."[33] Unable to leave the studio soundstage at the end of the day after imprinting a vision of domestic bliss on film, real housewives of the period often confronted terrifying social and emotional voids that left them both abandoned and disenfranchised. Warren goes so far as to argue that the individual "psychopathologies" of these women were in fact a socially symbolic prison, and she describes the "delusions and hallucinations" experienced by these schizophrenic women as "metaphors for their social place" (58). One woman, for example, "saw herself as having been hypnotized by her husband and her doctors, as punished for her offenses by [electroshock therapy], and as the victim of a master conspiracy to rob her of control of her own life" (58). Another subject in the study heard voices that accused her of not properly caring for her children, a condition that worsened to the point that she eventually set fire to her own home.[34]

Glorifying the virtues of the privatized family and bound more to narrative than social conventions, television's domestic sitcom had no language with which to engage the potential mental disintegration of Mayfield, Springfield, and the other well-scrubbed communities of "television-land." And although the fantastic sitcom often played on the temporary illusion of suburban schizophrenia (talking horses, Martian uncles, maternal automobiles, etc.), it was science fiction that presented the most expansive textual space in which to expose and explore this suburban psychopathology. Often presented in tandem with the vacuum of space and the vast electronic nowhere of television was an equally terrifying portrait of a more claustrophobic "emotional nowhere." In these domestic visions of oblivion, husbands and wives found themselves trapped, either metaphorically or quite literally, within the suffocating confines of the American home, often to the point of madness. Like much other science fiction of the period, *The Outer Limits* frequently portrayed the American home as a "domestic asylum," cultivating the ambiguity between the dominant conception of the household as a cozy "refuge" from the real world and a more critical view of the home as a place of the insane. As explored in *The Outer Limits,* the "domestic asylum" of the American suburbs was a zone of torpor and constraint, an emotional void every bit as alienating as the electronic oblivion to be found in television.

If the gendered schizophrenia of the 1950s, as Warren suggests, can be considered a symbolic response of women trapped by the constricting conventions of social reality, then *The Outer Limits'* numerous excursions into domestic dementia can be thought of as symbolic responses to the constrictive conventionality of familial representation found in American television. In tandem with *The Twilight Zone,* the series often called critical attention to the artificial, synthetic, and otherwise "fake" world of televisual domesticity itself, standing as the most disruptive resident in what Spigel has termed "the electronic neighborhood." Spigel argues that the mass exodus of postwar America to suburban communities led television to produce compensatory worlds that softened the alienation, competition, and conformism encountered by these families in their new preplanned communities. "Television provided an illusion of the ideal neighborhood — the way it was supposed to be. Just when people had left their lifelong companions in the city, television sitcoms pictured romanticized versions of neighbor and family bonding."[35] Frequently presenting an explicit critique of this idealized portrait of the American family so painstakingly molded by an alliance of governmental, advertising, consumerist, and television interests during the postwar period, *The Outer Limits* explored the "delusions and hallucinations" that might befall a June Cleaver, Margaret Anderson, or Donna Stone once the camera was turned off.

In "The Bellaro Shield," for example, an episode of *The Outer Limits* that first aired on 10 February 1964, a "deviant" housewife is driven insane by a literalized metaphor of her domestic confinement. In this episode a meek young scientist talks with his father about taking over the chairmanship of the Bellaro family's high-tech corporation. The scientist's wife, Judith, eagerly awaits the news of the promotion, hungry for the rise in status and power her husband's new position will provide. But the father decides his son is not fit to run the company and tells him he has picked another successor. Later, after the scientist forgets to deactivate a new laser technology he has been developing, its beam intercepts an alien, who is transported, much like "the galaxy being" before him, into the scientist's home.[36] When Judith discovers that her husband has "captured" an alien, she is sure this scientific triumph will convince the elder Bellaro to make her husband chairman. Even more enticing, the alien carries with him a small device in his hand that allows him to activate an impenetrable shield, a forcefield that can be expanded to any dimension. Judith realizes this technology would revolutionize the defense industry and make her husband's company the most powerful in the world, so she arranges for the father to return to see an amazing demonstration of his son's "new invention." She then steals the technology from the alien, striking the creature in the back of the head. When the father arrives, Judith demonstrates the wondrous new technology that she credits her husband for pioneering. Clicking the device, she activates the "Bellaro Shield," which she has named after both her husband and father-in-law. After demonstrating that the shield can withstand bullets and even laser fire, however, she discovers that she cannot deactivate the forcefield. She is trapped within its glass-like walls and is quickly running out of air. In the end the alien regains consciousness, returns to the lab, and deactivates the shield before expiring. But the experience of entrapment has been too much for Judith. She continues to flail away at the now phantom shield. She has gone completely mad and is convinced that she is still imprisoned within it and will be forever.

"The Bellaro Shield" is a rich and conflicted text in what it says about the relationship of marriage, gendered ambition, and domestic asylum in the early 1960s. On the one hand, Judith is clearly "punished" for having disrupted her prescribed role as the passive homemaker. She is marked early in the text as a suburban Lady MacBeth, aggressively pursuing her husband's corporate career even when he will not. For this alone she might be considered demented in the social context of postwar suburbia, where such ambition could easily be categorized as "crazy."[37] On the other hand, although portraying the harsh penalty of gender deviance, "The Bellaro Shield" also evokes the potential terror of domestic isolation through an exaggerated technological metaphor of the overly restrictive household. The Bellaro Shield, a device named (appropriately enough) after the patriarchal forces that contain her in the home on a daily basis, presents an intense and focused field of power that threatens to imprison Judith forever. One cannot help but be struck by how the "Shield" itself, as a box-like, glass prison within the home, stands as a metaphor for television. After activating the shield, Judith finds herself at the center of domestic space trapped behind suffocating panes of glass. The others look on in horror. Close-ups of the entombed housewife present the illusion that Judith is actually pressing against the glass of the viewer's home screen. This dynamic image of a woman flailing behind glass walls, at first real and then imaginary, is a dense and multivalent emblem that merges the period's visions of electronic and domestic oblivion. Women such as Judith were trapped by television in two ways, physically removed from the world and isolated within the home by this imperious domestic technology, while also trapped within its constricting conventions of representation. If the suburban home was truly a "domestic asylum," then television was the household's watchful warden, enforcing the housewife's solitary confinement while also instructing her in the desired behaviors for suburban assimilation.[38] As a televised housewife, Judith is perched between these electronic and domestic voids, trapped within a prison of brick and mortar on the one hand and of light and electricity on the other.

"The Bellaro Shield" aligns *The Outer Limits* with a larger cycle of period science fiction centering on mass society critiques of television, women, and the home. Keith Laumer's short story, "The Walls," first published in *Amazing Stories* in 1963, tells a similar tale of "domestic asylum," with a housewife in the not-too-distant future slowly driven to madness by her husband's desire for an ever more constricting television system in the home. The story begins with Harry replacing the couple's conventional TV set with a "full-wall," a new system that features a screen taking up an entire wall of the living room. Bored with this larger version of the same routine spectacle, Flora turns off the full-wall and is disconcerted to find that the deactivated screen, "the residual glow having faded now, was a perfect mirror."[39] Soon, Harry proudly adds a second "full-wall" unit adjacent to the first, transforming half of the living room into a giant TV screen. At this point Flora's fate becomes inevitable. A third full-wall unit is installed and then a fourth until finally the entire apartment is pervaded by an omnidirectional spectacle so strong that the room's doors and corners can no longer be perceived. The saturation of sound and image proves too much, causing Flora to panic one day while Harry is still away at work. Just before fainting, she deactivates the system. When she wakes up, she finds herself alone in the apartment surrounded, like Judith Bellaro, by four glass walls that now recede as mirrors into infinity. Also like Judith, she "misreads" her domestic situation through a video-induced psychosis:

> But how strange. The walls of the cell block were transparent now; she could see all the other apartments, stretching away to every side. She nodded; it was as she thought. They were all as barren and featureless as her own. . . . They all had four Full-walls. And the other women — the other wives, shut up like her in these small, mean cells; they were all aging, and sick, and faded, starved for fresh air and sunshine. She nodded again, and the woman in the next apartment nodded in sympathy. All the women were nodding; they all agreed — poor things. . . . She stood in the center of the room, not screaming now, only sobbing silently. In the four glass walls that enclosed her, she stood alone. There was no point in calling any longer. (67–69)

At the end of the tale, are we to believe that Flora is suffering a schizophrenic episode, watching her reflection in the mirror without realizing that it is herself that she sees? Or is she hallucinating, imagining that she can actually look into the apartments that surround her? In either case, Laumer's tale, like "The Bellaro Shield," revolves around the abandoned housewife whose existence becomes completely "mediated" by television. With their common themes of a "lost" reality within the home, these tales merge the electronic oblivion of television and the emotional oblivion of the home, not by pulling the victimized spectator into the television apparatus itself, but by having the void of television expand, both materially and symbolically, to become a totalizing and wholly simulated realm of electronic incarceration, one that concretizes a lonely emotional void already silently in place in the home. Both the Bellaro Shield and the full-wall system are manifestations of the emotional walls that already separate husband and wife in these tales and that no doubt divided many actual suburban homes of the decade.

Significantly, in these mass-society morality tales, television seems to drive women "insane" more frequently than it does men, suggesting that such stories have their roots in the prevailing cultural assumption that women watch too much television. "Common sense would indicate that women, since they spend more waking time at home than either men or children, would be the heaviest viewers, as a group," wrote Leo Bogart in the late 1950s, producing statistics to support this claim.[40] Along with this assumption, of course, is the perception that heavy TV viewers must be "continually diverted from the real world of people and problems to the fantasy world of the media."[41] In this sense, spotting a ghost or infinite selves on television is not far removed from a hysterical symptom. Women who watch too much television were bound to see something inexplicable, goes this line of reasoning, not necessarily because the image was truly paranormal, but because of their lack of masculine rationality.

Such a diagnosis evokes Andres Huyssen's contention that mass culture, at least since the nineteenth century, has been overwhelmingly perceived as feminine (and thus inferior) to the "masculine" qualities of modernist art. As Huyssen comments, "This line of argument invariably leads back to Nietzsche. Significantly, Nietzsche's ascription of feminine characteristics to the masses is always tied to his aesthetic vision of the artist-philosopher-hero, the suffering loner who stands in irreconcilable opposition to modern democracy and its inauthentic culture."[42] Early commentary on television abounds with such rhetoric. Spigel, citing Philip Wylie's venomous *Generation of Vipers,* argues that many in the 1950s believed television would join radio to "turn men into female-dominated dupes."[43] In a variety of contexts, television signified the invasion of feminine and thus "inauthentic" culture, presenting a direct threat to the taste, values, and autonomy of the "husband-philosopher-hero." In paranormal tales of television, the TV set not only stands as a symbol of this denigrated feminine culture; in some cases it actually becomes gendered as a sentient feminine being. Perhaps most remarkable in this regard is the 1953 film *The Twonky,* which tells of a college professor whose wife buys him a television set to keep him company while she is gone for the weekend. The TV set soon becomes ambulatory and assumes the feminized role of housekeeper, washing dishes, making coffee, and listening to banal pop records on the phonograph, all to the dismay and disgust of the husband.

Not truly a "fantastic" tale, Howard Nemerov's short story "Beyond the Screen" nonetheless depends on a similar equation of femininity, electronic presence, and the televisual apparatus as a form of stasis and oblivion. In this tale from the mid-1950s, a husband resolutely resists his family's appeals to buy a television set and stands fast until his wheelchair-bound mother-in-law comes for an extended visit. His wife complains that her mother is used to watching television and will be lonely without it. The husband relents, and soon a new television set is the focal point of the home, watched avidly by the mother-in-law, wife, and the couple's young son. The husband even agrees to climb the roof to connect the aerial and ground the lightning rod for the set. Eventually, the husband himself is snared into viewing, and after a few weeks he comes to an uneasy truce with the TV set. One day as the family sits watching a documentary showing the coronation of an African king (titled, interestingly enough, "Window on the World"), they view a young man being stoned to death for not kneeling and participating in the ceremony. Although the rest of the family passively watches the murder, the husband cannot believe what he has seen. He goes outside to think just as a major thunderstorm approaches from the west. The story ends with the man disconnecting the lightning rod. "Take your chance along with everyone else," he says before returning inside.[44]

This story revolves around an equation of television with femininity and of femininity with a loathsome passivity. The arrival of the television set, brought into the home by the doubly passive figure of the mother-in-law in a wheelchair, soon turns the entire family into passive zombies. Their passivity is so decadent that within the safety of their home, they watch without emotion as a boy is killed. Only the husband, of course, remains in touch with the real world, and his final act is to condemn the TV set as a living being, and by implication a woman, who wishes to survey the horrors of the outside world without emotion or consequence.

In a genre overwhelmingly dominated by men, it is not surprising that science fiction's critiques of marriage and domesticity in the early 1960s, although perhaps progressively motivated, so frequently cast women (and their TV sets) as an incarcerating "trap" within the home. A particularly hallucinatory episode of *The Outer Limits* provides another troubling meditation on the void of marriage and domesticity. In "The Guests" a young drifter (prominently coded as an independent bachelor who drives a convertible, wears a leather jacket, and dons sporty sunglasses) promises an injured elderly man that he will go to a nearby house for help. He makes his way to a gloomy, gothic-looking house at the top of the hill and soon finds himself surrounded by a most peculiar "family," one that consists of an older married couple, an aspiring movie actress, and a young woman named Tess. "The Drifter," as this family calls him for most of the episode, has been lured into this domestic trap by an alien creature in the attic. The alien uses those in the house as subjects of an experiment, probing their minds for information on human emotions. When the drifter tries to flee, he discovers that all the doors and windows are sealed and that there is no escape. Later he explores a maze of hallways and doors in search of an exit, only to return to where he started. When he sees Tess following him through this bachelor's nightmare, he accuses her of getting sadistic enjoyment from watching him wander like a rat through a maze. "I just didn't want you to be alone when you finally give up," she says in tears. A romance slowly develops between the drifter and Tess, and after a time she confesses finally that there is a way to escape the "prison-house." Each person has an individual "exit door" through which they may leave. The drifter begs Tess to escape with him, but she says she cannot leave the house. Vowing his undying love, the drifter says he will spend eternity with Tess in the house. But she will not allow this fate to befall him. She dashes out of her personal exit door and promptly dematerializes, leaving behind only a locket. "There is nothing for me out there either, Tess," says the drifter as he turns despairingly to go back into the house. But the alien is done with the experiment. The drifter has revealed to him the "missing emotion" in his study of earthlings — love. The alien lets the drifter go and then destroys the house with the other occupants still trapped inside.

Much like "The Bellaro Shield," "The Guests" also conducts a rather conflicted examination of love, marriage, and domesticity. Although the episode presents romantic love as the key for resolving the entire narrative, it does this only after portraying marriage and domestic life as little better than a waking death. The elderly wife in the house refers to their existence as a "dreamy nothingness." When asked why she stays in the home she replies, "A wife's duty is to share her husband's life sentence." She warns too that the drifter might also decide to "plunk right down here and dream a life. And live a dream." In the end the drifter is willing to "settle down" with Tess and continue their vigil in the suffocating, dark, gray, Victorian house, but Tess "frees" him by sacrificing herself. Once the prized object of display within the home, the housewife in this case becomes a vortex of stasis that threatens to draw the young bachelor forever into the domestic void. At the end of "The Walls," Flora realizes that "there was no point in calling any longer. No matter how she screamed, how she beat against the walls, or how she called for Harry — she knew that no one would ever hear."[45] Judith Bellaro, too, at the end of her story is doomed to remain forever on the other side, this time of sanity, imprisoned by a hallucinatory screen and unable to make contact with any other living being. But Tess receives the most severe verdict of all. The apparent epicenter of this domestic void, Tess can free the drifter only by destroying herself. Perhaps the most telling comment on the place of women within this binding ideology of privatized domesticity is Tess's fate on leaving the "safe" confines of the home — she instantly crumbles to dust.

Expanding the static borders of the "domestic asylum" to include an entire suburban neighborhood, a final and in many ways summarily emblematic episode of *The Outer Limits* is worth examining for its complex vision of "oblivion" as a melding of space, suburbia, and the American family. In "A Feasibility Study" (1964), an episode written by series creator Joseph Stefano, an alien spacecraft removes and then "telecasts," atom by atom, a six-block neighborhood from Beverly Hills to the planet Luminous ("It works very much like your television transmission," says an alien later in the episode when explaining the process to a bewildered human). In the morning residents of this community wake and prepare for the day unaware that their homes are now light years away from earth, having been telecast across the galaxy by an alien transmitter. Eventually, the humans learn that they are part of a "feasibility study" to see if humans can survive on Luminous to work as slaves. The Luminoids, as this race is called, have become literally petrified by an airborne virus so that they can no longer move. Slowly aging into rock-like creatures, they need a mobile species to do the more menial chores of running the planet. The humans discover that they too can become infected with the petrifying virus should they actually touch a Luminoid. In the episode's climax the human community gathers at the church to discuss their fate. Having come into direct contact with the Luminoids, an infected husband and wife stumble into the church already bearing signs of their imminent petrifation. After a passionate plea by one of their neighbors, the community decides to trick the Luminoids into thinking that humans are also vulnerable to the airborne form of the virus and are therefore unsuitable to work on the planet. In order to save the human race back on earth from the fate of intergalactic slavery, the entire suburban community lines up to infect themselves by touching the already diseased husband and wife.

Explicitly an allegory about the horrors of slavery (albeit an ironic racial reversal in which white suburbanites find themselves dispossessed, segregated, and in eventual solidarity), "A Feasibility Study" is equally remarkable for what it implies about the incarcerating dimensions of suburbia in the early 1960s. The story concludes with a heroic and uplifting sacrifice, but this resolution does little to address the depressing portrait of suburban isolation and domestic alienation depicted in the previous hour. At the opening of the story, for example, the narrative's central couple is on the verge of separating. After a year of marriage, the wife complains that she can no longer tolerate her husband's demands that she give up her career interests and remain in the house. As the alien plot unfolds, this couple gradually falls back in love and eventually leads the sacrifice made by the entire community. This is an uplifting ending, perhaps, both in terms of combating intergalactic slavery and rekindling romantic love. But there is still something rather sinister about a story that begins with an oppressed wife packing to leave her husband and then ends with the same wife acquiescing as she is turned into a rock. Similarly, the image of an entire suburban neighborhood marooned on a remote planet and hurtling forever through the void of space makes for an eerie yet apropos commentary on the state of suburbia in the 1960s. For this community of suburban exiles, lost in the stars yet permanently confined to a six-block patch of land, the decision to become infected by the petrifying virus may represent a brave sacrifice, but there is also the more nihilistic subtext that this final act of community is more of a suicide pact than a collective form of resistance.

"The World Is Unstable and May Collide and Blow Up"

As these episodes demonstrate, *The Outer Limits* and other science fiction texts, like the fantastic sitcom, frequently drew attention to the conventionality of domestic life. Also like the fantastic sitcom, they even re-affirmed on occasion romantic love and heterosexual marriage as the ideal resolution to certain textual and social problems. But the reliance on a separate set of narrative conventions and a profoundly different sense of the "fantastic" often placed the family, not as a site of (temporarily) renegotiated social roles, but as a source of violent disruption and a target of imminent extinction. Spigel notes that the fantastic sitcom operated through a logic of "displacement and distortion."[46] Compared to these sitcoms, the "fantastic" elements of *The Outer Limits* — its weird aliens and strange technologies — worked not so much to "displace and distort" anxieties about American life, but to *intensify* these anxieties by presenting the family with a series of apocalyptic crises that challenged the solvency and legitimacy of this social institution.

Perhaps no televisual oblivion of the early 1960s was as palpable and seemingly imminent as that of nuclear annihilation, another void continually rehearsed both by *The Outer Limits* and the medium in general. "The Premonition" (1965), airing a week before the show's final exile from network airwaves, opens with a bizarre and decidedly contrived domestic scenario. As a test pilot pushes record speeds in an experimental X-15 aircraft high above the American desert, his wife on the ground drives their daughter to the military base's day school. After surpassing a record speed in his jet, the pilot descends out of control and makes a crash landing. He emerges from his jet to find that the entire world is frozen in time. Out on the desert plains, a coyote chasing a rabbit stands as a still tableau, as do birds hanging in the air around him. Seeing his unconscious wife behind the wheel of her car, he revives her and she too quickly remarks that time seems to be standing still. Together they return to the base and find everyone absolutely frozen in place. In their explorations they meet the "limbo being," a man who long ago also entered this "black oblivion" of frozen time. "I am what you are. Trapped in this limbo-world between the present and the future." In perhaps the series' most vivid account of oblivion, he describes the hell that awaits them should they not escape. "Time will pass you by, and leave you where I am now, in the forever now, black motionless void . . . no light . . . no sun . . . no stars . . . no time . . . eternal nothing . . . no hunger . . . no thirst . . . only endless existence. And the worst of it? You can't die." The pilot and his wife also discover that their daughter will be killed immediately once time is unfrozen because her tricycle stands only feet away from a runaway truck. Working together, they finally devise a plan to both save their daughter and reemerge from the realm of the "limbo being." Once this is accomplished, they remember nothing of their experience outside of normal time. Nevertheless, they rush to the base with a strange premonition that their daughter might be in trouble. But they find her happy and at play, no longer endangered by the truck.

With its images of figures locked in time, the episode's lingering shots of frozen coyotes, static birds, and motionless human figures in the desert recall the unnerving imagery of the government's atomic tests at Yucca Flats in the mid-1950s and, by implication, the frozen moment of horror preceding the nuclear obliteration of Hiroshima and Nagasaki. In the Yucca Flats detonation, as is well known, the government built an entire town on the desert plains of New Mexico. "Survival City," as this outpost was called, featured a population of department store mannequins who occupied a row of houses on "Doomsday Drive." The entire experiment was staged as a high-profile media event, with CBS and NBC sharing the production costs in the hopes of capturing a vividly personal and highly rated encounter with the A-bomb. In a perverse attempt to "humanize" the story, reporters even went so far as to "interview" a family of these clothing-store dummies, the "Darlings," as they sat posed for destruction. "With the help of Kit Kinne, Foods Editor of the *Home* show," observed *Newsweek* in the midst of the bomb's preblast publicity blitz, "American housewives inspected the Darlings' cupboards and iceboxes and speculated on the effects of the blast on such items as baby food, dishwashers, and children's nightgowns."[47] Such "survival" coverage in the mid- and late 1950s helped precipitate the national mania for fallout shelter construction in the early 1960s, a campaign that once again placed the American home most palpably at the center of an impending oblivion. Civil defense literature evoked images of the suburban neighborhood as a final and lonely frontier. Faced with the prospect of nuclear annihilation, block after block of suburban families would be trapped, not just in their homes but in the even more tomb-like concrete shelters in their basements and backyards. In the midst of such nuclear oblivion, their only link to the outside world or to the neighbors next door would come through an even more remote and disembodied form of television: the Emergency Broadcasting System.

The Yucca Flat test experienced so many delays that the networks abandoned their extensive, in-depth coverage of the event.[48] Nevertheless, cameras were there to record the devastation as the bomb decimated "Survival City," the Darlings, and the other mute and motionless residents. These eerie images of postblast mannequins scattered across the desert appeared on a number of TV programs and made it in still form to the pages of *Life,* where all America could scrutinize at their own leisure their possible fate in the nuclear age.[49] With its images of the static desert, "The

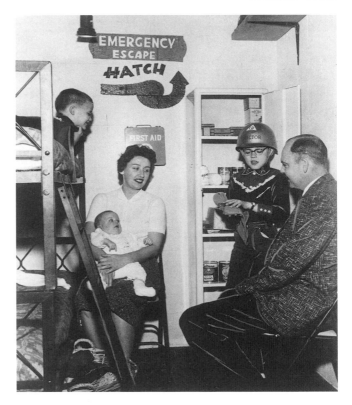

Domestic asylum and oblivion: a nuclear family of the late
1950s tests out their atomic bomb shelter. (U.S. Department
of Civil Defense)

Premonition" rehearsed this sense of nervous anticipation experienced
before any big blast, be it a desert test or an imminent enemy launch.
Vulnerable and helpless, the young married protagonists struggle, like so
many other Americans of the period, to save their child from the seemingly inevitable destruction that awaits her. Lost in this eternal moment of
anticipatory dread, their only contact is with "the limbo being," a creature
who himself is a specter of the atomic blast. Wearing shredded clothing
and deathly afraid of fire, the "limbo being" appears throughout the episode as a reverse negative. A black-and-white inversion of the world
around him, the "limbo being" wanders as a glowing, irradiated creature
doomed to "the forever now, the black motionless void."

As with so many other episodes of *The Outer Limits,* "The Premonition" ultimately returned the viewer to images of the reigning space age.

Test pilots, of course, were major cultural heroes of the time, seen as braving death to lay the groundwork for the eventual colonization of space. Breaking through a "new frontier" of speed, the pilot and his wife, like Shepard, Glenn, and the families of all other astronauts to follow, stand at the precipice of the greatest oblivion of all — the timeless and depthless expanses of outer space. The televised volley of rocket launches in the late 1950s and early 1960s not only made Americans more aware of their technological competition with the Soviets, but also produced a new understanding of the earth and its rather humble place in the vastness of the universe. Like the Copernican revolution centuries earlier, NASA's frenzied launching of monkeys and men into the black void of space could not help but tangibly remind human beings that they were very insignificant, incredibly vulnerable, and ultimately quite alone in the galaxy. "The growing preoccupation with outer space is one of the features of our present civilization," observed a psychiatrist writing in 1960. "It is not surprising that it should enter into the manifestations of certain neurotic symptoms."[50] Presenting a number of case studies in such neurosis, this psychiatrist discusses the plight of a thirty-three-year-old man who would no doubt feel quite at home in the world of *The Outer Limits,* a subject who felt "unsafe" because, as he put it, " 'the earth is a ball spinning round and I am on it.' " The psychiatrist comments:

> He became completely incapacitated and had to be admitted to [the] hospital with the fear "of going to disappear in outer space." He felt that his feet were on the ground and that the sky was above and he had to keep reminding himself that the force of gravity was keeping him down — "otherwise I would float into space." . . . Phrases which commonly occurred included: "it's space that's getting me — the curvature of the globe makes everything insecure." "We are surrounded by a hostile environment — if I think about it I want to run for cover." . . . His home was described as "a little small house on the globe and all the space above — and that is insecure." (1383)

Another patient reported a more specific fear of satellites and space stations, and still another admitted both fear and fascination with space programs on television. Describing her attraction-repulsion for these shows, she complained "It's a nuisance when you are interested in things and they frighten you." Living in the age of humanity's first tentative journeys into outer space gave her a general sense of anxiety over "peculiar things happening in the universe." Her biggest fear was that "the world is unstable and may collide and blow up." "She became worried," notes the psychiatrist, " 'about all the collisions there might be up in outer space because of all of this indiscriminate sending up of satellites.' She felt, 'there is no planning and it might affect the natural order of things' " (1386).

Emblematic of a particularly nihilistic strain of 1960s science fiction, *The Outer Limits,* of course, exacerbated such fears and did indeed suggest that earthling science could easily result in instability and disaster as slow-witted humans ventured into a realm with which they had no business interfering. At the disembodied mercy of the "control voice," the audience could do nothing but watch, powerless to intervene as any number of cosmic catastrophes befell the earth. Although viewers never actually see outer space in "The Premonition," it is space technology that opens this time rift, unlocking a hellish limbo that concretizes the terrifyingly abstract infinity of outer space by mapping it temporally onto the everyday world. Replicating the vast spatiotemporal rhythms of the heavens, the air base becomes an expansive void where humans remain separated, like stars and planets, by unimaginable gulfs of time and space. From this realm of suspended animation, the "black oblivion" of the limbo being, the parents must watch helplessly as their daughter "speeds" toward death at an uncannily slow pace, her temporally and spatially dislocated tricycle now as distant, imperiled, and helpless as the most remote *Mercury* capsule.

In a particularly vivid account of the impending oblivion of the early 1960s, the episode thus united two very different borders along the New Frontier: the infinitesimal yet potentially cataclysmic intricacies of the atom and the infinite expanses of outer space. Both the atom and outer space challenged Americans to imagine a fantastic terrain mapped by courageous scientists, powered by mysterious orbital mechanics, and somehow accessed through the equally mystifying workings of the television set. Between the spinning stars, planets, and galaxies of the universe existed a void beyond human imagination, a "final frontier" on a scale so vast as to be terrifying. Within the whirling protons and electrons of the atom, meanwhile, existed a power beyond human imagination, a destructive force so devastating that it was almost incomprehensible. In between these two perilous borders of New Frontier science stood the American family, plagued by its own often unstable dynamics and woefully unprotected from these other forces by feeble suburban homes. Vulnerable and withdrawn, families could nevertheless witness the continuing exploration of these often terrifying realms through their television sets.

All ends well in "The Premonition," as the encroachment of oblivion remains just that, a premonition. But even so, this episode demonstrates once again how frequently and often quite explicitly *The Outer Limits* disrupted the medium's characteristically self-congratulatory monologue on both the American family and the prospects of unlimited progress in American science and technology. *The Outer Limits* was remarkable for this consistent opposition to the new public celebration of the family, science, and technology that dominated the early 1960s. Playing on topical fears and anxieties that posed tangible threats to the family, *The Outer Limits* repeatedly sided with the alien's often cataclysmic critiques of the homogenizing inertia bred in American suburbia and the technological hubris bred in American laboratories. The series consistently implied that destruction and chaos lurked behind the gleaming facades of the new social and scientific order represented by television, and suggested that television itself, as a technology of cascading electrons, radioactive waves, invisible frequencies, distant transmissions, and other "strange" sciences, was a direct conduit for the domestic and electronic oblivions occupying the public mind in the early part of the decade.

"They're Heeeere"

Invading the home as a broadcast emanating from the more alienating encampments along the New Frontier, *The Outer Limits* confirmed that television was indeed an electronic oblivion, an eerie and imperious presence hovering over a number of "vast wastelands" in 1960s America. And this, perhaps, is what made the show too unsettling for its own historical moment yet such a success in the years following its cancellation. For the baby-boom generation that was the first to grow up with TV sets in its living rooms, *The Outer Limits* combines the pleasures of horror and nostalgia. It remains the only show to evoke so explicitly the dual sense of fascination and fear that attended the early years of television, a time when the TV set became the most ubiquitous, obsequious, and yet imperious of technologies to occupy domestic space and childhood memory.

Such memories clearly inform the 1982 blockbuster film *Poltergeist,* written and produced by boomer auteur Steven Spielberg. In a testament to the fixation of boomer consciousness on this haunted moment in television history, the movie updates the fears provoked by *The Outer Limits* to tell the story of a suburban family whose home is taken over by malevolent spirits and whose youngest daughter is kidnapped by the ghosts and held hostage in the electrical nowhere of the television set. In what is perhaps the film's most paradigmatic image of television and domestic terror, early in the story before the daughter's abduction, the soon-to-be paranormally beleaguered family sleep together in the parents' bedroom, illuminated by the blue light of the television they have forgotten to turn off before retiring. The camera slowly pans over to the set as it broadcasts the national anthem, a sign that the station is about to go off the air. When the anthem is complete, the image becomes pure static accompanied by a blast of white noise. The camera moves closer to the set and the shot rests for a few seconds on a close-up of the electronic blizzard occupying the TV screen. The shot is unsettling, not unlike the repeated shots of the mysterious photograph in Antonioni's *Blow-Up*. Even before the poltergeists manifest themselves, this intense close-up of the screen's shifting static suggests a sinister electrical presence to the apparatus, exploiting the ambiguity of television as a technology, a virtually sentient being, and a gateway to an electronic unreality. The implication in this shot is that if we look too long into the static, autonomous and perhaps terrifying images beyond human control will take shape (which of course is precisely what happens later in the film).

This tableau of the innocent family slumbering in front of the hissing presence of the TV set emblematizes the long history of cultural anxiety over the seeming vulnerability of the family before the unwavering eye of television. This early scene in particular dares the audience to stare into a field of potentially sinister electricity and confront the unknown presence within the set, the operating consciousness inhabiting the mysterious electronic space behind the screen's fading blip of light. Only the youngest child senses there is something more to the set's shifting fields of static. "They're heeeere," says Carol Anne in the film's most famous line of dialogue, evoking television's uncanny presence just moments before she is sucked into the haunted set's vast ghostland. While captive in the television set, Carol Anne cannot see her family, nor can they see her. Their only contact is through the child's disembodied and electronically processed voice, which can be heard swirling eerily in the family's living room.

Carol Anne of *Poltergeist* shortly before her abduction into televisual oblivion. (© 1982 MGM)

When questioned, the young girl cannot describe where she is in any detail, except to tell of a bright light she sees in the distance. Now lost on the other side of the television screen, Carol Anne is quite literally "nowhere."

This continuing narrative preoccupation with electronic technology as a gateway to oblivion suggests that television remains, even forty years after its introduction into the American home, a somewhat unsettling and alien technology. As a medium of powerful instantaneousness, television continues to display a perilously immediate relationship to public danger and disaster and is still believed to exert an ambiguous and unknown "control" over the American family. Following years of both fascination and disillusionment with the new medium, *The Outer Limits* and *Poltergeist* demonstrated that in extreme cases television could deliver families into an even more remote and terrifying "vast wasteland" than the one envisioned by FCC commissioner Minow. Implicit in the stories of *The Outer Limits* and made manifest in Speilberg's *Poltergeist* was the idea that the viewer is vulnerable to such assimilation simply by watching TV, thereby exploiting the medium's potential for terror to the fullest. Viewers who watch a horror film at a theater, after all, can return to the safety of their homes and put the experience behind them. The very premise of the "haunted TV," on the other hand, allowed fear to linger with the viewer. The unique electronic presence bound to this new medium suggested that even after a program was over and the receiver was turned off, the television set itself still loomed as a gateway to oblivion simply by sitting inert and watchful in the living room.

5 Simulation and Psychosis

In a novella for children, *Channel 10 from Nowhere,* a twelve-year-old girl has her television set fixed by repairmen from the "COSMIC REPAIR SERVICE." After these men work on the set, Rachel discovers that the TV, when turned to channel 10, can telecast the future. The author handles the accounts of the young girl's initial viewings of this strange TV set in an appropriately mysterious and vaguely sinister manner. "The room was dark but the light from the TV set gave the room a golden glow. When I switched to channel 10, the light became even stronger and seemed to pulse like the beat of a heart. . . . The glow filled most of the room, shimmering on the walls and ceiling. It was hypnotic. I couldn't take my eyes away."[1] At first, she sees only minor events from her own day-to-day life at school and at home, which she of course uses to her advantage. Rachel eventually becomes anxious about having such an explicitly paranormal force within her home. "For the first time in my life, I was really afraid. Afraid of what I'd see next on Channel 10. . . . How could anyone — let alone a 12-year-old — cope with a TV channel that shows the future?" (17).

Rachel later visits the office of the COSMIC REPAIR SERVICE. Taken into the backroom by a mysterious caretaker, she finds herself in a vast staging area of video reality. "When I looked up, I could see TV sets along the walls. There were dozens — maybe hundreds of sets — and the pictures on the screens were constantly changing." The caretaker of the COSMIC REPAIR SERVICE then gives Rachel a tour of the facilities. " 'The past and the future are both here,' " she says. " 'All events come and go — in time. The scenes are incidents that will occur, if nothing upsets the giant plan of the universe.' " On one screen Rachel sees a televisually impossible scene from the prehistoric past, "four short men wearing bearskins and preparing to fling spears into the mouth of a cave." Jumping into the future she next encounters a "magnificent city float[ing] on the surface of the ocean." Finally, Rachel has a privileged view of the ultimate media spectacle, watching on a monitor as "the entire planet flew into a million pieces" (52–53). As Rachel leaves, the caretaker refuses to answer the key mystery of these transmissions. Who or what is the agent recording and organizing these images? What entity controls this form of infinite vision, the most incredible electronic omnipresence ever imagined, one capable of witnessing and recording all of time and space. The story ends dramatically with Rachel's saving her mother from boarding an airplane destined to crash. A brief epilogue follows in which the men from the COSMIC REPAIR SERVICE return to deactivate the paranormal set. " 'You will no longer receive Channel 10,' " says one of them cryptically. " 'The error has been corrected.' "

Already banal enough to be explored within the province of children's fiction, the now seemingly ubiquitous theme of television's colonizing reality was also at the center of the 1998 blockbuster *The Truman Show,* identified by many critics as the most "intelligent" film of the summer movie season. In this parable of television's powers to counterfeit the real world, a man lives the first three decades of his life without realizing that all of America watches his every moment on live television. Unbeknownst to the hapless Truman Burbank, the town he inhabits is nothing more than a set. His wife, friends, and parents are all actors, the citizens of his tiny seaside community all extras, and the organizing power of his life a virtually omnipotent television director concealed within the town's artificial moon. Critics hailed the film as a provocative critique of the nation's unhealthy obsession with television and television's obsession with "false" emotions and staged realities. Of course, castigating the "unreality" of television has been a favorite (and some might say hypocritical) theme in Hollywood for many years, making *The Truman Show* not so much a startling innovation as a predictable installment in the tradition of *A Face in the Crowd* (1957), *Network* (1976), and *Being There* (1979).

The televisually mediated worlds of young Rachel and the deluded Truman must seem especially familiar to those scholars who ponder the complex relationships between electronic media and postmodern culture. "Everything that was directly lived has moved away into a representation,"[2] wrote Guy DeBord in *Society of the Spectacle,* a sentiment echoed in Jean Baudrillard's hyperbolic conception of postmodern reality as "that of which it is possible to give an equivalent reproduction."[3] Certainly, there could be few more striking examples of "the map preceding the territory" (to use Baudrillard's use of Borges's metaphor) than a story of omniscient television narration recording its own pre-electronic, prehistoric state, somehow capable of telecasting cavemen in pursuit of a woolly mammoth some four thousand years ago! Founding maxims of postmodern theory, DeBord and Baudrillard's words seem to capture in clinical

Truman Burbank of *The Truman Show,* trapped in the saccharine reality/ unreality of television. (© 1997 Paramount)

detail the plight of Rachel, Truman, and millions the world over who live in blissfully deluded states of absolute simulation.

Regardless of how one judges the ultimate value of postmodern theory and the political implications of its application, the Baudrillardian zeitgeist of proliferating "simulation" and an ever encroaching "hyperreality" unarguably resonates at many levels of contemporary cultural commentary about the media. Although it would be a gross oversimplification to say that Baudrillard's complex, incendiary, and ongoing repudiation of Marx, Freud, and Foucault can be reduced to the argument that all of life is gradually transforming into television, this is certainly the tact taken by both critics and acolytes of Baudrillard's project. Baudrillard himself, after all, cannot resist the temptation in *Simulations* to proclaim that the contemporary world is marked by the "dissolution of TV into life, the dissolution of life into TV" (55). At the very least, the Baudrillardian strain of postmodernity shares with these other more popular tales of omniscient electronic media the basic premise that "reality" is now inescapably mediated by spectacle, a form of covert attack in which an electronic mirage is gradually replacing the real world. Long a fixture of the lecture hall, these themes of electronically mediated (and usually alienated) societies have of late proliferated in popular culture as well. Television has pondered such themes in *Max Headroom, Wild Palms, The X-Files,* and a number of lesser known science fiction series; and the recent glut of films concerning the electronic mediation of subjectivity and society — movies such as *Videodrome* (1983), *Robocop* (1987), *Total Recall* (1990), *Lawnmower Man* (1992), *Virtuosity* (1996), *Strange Days* (1997), *The Truman Show* (1998), *Pleasantville* (1998), *Ed TV* (1999), and *eXistenZ* (1999) — testifies to the theatrical success of this once wholly theoretical paradigm.

One might offer two explanations for this increasingly prominent bridge between popular media and postmodern theory. On the one hand, we could interpret the various popular incarnations of *Simulations* as a sign that the once obtuse and radically disruptive theories gleaned from the pages of Semiotext(e) have now filtered down into the realm of the Scholastic Book Service. Twelve-year-olds, it would appear, are completely comfortable with the idea that all of human experience, be it their own birthday, the signing of the Magna Carta, or even the Big Bang, is somehow best accessed and ideally knowable through television. What could be more postmodern, after all, than a children's book that so effortlessly replicates such abstract postmodern logic? Hollywood has found success, meanwhile, targeting the now multiple generations of adults raised in the age of television who seem to enjoy entertaining the perverse suspicion that they might one day inhabit a media mirage. The idea that we live in a world created by television (as opposed to one simply *affected* by television) is so commonplace that this once scandalous intervention in media criticism serves now as a favorite stock plot of the entertainment industry.

On the other hand, the similarity of themes encountered in *Channel 10 from Nowhere, The Truman Show,* and Baudrillard's *Simulations* might also suggest, not a process of "popularization," but that postmodern theory is in itself simply another in a long series of occult fantasies inspired by electronic media. Considered in this respect, film, television, and mainstream fiction have not popularized postmodern theory so much as postmodern theory has rarefied a series of long-circulating superstitions bound to the historical imagination of electronic presence. Within the mythos of postmodernity, television often appears as a mystery box somehow capable of exorcising human subjectivity and conjuring a hallucinatory realm that hovers above the referential rubble of contemporary culture. Where there was once the "real," there is now only the electronic generation and circulation of almost supernatural simulations. Where there was once stable human consciousness, there are now only the ghosts of fragmented, decentered, and increasingly schizophrenic subjectivities. Where there once was "depth" and "affect," there is now only "surface." Where there was once "meaning," "history," and a solid realm of "signifieds," there is now only a haunted landscape of vacant and shifting signifiers. As Scott Bukatman describes this vision of postmodernity, it is a world marked by the "simultaneous over- and underevaluation of sign systems at a time when the sign *is* everything but *stands* for nothing."[4]

Recent discussions of television, both pop and postmodern, present one of the most elaborate fantasies of presence yet constructed around electronic media. In their more delirious articulations, popular accounts of incredible televisual worlds and postmodern meditations on proliferating media culture often share the premise that television produces a separate and wholly sovereign "reality." What unites stories like *Channel 10 from Nowhere* with the more ecstatic strains of postmodern theory is this mutual vision of a living electronic landscape, a product of television's cultural ubiquity and its capacity for uninterrupted simultaneity. Whether imagined as an illusion, an analogue, a surrogate, a recording, a mirage, or a parallel version of our reality, the electronic world of television has become the ultimate "elsewhere." As we have seen, in the earliest days of television the existence of such an elsewhere was only an intuitive suspicion (although one often made manifest in anxious science fiction of the era). Television's incredible success at colonizing both private and public life has enabled this once limbo-like "elsewhere" to grow and thrive as a wholly autonomous and ever expanding electronic universe. This new empire of the electronic, in turn, has translated easily into the emerging conceptual models of contemporary cyberculture. In the increasingly fantastic speculation about cyberspace and virtual reality, we encounter what appears to be the ultimation of this particular metaphysics of electronic media. Advocates of a cyberfuture the world over now wait for the mysteries of presence to deliver them from the material world and into the final and most transcendental of electronic spaces.

Whether diffuse in the ether or coursing through the wired networks of the world, electronic presence now thrives in the cultural imagination of an increasingly sovereign universe of escalating simulation. Joined in this vision of an autonomous electronic realm, pop and postmodern accounts of these media also frequently share a common model of the audience. Equally fantastic as the electronic elsewhere is the transformative effect electronic media are said to have on their publics. Inhabiting a world where "the sign is everything but stands for nothing," these spectators/ users of electronic media have become, for many, similarly ephemeral and phantasmagoric. The destabilizing metaphors of fragmentation and disassociation are especially favored in such fantasies. Academic circles, for example, often describe users of electronic media through the language of schizophrenia in a fable of the coherent subject's electronic dissolution. As with tales of the electronic elsewhere, however, popular narratives linking television and psychosis coexist with and even predate these more abstract discussions in postmodern theory. Both streams of schizophrenic speculation flow from a shared metaphoric wellspring.

The following pages provide a final study in the occult metaphysics of electronic presence, one that is important not only as a portrait of what remains our most pervasive media technology, but also in setting the terms of debate over the new telecommunications technologies predicted to replace television in the next century. Although the following discussion will center primarily on television, it should be clear that these metaphors of simulation and fragmentation, mirage and psychosis, continue to inform a range of cultural debates over the new cybertechnologies and their audiences. Cyberspace and virtual reality frequently present a strategic inversion of these metaphors. Often, the very dissimulative and disassociative properties that once made television such a dire threat to reality and subjectivity have become, in the era of new media, the foundation for a series of utterly fantastic narratives of disembodied liberation and emancipatory transcendence that once again recall the fantastic worlds imagined by the Spiritualists of the nineteenth century. Whether electronic media and spectatorship represent the "death" of human subjectivity (in the annihilating simulations of television) or its magical "rebirth" (in the ever expanding architecture of cyberspace), both accounts draw vividly on the uncanny animating presence so long perceived in electronic media. Behind our fascination with television's "confusion" of reality and virtual subjectivity's "liberation" of body and soul remains a highly adaptive metaphysics of electricity, one that continues to inspire supernatural accounts of live, living, and otherwise haunted media.

A Living Diegesis

Even though the practice of actual "live" broadcasting fell into industrial disfavor rather early in the medium's career, television has nonetheless continued to promote incessantly this sense of "liveness" throughout the medium's history, elaborating the simultaneity enabled by the technology into a larger metatextual aesthetic that pervades the entire medium.[5] "Don't go away, we'll be right back," rings the perpetual refrain of network broadcasting as it attempts to position us in a series of interpersonally live situations. From the local promotion of "eyewitness news" to that most synthetic convention of liveness — "canned laughter" — television works to maintain its status as a medium of unmediated spontaneity. As Jane Feuer argues, "Television's self-referential discourse plays upon the connotative richness of the term 'live,' confounding its simple or technical denotations with a wealth of allusiveness. Even the simplest meaning of 'live' — that the time of the event corresponds to the transmission and viewing times — reverberates with suggestions of 'being there' . . . 'bringing it to you as it really is.' "[6] Television's "liveness" appears to be a function of the technology itself. "In one sense, the television image . . . is effectively 'live,' " observe Heath and Skirrow in their study of TV textuality, "very different in this to that of film. Where the latter depends on the immobility of the frame, the former, electronic and not photographic, is an image in perpetual motion, the movement of a continually scanning beam; whatever the status of the material transmitted, the image as series of electric impulses is necessarily 'as it happens.' "[7] Television seems "live," in other words, because its scanned images are always in the process of "becoming" at the ultimately unrealizable terminals of transmission and reception, producing a "living" quality that pervades the medium and its programming. A function of both the technology and a variety of programming strategies, television's "power" emanates from this illusion of direct, personalized, and immediate contact with the audience, the medium consistently staging a form of simulated first-person address within a textual universe that always seems to be unfolding in the present, the now.[8] As Heath and Skirrow note, "The immediate time of the image is pulled into a confusion with the time of the events shown, tending to diminish the impression of the mode of presence in absence characteristic of film, suggesting a permanently alive view on the world; the generalized fantasy of the television institution of the image is exactly that it is *direct,* and direct *for me.*"[9]

Pivotal as well in this self-promoting aesthetic of "liveness" is the commercial practice of continuously intertwining segments of programming, promotion, and advertising into an uninterrupted "flow" that maintains a consistent velocity of address. As Raymond Williams writes in describing the concept of "flow," the now favored liquid metaphor of electronic textuality, "What is being offered is not . . . a programme of discrete units with particular insertions, but a planned flow, in which the true series is not the published sequence of programme items but this sequence transformed by the inclusion of another kind of sequence, so that these sequences together compose the real flow, the real 'broadcasting.' "[10] Critics often attribute the dominating influence of television to this forever-unresolved procession of audio/visual fragments, segment after segment accruing to produce the rival world and reality of television.[11] As Heath and Skirrow observe, "Like the world, television never stops, is continuous."[12] Indeed, TV is a world that is always there, at least in unrealized form, even when the set is turned off.

Broadcasters create and exploit the medium's illusion of simultaneity and its sense of unending flow through many strategies, hoping to craft the impression of immediate, intimate, and continuous contact with another world. Over television's history, for example, this sense of immediacy has made the "living medium" a prime conduit for the "living word." American televangelists have long integrated the uncanny living presence of television into their efforts to attract followers and raise money. Dallas evangelist Robert Tilton is exemplary in this regard. Tilton frequently invites viewers to touch the TV screen to make "direct" contact with the healing power of his cathode hand. Anticipating the skepticism of an increasingly media-savvy flock, Tilton takes care to assure viewers that his "teletouch" still works even if that day's particular episode is a rerun! Another favored strategy is for Tilton to suddenly interrupt his sermon as if he is seized with instantaneous telepathic televisual contact with a troubled viewer. "Someone who is watching me right now is experiencing pain in his left knee," Tilton will say with clinched eyes. "You need to send me $1000 right now and that pain will go away." A slightly more sophisticated version of *Romper Room's* "magic mirror" ("I see Tommy, I see Mary"), Tilton's scam plays on lingering adult superstitions (and spiritual hope) over the status of the televisual.

The impact of television's cultivated liveness and its unbordered empire of flow are no less fantastic in the realm of narrative programming. Once confined only to soap operas, the dominant narrative model in contemporary American television now strives, across all genres, to maintain the illusion that the diegetic time of a TV series is aligned with that of the

Repetition and simulated liveness make television characters and locations "real" in a fundamentally different way than do cinema and other media. Millions of American viewers "visit" Chicago each week during NBC's *E.R.* (© 1999 Warner Brothers)

viewer; that is, we experience seasons and holidays at the same time as the characters of *E.R.* or *NYPD Blue*. The effect of this illusion is to increase the verisimilitude of the series universe by allowing viewers to visit this parallel TV world on a weekly basis, suggesting that this other realm continues in its own cotemporal reality even when we are not watching. Combining this sense of parallelism with television's unique capacity for open-ended narrative runs, TV characters and their worlds become "real" in a way fundamentally different from that of the cinema and other media.[13]

The impact of liveness and flow is equally intriguing in the textuality of syndicated reruns. Shows that remain on the air year after year playing at various points throughout the broadcast schedule develop an even more resilient and convincing story world, one that becomes more complex and seemingly real through sheer repetition. The textual universe created by *Star Trek* (and its progeny) is undoubtedly the most pronounced example of this phenomenon. Through its nearly continuous thirty-year voyage through the broadcast schedule, *Star Trek* has accrued (for fans at least) the status of a compellingly real world with its own history, rules, and mythology. So powerful is television's ability to conjure sovereign electronic realms, apparently, that *Star Trek* reruns have managed to breathe life into an otherwise unconvincing world of dated cardboard sets, papier-mâché rocks, and extremely mannered acting styles. Images captured on film in a soundstage at Paramount in the late 1960s have thus become an autonomous universe and, for many fans, a "timeless" space.[14] The same might be said about much TV in its endless cycles of living repetition. The bar in *Cheers,* the 4077 compound in M.A.S.H., even the cramped, stage-bound apartment of the Cramdens in the *Honeymooners* all remain eternally real and temporally transcendent spaces.[15]

Pervasive in TV's narrative programming, the experience of "liveness" is perhaps most acute in television's news, information, and actuality genres. One of the few venues where "live" broadcasting remains in practice, television news, be it local, national, or international, succeeds according to its ability to convince viewers that it alone provides the most instantaneous access to events in the community, nation, or world. The capacity of television news to "cover" the globe, again articulated in terms of an implied omniscience, has reached its apotheosis in the competition among the twenty-four-hour cable news networks. The earliest TV newsreaders sat behind a desk and read copy, often without any visual support of any kind. News programs soon began to incorporate reports on film and then eventually videotape. Showcased by CNN in the 1980s, local and national newscasters now depend heavily on the "live remote," a convention that gives the impression of a network waiting in position to pounce on any scrap of news that might happen anywhere in the world at any time. This live network of global coverage (or at least its illusion) is so effective that many diplomats and heads of state are said to depend more on CNN than on their own intelligence agencies when monitoring international crises. The illusion created and heavily promoted is that TV's electronic eye is alive and ever ready to survey the whole of reality — be it a local police chase or a probe landing on another planet.

Considering the cumulative effect of this unending promotion of simultaneity, "liveness," and seemingly unmediated "reality" across all TV genres, it is easy to see why so many fantastic accounts of the medium collapse all of television — its sitcoms, news programs, soap operas, commercials, game shows, etc. — into one vast metatextual realm in which distinctions between real and unreal, true and false, cease to matter. This would seem to be the central fantasy of television elaborated by both postmodern and popular accounts of television culture. The entire medium becomes equally "real" (or equally "fake," depending on one's perspective); a textual galaxy that, like our own universe, is seemingly capable of expanding without end. Rachel's experiences in *Channel 10 from Nowhere* take this illusion to its ultimate end: the telecasting of all reality, public and private, across history and into the future.

What postmodern criticism typically describes in complex improvisations on "simulation" and "hyperreality," popular culture has often addressed through the more colloquial concept of "televisionland." Over the years, "televisionland" has also come to describe this ambiguous space that merges the real and the virtual, the living and the electronic. On the one hand, "televisionland" is that vast and largely domestic environment where viewers sit before the cumulative glow of a million television screens, the invisible nation hailed through television's familiar call, "Hello out there in TV-land." On the other hand, "televisionland" also describes the sustaining virtual realm of television itself as a metatextual electronic giant, the vast history of image and sound whose traces remain embedded in the circuitry of our sets and our minds. The mass marketing of Viacom's "Nick at Nite" and "TV Land" cable services is the most explicit example of this particular vision of "televisionland." Through relentless reruns and promos for reruns, "Nick at Nite" trades on the evocation of a shared "television heritage," an imaginary sitcom world that obeys its own logic and where each TV series stands as a distinctly real neighborhood within the larger electronic boundaries of the "televisionland" nation. Archie Bunker, Laura Petrie, and Beaver Cleaver all remain in a timeless suspension in a world where they never age and yet remain compellingly real as citizens of a cathode universe perpetually in the process of creation and expansion. Each new fragment, from a single commercial to the cumulative run of an entire series, adds to this sustaining virtual realm, helping to promote television's illusion of an alternate reality, one that resembles our own world in many ways and yet remains electronic and thus phantasmic. Televisionland is that rarest of principalities, an empire forged through a dissolution rather than a delineation of boundaries, a world where the Tidy Bowl Man and the president of the United States are equally "real" and enfranchised citizens.

Long a component in baby-boomer and postboomer cultural folklore, the concept of "televisionland" as an obviously "make believe" yet strangely "real" world has proved a durable premise in late 1990s cinema. The aforementioned *Truman Show* and films like *Pleasantville* and *Ed TV* address in different ways the common theme of collapsing the real and the televisual. *The Truman Show* visits these themes in rather predictable mass-elite terms. The "world" of television is saccharine and false—we hope that Truman will escape his video prison. *Pleasantville,* on the other hand, employs the familiar and more explicitly paranormal premise of viewers absorbed into their television set (an occult act facilitated by Don Knotts, no less). The story follows a brother and sister who enter the diegetic space of a 1950s domestic sitcom, where they find citizens baffled at the concept that something might exist beyond Main Street (as there is no precedent for this in the show's history). Others in this black-and-white world find it difficult to escape their routine patterns of thought and behavior (shaped by the endless repetition of restrictive sitcom conventions). In *Ed TV,* finally, a "regular guy" volunteers to have his day-to-day life broadcast live as it happens on cable TV. The premise provides the filmmakers with a platform to comment on both the shallowness of celebrity and television's ruthless appetite for using the problems of "real" people in order to generate the strangely detached universe of mass entertainment.

In addition to these films that feature rather extraordinary (and at times contrived) premises, a number of satirical films purport to engage in a more realistic critique of television's relation to public life. *Dave* (1993), for example, centers on a look-alike impostor forced to play the part of the president of the United States on television, giving narrative voice to the common political cynicism that the president's chief function *is* to be an actor on TV. *Wag the Dog* (1998), meanwhile, told the story of a TV producer hired to stage a war in order to distract the nation from a sexual scandal involving the president. The film's title, in turn, became a central part of the nation's political vocabulary when, shortly after its release,

A 1990s teen stuck in the diegesis of a 1950s sitcom in *Pleasantville.* (© 1998 New Line Cinema)

President Clinton authorized bombing raids on Iraq while mired in his own sexual scandal with Monica Lewinsky.

Wag the Dog provides an interesting point of contact between "televisionland" and postmodernity's more theoretical account of television's sovereign textuality. As a "fictional" media artifact commenting on a "real world" phenomenon that was, in turn, eventually acted out again in quite literal terms on the stage of national politics, *Wag the Dog* provides the type of serpentine anecdote so beloved by postmodern criticism (eclipsed only, perhaps, by the strange saga of would-be assassins, Arthur Bremer, Travis Bickle, and John Hinkley). Heavily influenced by Baudrillard's concept of simulation, this form of postmodernism revels in compiling evidence of an impending and irreversible collapse of the real. In an introductory primer on postmodernism, for example, John Storey writes that

> simulations can often be experienced as more real than the real itself. . . .
> Think of the way in which *Apocalypse Now* has become the mark against
> which to judge the realism of representations of America's war in Vietnam. . . . Thus we inhabit a society of hyperrealism in which people write
> letters addressed to characters in soap operas, making them offers of mar-

riage, sympathizing with their current difficulties, offering them new accommodation, or just writing to ask how they are coping with life.

Television villains are regularly confronted in the street and warned about the possible future consequences of not altering their behavior. Television doctors, television lawyers and television detectives regularly receive requests for advice and help.[16]

Somewhat caricaturing postmodernism's complexities for the purposes of a broad introduction, Storey's anecdotal description nonetheless captures the theory's recurring critical fascination with individuals and societies that seem increasingly unable to distinguish the lived real from the media real. For those who decry postmodernity, such confusions present evidence of power and capital's final victory over the forces of rational humanity. Television lives up to our worst expectations by transforming the public into a mass of deluded (and subjugated) morons. The more ecstatic celebrations of postmodernism, meanwhile, castigate as idiots those who would attempt at this point in history to cling to such antiquated distinctions between "authentic" and "mediated" realities.

In either case, critical meditations on postmodernity frequently center on similar examples of a seductive vacillation between the real and its simulated double. Again, Baudrillard is the key figure here, not just conceptually but rhetorically as well. For example, when Baudrillard writes that the contemporary world exhibits the "dissolution of TV into life, the dissolution of life into TV,"[17] he foregrounds a strategy of argumentation encountered across his work on electronic media, one that has become an immensely influential trope cleverly repackaged for maximum shock value in each new context. For lack of a better term, we might call this rhetorical flourish of postmodern criticism the "infinitely reversible binary." Is life becoming more like television, or television more like life? Is it either, neither, or both? Elsewhere in *Simulations* Baudrillard presents an extended discussion of the PBS documentary *An American Family*. In this televisual experiment from 1973, the Loud family of Santa Barbara, California, allowed a documentary team to record and then broadcast their day-to-day life in a form of "TV-Verite." "Admirable ambivalent terms," writes Baudrillard of TV-Verite, "does it refer to the truth of this family, or to the truth of TV?" (51). Perhaps the single most well-known passage of *Simulations* involves Baudrillard's reading of Disneyland, in which he again invokes a series of reversible binaries between the "real" and "unreal." "Disneyland is presented as imaginary in order to make us believe that the rest is real," writes Baudrillard, "when in fact all of Los Angeles and the America surrounding it are no longer real, but of the order of the hyperreal and simulation. . . . The Disneyland imaginary is neither true nor false; it is a deterrence machine set up in order to rejuvenate in reverse the fiction of the real" (25). Revisiting these themes in *The Perfect Crime,* it takes only two pages for Baudrillard to cut to the conceptual chase: "The great philosophical question used to be 'Why is there something rather than nothing?' Today, the real question is: 'Why is there nothing rather than something?' "[18] Finally, when Baudrillard opines in recent work that "the Gulf War did not take place," his polemic mobilizes the now routinely accepted premise that the media real is increasingly the "real" real. Taken as a set, the three essays on the Gulf War ("The Gulf War Will Not Take Place," "The Gulf War Is Not Taking Place," and the eponymous "The Gulf War Did Not Take Place") rehearse a variation of this "fiction of the real" in slow motion (as published in a series of installments in the French press): what everyone thinks will happen will not happen, what you think is happening is not happening, what you thought happened did not happen. The real and the unreal merge in their infinite reversibility.

Like so much of Baudrillard's work, the essays on the Gulf War are meant to be hotly polemical (nothing enrages old-school leftists more than the suggestion that this bloody first-world intervention didn't really happen!). Nurtured in the high-stakes competition of French intellectual culture, Baudrillard's role in the academy has frequently been that of bomb thrower, and his argument about the Gulf War is both provocative and persuasive. The notion that the conflict in the Gulf was first and foremost a "TV war" resonates on many levels: the military's promotion of "pool footage" showcasing the accuracy of its smart bombs and the simultaneous suppression of footage featuring "collateral damage" (i.e., dead Iraqis); the news networks' use of elaborate graphics packages and familiar narrative conventions to transform the event into an exciting miniseries; the realization that the electronic space of the world's media was a more significant battleground than the Iraqi desert where the actual conflict took place. Indeed, the idea of a television war (or Nintendo War, as it was sometimes called) achieved such cultural currency that television itself eventually took up the discussion to fill dead airtime between carefully managed press conferences and impending SCUD missile attacks. Television's ability to incorporate even critiques of its own ability to incorporate testifies to the validity of Baudrillard's cosmology, demonstrating how these collapsed binaries and reversible realities have been invaluable in pushing critics to rethink the boundaries of mass mediation and social reality.

As with every high-profile intellectual, however, Baudrillard's texts have bred a certain author-centered mythos (true of any thinker whose name becomes an adjective: Baudrillardian), which has led as well to a host of more earnest imitators. This has created a strange situation in media theory, where many of Baudrillard's acolytes and interpreters have taken the author's hyperbolic polemics and tried to apply them to cultural analysis as if they were, ironically enough, "true" in some scientific sense. Arguably, the most thriving form of the postmodern occult has arisen from this gradual reification of Baudrillard's enigmatic maxims and reversible binaries, producing a mediascape that is no longer seen as metaphorically more real than the real — but is addressed as a genuinely paranormal replacement of the real, as if simulation were a material transformation rather than a semiotic process. The verbal play of this form of postmodernism delights in figure-ground exercises that portend a collapse of binaries and an implosion of the sign. In this new world of Baudrillardian prophecy, television remains the primary fountain of "bad" simulation (as opposed to the pomo-ecstacy of cybersimulation). For Baudrillardism, television has collapsed public and private, interior and exterior, medium and audience, and just about any other binary one cares to invoke. It leaves behind a phantasmagoric landscape of simulation, an imploded real now wholly interpenetrated by the electronic circulation of another "reality" where anything can seemingly become anything else. Or, as Baudrillard himself writes (invoking McLuhan), "The medium is no longer identifiable as such, and the merging of the medium and the message is the first great formula of this new age. There is no longer any medium in the literal sense: it is now intangible, diffuse and diffracted in the real, and it can no longer be said that the latter is distorted by it."[19] As a theoretical salvo, this is a provocative tool for confronting the cultural dynamics of electronic media's growing presence in social life. To believe it as literally true demonstrates nothing less than faith in the supernatural.

The Surfing Schizophrenic

In *Channel 10 from Nowhere,* Rachel's vision of infinite monitors screening ephemera from across recorded time implies that the "scope" of history, both the grand events of public life and the minutia of private memory, is entirely mediated by an electrical omniscience now imprecated in the staging of all reality, or at least in providing the transhistorical "sight" through which we can review that reality. Just as wireless suggested a sense of consciousness in the air, "thoughts" of spirits, ghosts, and telepaths that could be snared by the radio antenna, television transmission implies a form of "vision on the air," an electronic envelope around the world capable of a God's-eye view. Encountered throughout the history of television, such stories combine qualities of "liveness" with the medium's apparent sentience to imbue television with the power of spatially and temporally infinite vision. All of human experience is now apparently subject to the logic of a vast and divine program schedule, where life and history are accessed through the conventions of classical continuity editing and the immediacy of "live" telecasting. God (or the "giant plan of the universe" as Rachel's story says in more secular fashion) now prefers the convenient surveillance offered by video over the outmoded graphemes of the Book of Life as a means of recording human history.

The emergence of television as the privileged surveyor of all reality implies a popular shift in media consciousness, suggesting that the seemingly "infinite" vision of television has replaced the previously "perfect" view of the cinema as our dominant cultural model of the ideal visual record. In the offices of the COSMIC REPAIR SERVICE, for example, had Rachel encountered an infinite number of Bell and Howell film projectors screening film loops of past and present, it would have made for a less than convincing illusion of a central staging area of all reality. This fanciful tale, like much postmodern theory, creates its effect by elaborating the electronic presence of television into a larger fantasy of omniscient surveillance and proliferating simulation. As objects taken from a can and temporarily illuminated by a stream of light, films can provide only momentary illusions of alternate worlds frozen in history. A boundless and constant empire of "live" transmission, television appears to *be* its own world: coterminous, contemporaneous, and even stretching into the future.

In this process of transition, one might argue also that televisual transmission has replaced cinematic projection as the dominant metaphorical basis for conceptualizing consciousness and subjectivity. The mind's eye, once a screen for projected mental imagery, is now more frequently conceived in cybernetic terms of circuitry, scanning, and electronic storage. The implication in *Channel 10 from Nowhere* is that Rachel's most private memories can be easily translated by an electron gun, mysteriously transmitted and made visible on a bank of television sets. Memories are no longer dusty reels of film resting on the shelves of the mental archive. They now exist as data ready for instantaneous retrieval and transmission on either internal or external monitors. The once stately "theater of the mind" has thus lost its lease to a consortium of electronic brains, electronic subjects, electronic visions, and electronic realities.

Although any model of mind, vision, and memory is by necessity rooted in the shifting historical soils of metaphor, this has not prevented such metaphors from serving as the more concrete foundation for larger theories of media spectatorship and even subjectivity itself. This has been especially true in certain academic discussions of the televisual spectator (or, more often, in theorizations of the more abstract state of televisual spectatorship). Here we enter the often contentious debates that argue television technology and its characteristic forms of flow produce a form of spectatorship (and spectator) that differs greatly from that posited for cinema. John Ellis organizes this speculative dichotomy in the two media around a difference between the "gaze" and the "glance." Psychoanalytic theories of film spectatorship, of course, emphasize the cinematic experience as organized around the "gaze," the film image providing the viewer with the intense, almost hallucinatory pleasures of a regression into the Imaginary. In this line of theory, the appeal of the cinematic image depends on the process of "primary identification." Here, the viewer identifies with what Christian Metz describes as the "invisible seeing agency of the film itself as discourse, as the agency which puts forward the story and shows it to us."[20] This allows the viewer to enjoy the illusion of being "all-perceiving" (48). "In other words," writes Metz, "the spectator identifies with himself, with himself as a pure act of perception" (49). To facilitate such identification, the cinema has developed primarily as a voyeuristic medium, one in which the film unfolds without acknowledging the presence of its viewing audience. A film does this, so the argument goes, by hiding the markers of its "enunciation" and thus disguising its status as "discourse." Confronted in a darkened theater with a larger-than-life image, one that seems to be without enunciative origin, the cinematic spectator is thus "maintained in a position of mastery in relation to the film" (61). As Metz writes, "The cinematic spectator is separate from the film's fiction, able to judge and to assess; separate from the filmic image, which is absent even whilst it presents itself as present" (62).

Television spectatorship, on the other hand, appears to differ radically from this model. A domestic medium hypothetically consumed in an environment of distraction, television depends on the "glance" — fleeting and intermittent attention to a smaller screen. Also, whereas the cinema has developed primarily as a narrative medium, television continually mixes its genres, moving vertiginously from news to talk show to sitcom to drama. Each genre, in turn, has a different mode of address, assuring that television can never be characterized by a single form of enunciation. In the American model, even programs that emulate the cinema's mode of address are periodically interrupted by commercials that refocus the spectator as a subject of direct contact. Throughout the broadcast day, in fact, television continually acknowledges and even confronts the viewer, thereby compromising many of the voyeuristic pleasures of the cinema.

Taken together, television's smaller screen, mixed modes of address, and prevalence of the "glance" are said to thwart any possibility of primary identification. TV's constant fragmentation prevents the viewer from taking the image as a function of his or her all-perceiving mastery. "Because there is no artificial regression, primary voyeuristic identification is not engaged. The source of enunciation is dispersed (and made problematic) and, with that, its terms of address."[21] Or, as Ellis writes, "Broadcast TV does not construct an image marked by present absence, its regime is one of co-presence of image and viewer. The image is therefore not an impossible one, defined by the separation of the viewer from it, but rather one that is familiar and intimate."[22] Theorists differ as to the ultimate effect of this relationship in television. John Caughie argues that the viewing subject occupies numerous fleeting positions in relation to the changing fragments of televisual textuality.[23] Mimi White, on the other hand, proposes that the continual fragmentation of television ultimately coheres to produce a unified subject across the grand metatext of television.[24]

In actual practice, of course, the distinction between the gaze and the glance in the two media is not absolute (there are, after all, disengaged cineastes just as there are transfixed video viewers). At its best, this body of theory challenges us to examine the historical specificity of signifying practices and spectatorship in both media. At its worst, such theory engages in a form of rank technological determinism that essentializes differences in the social experience of the two media as somehow intrinsic to the technologies themselves. I would argue, for example, that television's perceived lack of "primary identification," the experiential component postulated from the medium's perpetually unfolding "flow," has become the essentialized foundation for one of the most supernatural constructions in all media criticism: the "ungrounded" televisual subject. In this scenario, the solid, substantial subject produced by the cinematic apparatus has been demolished, replaced in the age of television by more distracted, ephemeral, and postmodern subjects who seem perpetually at the brink of psychic disintegration. This conflict is perhaps best expressed in the familiar metaphors used to theorize the two viewing experiences: suture vs. surfing. In academic film and television theory, a whole series of assumptions (many based on no more than the differing cultural status of the two media) proceed from the questionable premise that the cinema "sutures" viewers snugly into subjective place, whereas television transforms them into fragmented, channel-surfing schizos.

Once again, interesting parallels of this debate can be found in popular culture. Like its academic cousins, popular accounts of extraordinary vision in the cinema have usually focused on the powers of exaggerated "identification" through projection, whereas paranormal treatments of televisual spectatorship emphasize flow and fragmentation. Occult fictions surrounding the two media have thus shifted from a spectacle of absorption, the viewing subject "tricked" into taking the cinematic image as his or her own field of vision, to a spectacle of electronic vertigo, a preexistent subject drawn into the televisual apparatus and subjected to the disorientation of television's fragmentation and flow. *Uncle Josh at the Moving Picture Show* (1902), for example, remains a paradigmatic example of extraordinary identification in the cinema. In this early silent short, an uninitiated film viewer mistakes a series of projected images as "real worlds" and attempts with comic effect to enter these various projected realities only to find himself repeatedly confronted with the unyielding two-dimensional reality of the screen. Other films have imagined this fantastic transfer actually taking place, a flesh-and-blood viewer allowed to enter the projected diegesis of the motion picture. In these tales of extraordinary projection and identification where the screen itself becomes a permeable boundary between the real world and the projected reality of the motion picture, the subject journeys to the otherside of the screen to occupy a singularly fantastic (and yet equally stable) world.

Stories of viewers transported to the otherside of the television screen are equally common, but portray this journey in quite different terms. In the 1992 release *Stay Tuned,* a representative of Satan cons a man into

Husband and wife trapped in their television set and forced to compete on a moronic game show in *Stay Tuned.* (© 1992 Morgan Creek Productions)

trying a new television system and satellite dish free of charge. One night, as the man and his wife fight in the backyard over the new TV system, they are "electrified" and then swept up by the satanic satellite dish (their entire existence quite literally transformed into a type of transmission). Once in this electrical otherworld, they free-fall past hundreds of cable and wire bundles, apparently descending to the "heart" of the television. They land, finally, on the set of a game show that initiates an adventure through many TV genres as the couple attempts to escape the demon set with their souls intact. When traveling from program to program (and presumably from channel to channel), the couple falls into open doorways of static that deliver them to their next video destination. Significantly, those who enter the televisual fantastic most often find themselves in a vertiginous, fragmented world that, like television itself, has no single, stable diegesis. Whereas paranormal film viewers find themselves immersed in the intense reality of a single diegetic world, video spectators find themselves dropped into the river of "flow" that rolls through "televisionland."

Given these often essentialized dichotomies in the two media — unity vs. fragmentation, depth vs. surface, attention vs. distraction — it is perhaps not surprising that the metaphor of "schizophrenia" should become so prominent in discussions of television. In his influential essay on post-modernity, Fredric Jameson links this sense of "fragmentation," seemingly endemic to postmodern culture and epitomized in the flowing "imagescape" of television, to Lacan's theories of schizophrenia. Jameson specifically invokes Lacan's theories to help describe the intensity of an "undifferentiated vision of the world in the present," a characteristic he sees as central to the postmodern experience and that others identify as the very essence of the televisual. Schizophrenia for Lacan results from an inability to process correctly the signifying chain that unifies past, present, and future. The schizophrenic thus experiences reality, in Jameson's words, as "a rubble of distinct and unrelated signifiers." The ultimate effect is that the schizophrenic subject eludes the temporal unification enabled by language and thus exists in a perpetual present. "The schizophrenic," writes Jameson, "is reduced to an experience of pure material signifiers, or, in other words, a series of pure and unrelated presents in time." "This present of the world or material signifier," he continues, "comes before the subject with heightened intensity, bearing a mysterious change of affect . . . which one could . . . easily imagine in the positive terms of euphoria, a high, an intoxicatory or hallucinogenic intensity."[25]

Jameson's words seem to diagnose in clinical detail the emergence of a giddy pop-cult figure who would become, in the late 1980s and early 1990s, the poster boy of postmodern media theory. "Born" in England and brought to America on a multimedia wave of hype, *Max Headroom* debuted on American television in the spring of 1987. "Max" was the spastic, chattering, computer-generated alter ego of video journalist Edison Carter, "brought to life" when sinister forces downloaded the nearly dead Carter's mind and memories into a computer mainframe. In a dystopic urban wilderness set "twenty minutes into the future," Carter and his cyberdouble, Max, sought to expose injustice in a noirish world dominated by media conglomerate Network 23 and its nefarious patron, the Zik Zak Corporation. Co-starring in the ABC series with humanoid Carter, Max also hosted solo his own talk show on Cinemax and served briefly as a pitchman for Coca-Cola.

On the surface (and Max, of course, was nothing but surface), *Max Headroom* appears to be an irrefutable confirmation of postmodernity's ascendancy as a cultural dominant. Max certainly embodies (or more preciously, [dis]embodies) the favored thematic inventory of postmodern media theory: telematics, simulation, fragmentation, surface, pastiche, and of course schizophrenia. As a result, *Max Headroom* quickly became a favorite critical object of media theory and criticism in the late 1980s and early 1990s. Here at last was a faithful portrait of postmodernity rendered in the era's most postmodern medium. *Max Headroom* was for many the very distillation of the televisual and emphatic evidence of the medium's privileged position in postmodern culture. Such enthusiasm, in turn, often made the series a foundational text in theorizing the media universe. Although authors approached Max with a variety of critical questions and agendas, there was nevertheless an unstated assumption linking much of this work that the series was in some way emblematic of television as a whole, either as an institution, a textual environment, or a mode of spectatorship.

Max's centrality was not to last, however. "As the fashion of postmodernism passed through academic circles," notes John Caldwell in his study of television style, "shows like *Max Headroom* faded from the theoretical spotlight."[26] With benefit of historical hindsight, we can see certain fallacies working to undermine such totalizing claims about the series and its relation to television and postmodernity. For one thing, in the grand scheme of television history and culture, *Max Headroom* was simply not very important. Cancelled after thirteen episodes, Max did live on briefly in ads and guest appearances on other shows, but overall, his impact and significance as a defining vision of American culture lies somewhere between *Joanie Loves Chachi* and *Fantasy Island*. More important than Scott Baio, certainly, Max nonetheless remains a less recognizable icon for the American populace than Herve Villechaize's Tattoo. The program's chief legacy, as Caldwell points out, has been in terms of a more aggressive visual style in television (one that ultimately transcends genre and thematics). Interestingly, *Max Headroom* demonstrated that what would eventually prove to be a successful genre in film (*Robocop, Total Recall, The Running Man,* etc.) did not fare so well in television. Audiences may have enjoyed critiques of electronically mediated dystopias in the cinema, but they apparently turned to television for something else.

Max's extraordinary popularity with a small audience segment (science fiction fans and media scholars) suggests that the series, rather than capturing a grand "reality" of television, epitomized a certain fantasy about television held by this more limited audience group. Max, in short, confirmed postmodernity for those who already had contact with and believed in the premises of postmodernity. This explains, perhaps, how the series

Max Headroom: Postmodern poster boy. (© Warner Brothers 1987)

assumed such theoretical importance in the academy. In their understandable enthusiasm for the series, critics often approached *Max Headroom* as if it were a documentary artifact of a real postmodern world rather than a highly mediated fiction *about* television and postmodernity. Lost in the zeal was the realization that *Max* was not a "reflection" of our electronic culture (despite occurring "twenty minutes into the future"), but was instead a science fiction *fantasy* about the world of television. *Max* was a very clever (and thus already atypical) television series that, in an attempt to attract younger, more upscale and educated viewers to ABC, drew on the then hip dialogue between cyberpunk and cybertheory to marry a familiar mass society nightmare with postmodern thematics, a vision outfitted, in turn, with the bells and whistles of cybernetic fashion. Max became a very effective salesman during his brief run, not only for Coke, but also for postmodernism as a certain fashionable sensibility, one that had very little to do with how the populace actually experiences the media and world but that captured vividly the metaphysical fantasies of surface, simulation, and schizophrenia so endemic to more educated visions of the media occult.

Presented in pop culture as the ideal TV character (the ultimate "talking head") and positioned in academic circles as the ideal televisual subject, Max was in the end only another ghost in the machine. As interiorized visions of simulation, such portraits of fragmented, disassociated, and otherwise "schizophrenic" subjects, be they Max's cyberecho of Edison Carter or the ungrounded, fleeting, fragmented subjects theorized on the couch, present yet another fantastic narrative of disembodiment in electronic media. Once again, such accounts imbue electronic telecommunications with the inexplicable power to unmoor consciousness from space, time, and the body, in this case through disembodying metaphors of surface and psychosis. Whereas psychoanalytic theories of film spectatorship imagined the cinematic apparatus as "productive" of subjectivity, models of spectatorship in television regard the apparatus as a means toward the estrangement and disassociation of the subject. Television divorces the subject from reality, not in an ideological form of "imaginary relations" or "false consciousness," but through a seemingly literal electronic intervention that displaces the real and scrambles the mind of the subject. As Vivian Sobchack argues in distinguishing electronic presence from that of the cinema, "Saturation of color and hyperbolic attention to detail replace depth and texture at the surface, while constant action and 'busyness' replace the gravity that grounds and orients the movement of the lived body with a purely spectacular, kinetically exciting, often dizzying sense of bodily freedom. In an important sense, then, electronic space *disembodies*."[27] But what does it mean, short of teleportation, for a technology or its signifying practices or even the very texture of the image to disembody? Although this sense of ungrounded fragmentation felt by so many in television is clearly a function of specific historical applications of the technology and is linked to a larger metaphysics of electronic media, these metaphors of simulation and psychosis often intertwine to produce a seemingly immutable model of textuality and spectatorship in television, one that invokes a loss of the real as the medium's fundamental, intrinsic, and defining characteristic.

Seemingly imbued with an uncanny electrical consciousness that mirrors our own, as well as the ability to counterfeit our real world, the animating presence of television has long been regarded as a potentially invasive psychic threat to the viewer. There is in popular fiction a long tradition that similarly associates television with themes of simulation, psychosis, and a loss of the real. This popular tradition predates contemporary theoretical musings on electronic media and postmodern culture, suggesting once again that certain varieties of postmodern media theory may be only more specialized incarnations of a popular form of occult fiction. Bruce Jay Friedman's "For Your Viewing Entertainment," for example, a short story first published in *Playboy* in 1960, anticipates the disembodying dimensions of televisual psychosis posited in postmodern theory, centering in this case on a flesh-and-blood viewer who becomes a target of direct attack by his TV set. Friedman's story centers on a Mr. Ordz, a middle-aged husband who appears to receive a death threat via television one night as he watches a variety program. The show's malevolent emcee addresses Ordz directly in a telematic nightmare,

> I've got exactly one week to kill you or I don't get my sponsor. . . . I don't mean I can reach out and strike you down. That's the thing I want to explain. I can't shoot you from in here or give you a swift, punishing rabbit punch. It isn't that kind of arrangement. In ours, I've got six days to kill you, but I'm not actually allowed to do it directly. Now, what I'm going to do is try to shake you up as best I can, Ordz, and get you to, say, go up to your room and have a heart attack.[28]

Mr. Ordz tries to convince various people in his life that the television is plotting against him, but no one is willing to listen. During the week, the emcee returns on TV night after night, baiting Mr. Ordz and reminding him of how much time is left. Mr. Ordz's personality undergoes a gradual breakdown until one night in anger he finally smashes the TV screen with his fist, "obliterating the picture and opening something stringy in his wrist." At the hospital Ordz loses consciousness. When he "awakes," he finds himself surrounded by mysterious technicians. "Out of the corner of one eye, he saw his m.c., and two distinguished executive-type gentlemen soar out of the top of the building. . . . The executives were holding the m.c. by the elbows and all three had sprouted wings. Then Mr. Ordz was shoved forward. Hot lights were brought down close to his face and cameras began to whir" (22). Cue cards are lowered for Ordz, and he is told to read them aloud. He tries vainly to resist. "The lights got hotter. Then he looked at the card, felt his mouth force into an insincere smile, and heard himself saying to a strange man who sat opposite him in a kind of living room, munching on some slices of protein bread, 'All right now, Simons, I've got exactly one week to kill you' " (22). In this disassociative experience, Mr. Ordz "feels" his mouth force an insincere smile and "hears" himself talking to the next victim. The circular tale ends with Ordz in complete collapse and the reader uncertain as to the status of the real and the televisual, actor and spectator having apparently switched electronic places.

But schizophrenia is not the only psychic hazard awaiting the televisual spectator. Television has also been long suspected as a facilitator of fantastic affective disorders. Indeed, just as there are many popular examples linking television and psychosis that anticipate the use of schizophrenia as a media metaphor, other tales anticipate critiques of postmodernity in terms of a "waning of affect." Describing the Western world's cultural odyssey in painting from Van Gogh to Warhol, Jameson charts what he sees as the dissipation of a modernist aesthetic of depth into a postmodern play of surface. He identifies four depth models that have been both repudiated by contemporary cultural theory and collapsed by postmodern culture — "essence and appearance," "latent and manifest," "authenticity and inauthenticity," and finally, "signifier and signified."[29] For Jameson, postmodern culture has effaced each of these binaries to produce a new cultural environment of "depthlessness." Such depthlessness testifies in turn to the death of the monadic subject so pivotal to both high modernism and high capitalism. Jameson concentrates on a comparison between Van Gogh's *A Pair of Boots* and Warhol's *Diamond Dust Shoes,* reading in these two images of footwear a larger crisis of the subject, lamenting that postmodernity's "waning of affect" may eventually erase the category of the critical human subject. "As for expression and feelings or emotions," notes Jameson, "the liberation, in contemporary society, from the older anomie of the centered subject may also mean not merely a liberation from anxiety but a liberation from every other kind of feeling as well, since there is no longer a self present to do the feeling" (15).

Popular writers of the fifties and sixties also implied that the new media culture was slowly effacing the "authentic" emotional world formerly available to a more centered human subjectivity, replacing it with the accelerated, ephemeral, and ultimately "inauthentic" sensations of television. Indeed, much science fiction of the period explicitly addressed television as an enemy of affect, whether such affect was conceived in terms of artistic sensibility or political subjectivity. L. Sprague de Camp's short story, "Corzan the Mighty," first published in 1955 by *Future Science Fiction,* tells of a mammoth television production using a revolutionary new process to produce video "affect." Describing the project, the narrator writes, "Not only was it designed for alethochromatic three-dimensional wide-screen high-fidelity binaural dual-modulation broadcasting, but also it represented the first commercial use of the consiline hypnosis on the actors." This form of hypnosis involves injecting the actors with a drug that makes them believe, "while they were acting the parts, that they actually were the characters whom they portrayed."[30] The story imagines television in search of a cure, writing prescriptions for itself to remedy the medium's affective vacuum. In a world where television is all pervasive, only psychotropic drugs can overcome the medium's shallow surfaces and inauthentic emotions. The scientist has a second idea, however, that is even more radical, a drug he calls "somnone-beta." "With that I indoctrinate, not the actors, but the customers." An incredulous coworker asks if that means the viewer gets a shot and then dreams the show. "Is right," says the scientist. "No actors, no sets, no engineering, no nothing. Customer makes up his own story according to the directions on the tape. He can be a participant or onlooker. The entertainment is much more vivid than anything you can get watching a stage or screen" (146). With "somnone-beta" he envisions the final transformation of electronic spectacle into biochemical illusions in the minds of the audience, a final and ultimate collapse of media, reality, and consciousness. So absolute are the imperious powers of control in television, however, that the institution cannot accept being displaced as the prime supplier of mass hallucination. The story ends with the television industry paying the scientist millions of dollars to suppress "somnone-beta," thus insuring the keeping of its audience in electronic rather than chemical incarceration.

In Kate Wilhelm's mid-sixties tale "Baby, You Were Great," viewers plug in to the network to experience the transmission of authentic emotions. "The gimmick was simple enough. A person fitted with electrodes in the brain could transmit his emotions, which in turn could be broadcast and picked up by the helmets to be felt by the audience. No words, or thoughts, went out, only basic emotions — fear, love, anger, hatred."[31] A camera shows what the program's electro-brained "star" is seeing, but many users of the system consider this a redundant distraction. "You didn't really need the camera and the sound track; many users never turned them on at all, but let their own imaginations fill in the emotional broadcast" (27). In this future, television becomes an affective vampire, preying on the emotional turmoil of the network's main star, Anne Beaumont, who (like Truman Burbank) is doomed to live her life being continually harassed, tricked, surprised, disappointed, threatened, and terrified by television producers, all so that she will continue to broadcast vivid and novel emotions for her audience. Wilhelm, in turn, conceives of this audience as drained of all affective capacities, presumably by years of such television, to the point where a TV producer describes them as not even alive "unless they're plugged in" (26). Having dulled its audience through years of superficial sensationalism, TV can ultimately only produce affect by hardwiring it into the audience.

The ultimate endgame in such logic, of course, is the absolute and irrevocable electronic mediation of consciousness, a "virtual reality" of no return. Thus, in the story "Spectator Sport" a Dr. Rufus Maddon receives a lobotomy for disrupting the "status quo" of a futuristic society. When technicians involved in his "lobe job" realize they have made an error, they decide to hook up Maddon to a "perm" to cover their mistake. A perm can best be described as a self-contained virtual reality unit in which one remains for life. Buying a perm is the ultimate status symbol in this society of the future:

> The bored technicians worked rapidly. They stripped the unprotesting Rufus Maddon, took him inside his cubicle, forced him down onto the foam couch. They rolled him over onto his side, made the usual incision at the back of his neck, carefully slit the main motor nerves, leaving the senses, the heart and lungs intact. They checked the air conditioning and plugged him into the feeding schedule for that bank of Perms.
>
> Next they swung the handrods and the footplates into position, gave him injections of local anesthetic, expertly flayed the palms of his hands and the soles of his feet, painted the raw flesh with the sticky nerve graft and held his hands closed around the rods, his feet against the plates until they adhered in the proper position.[32]

Having converted Rufus into the ultimate couch potato, one technician sighs enviously, "Nothing to do for as long as he lives except twenty-four hours a day of being the hero of the most adventurous and glamorous and exciting stories that the race has been able to devise. No memories. I told them to dial him in on the Cowboy series. There's seven years of that now. It'll be more familiar to him. I'm electing Crime and Detection. Eleven years of that now, you know" (7). Such a passage seems to realize most literally Baudrillard's cybernetic assertion that the media "transforms our habitat into a kind of archaic, closed-off cell, into a vestige of human relations whose survival is highly questionable. . . . As soon as behavior is focused on certain operational screens or terminals, the rest appears only as some vast, useless body, which has been both abandoned and condemned."[33]

This account of the ultimate postmodern subject, however, is not from the annals of cyberfiction or cybertheory but comes instead from mass-market spy writer John MacDonald. The story dates from 1950 — at the dawn of television's arrival in the American home and a full thirty years before the appearance of Baudrillard's *Simulations.* Clearly, the fear that television would eventually replace reality prefigured the theoretical paradigm that would so often argue that television has in fact simulated reality; indeed, MacDonald's story is not *informed* by television so much as it *anticipates* both the arrival of television and the critical fears that would accompany its mass dissemination. Tales like "Spectator Sport" suggested that the then emerging spectacle of the televisual age would be not merely a deceptive illusion fooling us into temporarily misapprehending reality (like the cinema), but would be instead an invasive form of electronic presence emulating and commandeering both reality and consciousness. In MacDonald's brief tale of sinister simulation, then, we have an early example of the ultimate fusion of psychosis and simulation, and a dystopic precursor to the vast electronic environments of "cyberspace," "the Net," the "matrix," "simstin," and all other occult visions of transmutable bioelectric subjectivity that would follow.

The Logic of Transmutable Flow

These tales from the fifties and sixties demonstrate that popular culture was equally engaged with the questions of contemporary electronic media that would occupy postmodern criticism in the seventies and eighties. These fantastic portraits of "televisionland" as a world that simulates through destruction and mediates through infiltration would find a theoretical voice in DeBord, Baudrillard, Jameson, and the other significant architects of postmodern theory. Still, one is left to wonder why we are so willing to assume television (and subsequent electronic media) — whether presented in pop or postmodern form — have the incredible power to actually replace reality and displace subjectivity? Why do the polar extremes of simulation and psychosis seem so much more plausible in discussing television than in other media?

196

Paranormal accounts of simulation and psychosis in television represent the culmination of the fantasies of electronic presence that began with the telegraph. One last example drawn from popular culture may help explain the continuing dominance of this fantasy. In a rather marginal horror film from 1989, *Shocker,* a community suffers a series of brutal murders committed by a demented and sadistic television repairman named Horace Pinker. Once captured, Pinker is sentenced to death in the electric chair. When the guards come to his cell to take him to the death chamber, they find Pinker connected to a TV set in his cell with some jumper cables. Electricity spewing from the set, the cables, and Pinker's body, the killer makes a pact with Satan (we can only assume), who appears as a pair of electronic lips emanating from the television. Once in the chair, Pinker is jolted with incredible amounts of electricity, but this only appears to make him stronger (at least for a few moments). After the execution a prison doctor tries to take his pulse, but she is knocked backwards by a powerful shock. Inexplicably, Pinker's body suddenly crumbles to dust. In typical low-budget horror logic, however, everyone leaves thinking justice has finally been served. The film then cuts to the prison doctor, now on her way to the hospital in an ambulance. The doctor, who had seemed injured by her "shocking" encounter with Pinker, suddenly rises up malevolently from her stretcher and kills her police escort. Thus, we discover that Horace Pinker's pact with Satan has allowed him to become a wholly electrical being, capable of transferring his consciousness from body to body by simple physical contact.

Such a premise, of course, follows a cultural logic reaching back to the Spiritualists of the nineteenth century. Like John Murray Spear, Horace Pinker also has faith (albeit satanic) in the fantastic powers of electrical disembodiment and transmigration. The middle section of the film follows Pinker as he switches electrically from body to body in pursuit of the film's teen hero, Johnny, who becomes the primary focus of his murderous anger. During this chase we find that the electrical Pinker can exist outside of his host body, but only for a few moments. When Pinker does emerge from the host body, he assumes the form of a video image; that is, his body is semitranslucent and filled with static! Unable to find a host body during a crucial fight, Pinker instead transfers his body into an electrical outlet. This gives him the power to emerge from any other electrical outlet in the city, a power he of course uses to commit more crimes. Finally, in another body Pinker chases Johnny to the top of a television broadcasting tower

Horace Pinker's electrocution allows for a series of extraordinary substitutions and transmutations of electronic flow in *Shocker*. (© 1989 Universal City Studios)

and during a struggle transfers his electrical body into the transmission dish. "I'm nationwide now," laughs Pinker as he disappears into the ether. Appropriately, *Shocker* concludes with a long chase and fight sequence between Pinker and Johnny in the ambiguous realm of "televisionland." Having turned himself into a broadcast signal, Pinker can now enter the diegetic space of any TV program and the domestic space of any living room with an activated TV set. By using a special amulet, Johnny is also able to enter this virtual realm, and the two chase each other through a variety of programs. Johnny finally pursues Pinker into a "TV room" equipped with a monitor and a video camera. Once in the room, Johnny uses a remote control to "freeze" Pinker and then employs its fast forward and reverse functions to make him bang his head against the wall repeatedly. More fighting ensues until finally Johnny escapes the "TV room" leaving Pinker trapped within. Johnny exits this world via his home TV set, but before Pinker can follow him, Johnny's friends shut down the power plant for the entire city. Unable to access his electrical lifeblood, Pinker at last perishes.

Described in such fashion, *Shocker* seems a film held together by a narrative logic that verges on the insane. The viewer is asked to accept, without question, that one might transmute into a wholly electrical being. With the premise established, it is then assumed the viewer can follow a rapid series of surreal transformations — Pinker becomes a woman, a little girl, a murderous lamp, a deadly vibrating chair, a broadcast signal, and a television image. Overall, the film follows an incredibly "liquid" narrative logic, one governed by a metaphysics that can effortlessly convert flows of electricity, consciousness, television signals and programming into interchangeable analogues. The movie can only "make sense" because these ideas about electronic media, long in circulation, are now free-floating in the cultural imagination.

When the viewer turns on the television and engages its "stream" of images, four distinct types of "flow" appear to intersect. There is the electrical "current" that powers the apparatus and the "galvanic" energy that powers the body. There is the "flow of programming" or information that occupies the medium and the "stream of consciousness" that occupies the mind. The convergence of these rivers of flow, streams of electricity, programming, and consciousness, produces a fantastic arena where these forces and entities can seem interchangeable. Both pop and postmodern fictions of electronic media revel in the exchange and confusion of these terms. Whether encountered in *Shocker* or *Simulations,* this logic of transmutable flow seems so naturalized as to be common sense (one must be well versed in this mythology to make sense of either text). This enduring logic of transmutable flow allows simulation to replace reality, information to become consciousness, the human to become mechanical, and the technological to become sentient. But, as we have seen with telegraphy, wireless, and radio, the quality of "living" electronic presence that informs so much thought about television is only a recent articulation of a longstanding theme in the cultural history of telecommunications. This sense of "presence" that now seems to be an innate property of television is in fact the product of a series of historically specific intersections of technological, industrial, and cultural practices. The animating pulse of electricity powers a machine promoted by its industry as a "live" gateway to an expanding electronic universe, a cosmos that often seems as tangible and real as the material world. The "ideology of liveness" that pervades television is thus precisely that: a historically specific way of thinking about the media within the context of a particular social formation, certain industrial strategies, and a cultural tradition significantly informed by occult accounts of the media. Postmodern metaphors of simulation and psychosis are equally a part of this "ideology of liveness," articulating in the historical debates associated with television's technical development, social diffusion, and critical evaluation a now centuries-old metaphysics of electricity and telecommunications.

Fantasies of electronic disembodiment began as a belief in the social deliverance to be achieved through the spiritual telegraph. These discorporative wonders continued in wireless and radio, culminating in television with a belief in an autonomous electronic reality. In the foundational debates of postmodernity waged in the 1960s, 1970s, and 1980s, television was often nothing more than a cruel inversion of the spiritual telegraph. Television also promised to teleport viewers to another space and time yet in the end only delivered them to the disassociative empires of simulation and psychosis. In this respect Baudrillard's *Simulations* functioned as a twentieth-century rewriting of Shelley's *Frankenstein.* In the postmodern version of Faust's tale, the electric spark provided by Mary Shelley's God to animate a constructed homunculus now powers a vast electronic network where humankind's soul and subjectivity are just as equally "constructed" and just as irretrievably lost.

Consensual Hallucinations

"If a spiritually endowed human agent, while hampered by his material environment, can perform acts independent of material limitations, is it not fair inference that he can do more and better when the same spiritual powers are released by the dissolution of the physical husk?"
— Epes Sargent, *The Scientific Basis of Spiritualism*

A common conceit in historical writing is to end where one began. Cyclical returns in history imply the existence of immutable forces, powers brought to light and made predictable by the insight of the author's historical analysis. "History repeats itself" goes the well-known aphorism, and so it would seem in the histories of electronic presence and haunted media, especially as the world enters the much heralded cyberage of the new millennium. Compare Spiritualist Epes Sargeant's comments, made in 1891, with those of cyberbooster Michael Benedikt in 1991:

> Cyberspace: The realm of pure information, filling like a lake, siphoning
> the jangle of messages transfiguring the physical world, decontaminating
> the natural and urban landscapes, redeeming them, saving them from the
> chain-dragging bulldozers of the paper industry, from the diesel smoke of
> courier and post office trucks, from jet fuel fumes and clogged airports,
> from billboards, trashy and pretentious architecture, hour-long freeway
> commutes, ticket lines, and choked subways . . . from all the inefficiencies,
> pollutions (chemical and informational), and corruptions attendant to the
> process of moving information attached to things — from paper to brains —
> across, over, and under the vast and bumpy surface of the earth rather than
> letting it fly free in the soft hail of electrons that is cyberspace.[34]

Here we have two visions of electronic technology's liberating humanity
from the constraints of the body and the drudgery of the physical world,
two predictions of a utopian spiritual age ushered in by "scientific" principles and magical machinery. As another writer rhapsodizes, virtual reality
"revealed a state of grace to us, tapped a wavelength where image, music,
language and love were pulsing in one harmony."[35] Described in such
terms, virtual reality truly is the new "seventh heaven."

At the threshold of the new millennium, a number of writers are making
connections between these two utopian moments. "Today the Internet is
often described as an information superhighway," notes Tom Standage in
his book, *The Victorian Internet;* "its nineteenth-century precursor, the
electric telegraph, was dubbed the 'highway of thought.' "[36] John Durham
Peters, meanwhile, argues that the act of "communication" has long been
conceptualized in spiritual terms, even before the advent of electronic
technology.[37] In her article "Ghosting the Interface," Sarah Walters draws
out the many parallels between Spiritualist thought and the discourses of
cyberspace.[38] Tom Gunning, finally, notes an affinity between nineteenth-
century interest in "spirit photography" and our own era's fascination
with the simulations of postmodernity. In the spirit photograph, he writes,
"we uncover a proliferating spiral of exchanges and productions of images, founded in a process of reproduction for which no original may ever
be produced. Spooky, isn't it?"[39]

What are we to make of the uncanny parallels between late-nineteenth-
and late-twentieth-century thought on uncanny technologies? Is this parallelism the product of a genuine historical cycle or a projection backward
of certain obsessions in contemporary media historiography? As should

be clear by now, this book argues that the similarity between the Spiritualist occult and the current explosion of supernaturalism in cyberspace is less an example of a historical "return" than of a historical trajectory. By traversing time and space at the speed of light, electronic media have always indulged the fantasy of discorporation and the hope that the human soul, consciousness, or subject could exist independently of his or her material frame. Related to the discorporative fantasy is that of the electronic elsewhere—the media's occult power to give form to sovereign electronic worlds. These remain the fantasies informing accounts of fantastic media, even today, be they in the form of paranormal anecdotes or postmodern prognostications.

But, as argued in the introduction of this book, we should not take this paranormal continuity as a sign of some transcendental, ahistorical essence within electronic media. As we have seen, although fictions of transmutable flow in electronic media remain constant, their actual historical content and social significance have changed dramatically from decade to decade and technology to technology. As Walters argues in her study of cyberspirits, "If virtual and occult experiences are both part of some 'ancient' transcendental project, then that project is a crucially variable one, with a shape and significance susceptible to inflection by cultural and ideological change."[40] As a historically specific phenomenon, what are we to make of the occult discourses currently proliferating around the emerging computer technologies, especially in relation to the truly fantastic futures imagined for virtual reality? As cyberspace replaces television as postmodernity's technological dominant, how have these occult logics of flow and transmutability changed once again?

In the high age of televised spectacle, cultural critics often decried the evaporation of the real and the phenomenon of simulation as an endpoint for human subjectivity. Rendered in metaphors of simulation and psychosis, television was the most viral and virulent form of mass mediation ever encountered. More recently, however, a certain ecstatic celebration of both simulation and fragmented subjectivity has replaced this once dour saga of video alienation. In the zeitgeist of cyberculture, promoted by both new-tech gurus in the academy and the editorial board of *Wired,* electronic postmodernity is no longer a lamentable "condition," but is instead a hip and exciting lifestyle in which those who are willing to shed the illusion of the "human" will be rewarded in the emancipating splendor of techno-bodies and the enlightened consciousness of "virtual subjectivity."

Having transcended the illusion of the "human" and the lie of innate "subjectivity," these apostles rewrite what had been a dead end in television as the point of departure for a wholly polymorphous electronic future. In this new world, technology allows one to escape traditional (and now increasingly boring) social markers of gender, sexuality, race, age, and class to fashion entirely new identities. Beginning with tentative excursions under assumed personas in MUDs, this future is to one day culminate in the fully realized fantasy of virtual reality environments where individuals can be anyone or anything they care to be. Allucquère Rosanne Stone dubs this emerging age nothing less than a "fourth epoch," a new form of human communications that will become the foundation of a new form of reality. Scott Bukatman, in turn, labels this emerging subjectivity as "terminal identity: an unmistakably doubled articulation in which we find both the end of the subject and a new subjectivity constructed at the computer station or television screen."[41] Accompanying this new sense of identity is a new sense of space. "Whether Baudrillard calls it *telematic culture* or science-fiction writers call it *the Web, the Net, the Grid, the Matrix,* or, most pervasively, *cyberspace,* there exists the pervasive recognition that a new and decentered spatiality has arisen that exists parallel to, but outside of, the geographic topography of experiential reality."[42]

What is the conceptual foundation for this new vision of identity and space? Stone argues the founding event in the creation of her "fourth epoch" was the 1984 publication of William Gibson's sci-fi novel *Neuromancer,* a work that gave the world the most developed and influential model of cyberspace's future terrain.[43] An originally ambivalent term used by Gibson to describe the 3-D telematic electronic infrastructure seen as replacing the collapsing material edifices of advanced capitalism, "cyberspace" in its most giddy incarnation now describes a potentially exhilarating virtual world produced by networks of telecommunications media and accessed by human subjectivities "plugged in" to a global electronic matrix. Bukatman, meanwhile, locates the critical articulation of his "terminal identity" in the postmodern fiction of figures such as Gibson, J. G. Ballard, and William S. Burroughs, as well as in the work of cultural theorists such as McLuhan and Baudrillard. This mixture of fiction and theory is significant. Bukatman's book argues that the concerns of postwar science fiction and contemporary media theory have gradually merged to the point that the two discourses are increasingly indistinguishable. This is undeniably true (a phenomenon epitomized in the 1999 Hollywood re-

Looking cool while you duel: Ostensibly a dystopic film about the "horrors" of virtual imprisonment, *The Matrix* (1999) nevertheless contributes to the reigning romance of cyberspace by presenting virtuality as a hipster playground of high-action and high-fashion. (© 1999 Paramount Pictures)

lease *The Matrix,* in which the film's cyberhero keeps a stash of illegal VR programs in a hollowed-out edition of Baudrillard's *Simulations and Simulacra*). If we accept Bukatman's premise that theory and science fiction have merged, however, the question remains as to what conclusion we should draw from this implosion of discourses. Should we take this collapse as mutual corroboration, evidence that virtual subjectivity is in fact an emerging and ever more "real" phenomenon? Or should it suggest to us instead that "virtual subjectivity" is such a compelling fantasy of electronic presence that its metaphysic has colonized both fiction *and* theory? Whether personified as virtual subjectivity or spatialized as virtual reality, virtuality itself remains a construct more of the imagination than of technology. No one has ever or is ever likely to confuse the electronic world for that of the real. As a culture, however, we remain profoundly invested in the fantasy that such substitutions might take place. When discussing the emerging virtual technologies, many commentators invoke Gibson's definition of cyberspace as a "consensual hallucination." But, we might ask, is cyberspace a consensual hallucination, or is it the *concept* of cyberspace that is the consensual hallucination?

Brains on Ice

As incredible as these fantasies of subjectivity, cyberspace, and virtual reality may be, they are eclipsed by what is possibly the ultimate cyberfantasy. "Kill Switch," an episode of *The X-Files* cowritten by William Gibson and Tom Maddox, provides a concise example of this transcendent digital dream. Investigating a shoot-out at a diner, agents Mulder and Scully cross paths with Esther Nairn, a prototypical cyberpunk heroine (i.e., a beautiful, tough-as-nails, romantic outsider-computer-genius with unusual makeup). Esther leads the agents through a typically serpentine cyberworld of illusion and conspiracy in a plot involving a Net-borne form of artificial intelligence. Hounded by the "evil" AI entity as it fights to maintain its sentience and autonomy, the agents' search eventually leads to a trailer on a remote farm where Esther hopes to find her colleague and lover. They instead find his lifeless body wearing a virtual reality helmet and surrounded by complex computer components. The episode concludes with Esther's loading a secret program into the computer and donning the VR helmet from her dead lover. On screens all around her, dizzying displays of data accelerate as her body shakes violently in the apparatus. And then in silence, with only a puff of smoke rising from her terminal contacts (signifying that the computer has worked really, really hard to effect this program), she is reunited with her lover in the Net. Having shed their mortal coils, both now exist forever as pure electronic data.

Two fantasies of flow here are obviously interrelated. On the one hand, we have the familiar conceit of the sentient computer, the self-aware, living form of artificial intelligence that manipulates cybersystems to maintain its autonomy and expand its influence. On the other hand, we have the dream of leaving the human body behind and downloading consciousness into a computer system. Here, Gibson and Maddox's script provides another tale of lovers disappearing into the telegraph wire. A concise treatment of these reigning cyberthemes (so truncated, in fact, that one wonders if it wasn't meant as a parody of these now ubiquitous conventions), "Kill Switch" demonstrates economically that these two fantasies are in fact a product of reciprocal exchange within a larger cultural logic. Once again, electricity facilitates transmutations of flow between mind and media, allowing the inanimate to become sentient and the sentient to become a ghost in the machine.

Like much other science fiction, this story encourages us to think of the brain as a living computer and the computer as a mechanical brain. So naturalized is this assumption now that it is easy to forget this comparison is a function of metaphor. In some sense brains and computers both "think," certainly, and both are animated by electricity. But this does not mean that they are compatible hardware systems ready to share various forms of software. The fantasy of the brain as "wetware," however, is persuasive enough that several hundred people in the world today are awaiting "cryonic neurosuspension." At death, they plan to have their heads severed and then frozen in liquid nitrogen. There they will remain in suspension until future scientists develop the necessary technology to thaw their brains out, and then either reattach them to a new body or download their neural net into a computer system. Thus will immortality, or at least virtual immortality, be achieved at last.

It is easy to dismiss the cryogenic crowd as a bunch of kooks, only one step behind the Heaven's Gate cult that believed a spaceship awaited them in the tail of the Hale-Bopp comet. Given the current state of discussion around the new cybertechnologies, however, their assumptions seem at least plausible, perhaps even reasonable. If a thousand years from now these eccentrics somehow awake as sentient beings in the computer networks of the future, they will have at last realized a dream begun in the mid–nineteenth century. They will truly be in the "Summerland," that Spiritualist haven of eternal light and beauty where, unfettered by material concerns, they can look back in sorrow at all the mortal fools who did not have the forethought to put their brains on ice. Will this ever happen? Probably not. Unless, of course, some inconceivably brilliant mind in the future finds a way to literalize a two-hundred-year-old metaphysical metaphor.

Science fiction is in the business of fantastic speculation. We should not be surprised to find accounts of electronic reality, artificial beings, and frozen brains next to those of universal translators, time warps, and flying cars. But how can we explain contemporary media theory's enthusiastic and often naive investment in the discorporative fantasies of cyberspace? One gets the impression reading Gibson that the author himself is skeptical or at least ambivalent about his own vision of this future world. Reading some of the more delirious forms of contemporary cybertheory, on the other hand, one gets the impression that Gibsonian cyberspace is a cultural and technological fait accompli, a place regarded as more "real" than the "real" itself.

Simulation and Psychosis

In many respects, academic culture's investment in cyberfantasy is a function of the vicissitudes of academic fashion. Here lies a whole new field of jargon and a ripe terrain for generating even more (paren)thetical paper titles. Moreover, virtual subjectivity is a particularly seductive figure in the academy in that it represents a perhaps inevitable coda to a certain trajectory in recent critical theory. One might argue that the dominant philosophical/theoretical project of this century has been the historicization of human subjectivity. No longer regarded as an innate quality of the human mind (linked to a metaphysics of the "soul"), subjectivity became in the twentieth century a "construct," the end product of sociohistorical discourses that provide the ideological illusion of autonomous, innate subjectivity. A guiding project in the melding of Marxist and psychoanalytic theory, such models of constructed subjectivity were particularly pervasive in film theory during the 1970s, which then became a foundational moment for all media studies. Having theorized the subject's construction, critics in the turn to postmodern theory contemplated this same subject's fragmentation and dissolution. The shift from capitalism to late capitalism, many argued, presented the death knell of the conventional bourgeois subject and the rise of fragmented and fleeting subjectivities. Fredric Jameson describes this "death of the subject" so central to postmodern criticism as one of the more "fashionable themes in contemporary theory . . . , the end of the autonomous bourgeois monad or ego or individual — and the accompanying stress, whether as some new moral ideal or as empirical description, on the decentering of that formerly centered subject or psyche."[44] But metaphysics do not die so easily. Having dethroned the bourgeois subject and reveled in the decentering of the postmodern subject, contemporary theory latched onto the exciting fantasy of the malleable cybersubject. For an intellectual circle devoted to the idea that subjectivity is ultimately a fragile and variable historical concept, technologies that promise to craft, exchange, transmute, and otherwise conjure subjectivity would of course have immense appeal. Thus were the humanist illusions of traditional metaphysics replaced by the technological illusions of electronic presence. It is almost as if, unsettled by the subject's historical variability, contemporary theory looked to the cybertechnologies as both a validation of its model of the constructed subject and as a means of deliverance from that model's potentially alienating implications.

The irony here, of course, is that to accept the power of these technologies to engineer so effortlessly new subjectivities and realities threatens to trivialize and dismiss the profoundly important political mechanisms originally posited as producing subjectivity in the first place. Are the experiences and categories of gender, race, sexuality, and class really so disposable that they can be escaped or even significantly disrupted by a few hours in cyberspace? Even if we can imagine the existence of a *Star Trek*–like vision of the holodeck, an absolutely verisimilitudinous and completely programmable interactive virtual realm, will the occupants inside really be able to leave behind so easily the years of intertwined personal experience, social history, and ideological formation that shaped their minds and identities in the first place? For that matter, can cyberspace and VR ever provide "identities" and "elsewheres" not already present in the sociopolitical psyche of the culture that perfects such technology? Until the majority of lived life takes place in cyberspace (a highly unlikely prospect in any age), there seems little evidence that electronic technologies, no matter how convincing their illusions, will actually restructure identities and subjectivity in any meaningful way. Or, to put it more simply, if I'm a fifty-year-old man who likes to assume the identity of a teenage girl, either in chatrooms or in the illusions of VR, such impersonation may say much about the complex structure of fantasy and desire in my fifty-year-old male mind, but it certainly does not mean that I have somehow become a teenage girl simply by putting on a visor. And yet much cybertheory approaches the technology as if *subjectivity, identity,* and *fantasy* were equivalent and interchangeable terms (when, of course, they are not). Strange, too, that theories with a lineage in Marxism (however distant) would so frequently ignore that, given the current trajectory of late capitalism, it is more than likely that only 10 percent or so of the future first world will be able to escape into VR programs while the other 90 percent flip hamburgers, take nightshifts, and work other service jobs to maintain the infrastructure that supports the electronic bliss of the ruling class.

Having such delusions is not necessarily harmful. Everyone has recourse to some form of fantasy to help them cope with life (and death). Cyberenthusiasts are no more insane than Christians, Buddhists, Muslims, or any other practitioner of mystical belief. As is the case with all religion, however, society can only benefit by remaining vigilant at the prospects of an impending theocracy, be it of the church or the computer. It is true that the signifying environment created by electronic media is complex, dense, increasingly invasive, and truly relentless. When confronted by its sheer volume and audacity, one is tempted to ignore the social and economic structures that give it shape and instead abstract it into a religious vision of virtual omnipresence, one capable of forcing absolute enslavement or delivering discorporative immortality. We would do well to remember, however, that 150 years from today, it is doubtful anyone will be discussing or even remember our current debates over simulation, hyperreality, cyborgs, cyberspace, techno-bodies, or virtual subjectivity, except perhaps for a few baffled historians interested in the peculiar mystifying power that a certain segment of the intelligentsia invested in their media systems. What remains to be seen from this future vantage point is whether cybertechnologies truly prove to be the first in a series of innovations to reconfigure reality and redefine human subjectivity or whether, instead, our current visions of media disembodiment are simply the last round of fantastic folktales generated by the modern world's most uncanny innovation: electronic media.

Notes

Introduction

1 "Obviously Self-Defense: Long Islander Puts Bullet into TV Set as 7 Watch," *New York Times,* 21 October 1952, 31.

2 See "An Irate Video Owner Has Come Up with an Unusual Solution to Your Chief TV Bete Noir," *New York Times,* 22 October 1952, 37; and "Quiz Shows," *New York Times,* 29 October 1952, 41.

3 "Crazed Knife-Wielder Invades a TV Studio, Stabs Cameraman, Fells Actor with Pitcher," *New York Times,* 1 July 1953, 39.

4 "Haunted TV Is Punished; Set with Face That Won't Go Away Must Stare at the Wall," *New York Times,* 11 December 1953, 33.

5 "Face on TV Set Goes, Mystery Lingers On," *New York Times,* 12 December 1953, 16. See also *Television Digest,* 12 December 1953, 11.

6 Jane Feuer, "The Concept of Live Television: Ontology as Ideology," in *Regarding Television,* edited by E. Ann Kaplan (Los Angeles: AFI, 1983), 14.

7 Sherry Turkle discusses such phenomena (termed the "Julia effect" and the "ELIZA effect") in her book *Life on the Screen: Identity in the Age of the Internet* (New York: Simon and Schuster, 1995), 101.

8 For a typical case study, see "A Note on the Meaning of Television to a Psychotic Woman," *Bulletin of the Menninger Clinic* 23 (1959): 202–203.

9 Jean Baudrillard, *Simulations* (New York: Semiotext(e), 1983), 55.

10 Mary Ann Doane, "Information, Crisis, Catastrophe," in *Logics of Television,* edited by Patricia Mellencamp (Bloomington: Indiana University Press, 1990), 222.

11 Of the various terms that might be used to describe this quality of the media, I will use *presence* most frequently because it seems the most inclusive term for describing the many varieties of this phenomenon.

12 See W. E. Steavenson and Lewis Jones, *Medical Electricity: A Practical Handbook for Students and Practitioners* (London: H. K. Lewis, 1892), n.p.

13 William James, *Principles of Psychology* (New York: H. Holt, 1890), 239.

14 Raymond Williams, *Television: Technology and Cultural Form* (London: Wesleyen University Press, 1992), 80–112.

15 See Jean Baudrillard, *The Ecstasy of Communication* (New York: Semiotext(e), 1987), 15.

16 For this perspective see Donna Haraway's "A Cyborg Manifesto: Science, Technology, and Socialist-Feminism in the Late Twentieth Century," in

Simians, Cyborgs, and Women: The Re-Invention of Nature (New York: Routledge, 1991), 149–182.

1 Mediums and Media

1 "Telegraphic Meeting," *Tiffany's Monthly* 3 (1857): 142.

2 Ezra Gannett, *The Atlantic Telegraph: A Discourse Delivered in the First Church, August 8, 1858* (Boston: Crosby, Nichols, 1858), 13.

3 Through a series of yes-no questions, the family learned that the eerie interlocutor was the ghost of a peddler who had been murdered by a former occupant of the house years earlier. Later, by rapping out the alphabet, the spirit identified himself as "Charles Rosma" and claimed that his bones could be found buried in the basement of the home. Intriguingly, excavation of the Fox house many years later did indeed reveal an adult skeleton behind a wall in the basement.

4 Period articles and individual statements by the concerned parties in the "Rochester knockings" can be found in several sources, including M. E. Cadwallader, *Hydesville in History* (Chicago: Progressive Thinker Publishing House, 1917); Emma Hardinge, *Modern American Spiritualism* (1869; reprint, New Hyde Park, N.Y.: University Books, 1970). For period accounts, both pro and con, see E. E. Lewis, *A Report of the Mysterious Noises Heard in the House of Mr. John D. Fox* (Canandaigua, N.Y.: by the author, 1848); *The Rappers: or, the Mysteries, Fallacies, and Absurdities of Spirit Rapping, Table-Tipping, and Entrancement, by a Searcher after Truth* (New York: Long, 1854); *Rochester Knockings! Discovery and Explanation of the Source of the Phenomena Generally Known as the Rochester Knockings,* reprinted from *Buffalo Medical Journal* (March 1851).

5 Some Spiritualists claimed that Lincoln's contact with the movement and its socially progressive spirits guided the president into issuing the Emancipation Proclamation. A young medium and trance speaker, Nettie Colburn Maynard, allegedly instructed the president in the necessity of freeing southern slaves, a position Lincoln did not support at the beginning of his presidency.

6 Hardinge, *Modern American Spiritualism,* 39.

7 J. H. Powell, *Mediumship: Its Laws and Conditions; with Brief Instructions for the Formation of Spirit Circles* (Boston: William White, 1868), 21.

8 *The Spirit World, Its Locality and Conditions, by the Spirit of Judge John Worth Edmonds, Late a Prominent Citizen of New York, Given through the Mediumship of Wash. A. Danskin, and Published at the Request of the First Spiritualist Congregation, of Baltimore* (Baltimore: Steam Press of Frederick A. Hanzsche, 1874), 7.

9   Ann Braude, *Radical Spirits: Spiritualism and Women's Rights in Nineteenth Century America* (Boston: Beacon Press, 1989), 23.

10 John Murray Spear, *The Educator: Being Suggestions, Theoretical and Practical, Designed to Promote Man-Culture and Integral Reform, with a View to the Ultimate Establishment of a Divine Social State on Earth,* edited by A. E. Newton (Boston: Office of Practical Spiritualists, 1857), 163.

11 James Carey, "Technology and Ideology: The Case of the Telegraph," in *Communication as Culture* (Boston: Unwin Hyman, 1989), 204.

12 Andrew Jackson Davis, *The Present Age and Inner Life: Ancient and Modern Spirit Mysteries Classified and Explained. A Sequel to Spiritual Intercourse Revised and Enlarged* (Rochester: Austin Publishing, 1910), 101–102. Originally published in 1853.

13 Davis, *Present Age and Inner Life,* 88.

14 Edward Tatnall Canby, *A History of Electricity: The New Illustrated Library of Science and Invention* (New York: Hawthorn Books, 1963), 22.

15 Alfred Vail and J. Cummings Vail, *Eyewitness to Early American Telegraphy* (New York: Arno Press, 1974), 119. This volume incorporates publications on the telegraph dating from 1845 and 1914.

16 Canby, *History of Electricity,* 38.

17 Such trepidation reflected a longer theological history of electricity as a divine substance. For a more detailed account, see Ernst Benz, *The Theology of Electricity: On the Encounter and Explanation of Theology and Science in the Seventeenth and Eighteenth Centuries,* translated by Wolgang Taraba (Allison Park, Penn.: Pickwick Publications, 1989).

18 Galvani's work, as well as a summary of period experiments by other scientists, can be found in Luigi Galvani, *Commentary on the Effects of Electricity on Muscular Motion,* translated by Margaret Glover Foley (Norwalk, Conn.: Burndy Library, 1953).

19 John Bostock, *An Account of the History and Present State of Galvanism* (London: Baldwin, Cradock, and Joy, 1818), n.p.

20 See Fernand Papillon, "Electricity and Life," *Popular Science Monthly,* March 1873, 532–533.

21 Mary Shelley, *Frankenstein,* in *Three Gothic Novels* (New York: Penguin, 1968), 262–263.

22 Ibid., 263.

23 James Apjohn, "Spontaneous Combustion," in *Cyclopaedia of Practical Medicine,* edited by John Forbes, Alexander Tweedie, and John Conolly (Philadelphia: Lea and Blanchard, 1849), 475.

24 For an account of phrenology's impact in this period, see Roger Cooter, *The Cultural Meaning of Popular Science: Phrenology and the Organization of Consent in Nineteenth-Century Britain* (Cambridge: Cambridge University Press, 1984).

25 The "vagueness" of animal magnetism and animal electricity as physical forces was not lost on period commentators. Many critics lampooned the often inarticulate theories of these emerging "sciences" in cartoons, editorials, and popular literature. For example, in Elizabeth Inchbald's play *Animal Magnetism: A Farce in Three Acts,* written in 1792 and performed well into the next century, an inept doctor hopes to learn the science of animal magnetism from a visiting expert, La Fluer. In the following exchange, La Fluer explains the principles behind mesmeristic science.

La Fluer: You know doctor, there is an universal fluid which spreads throughout all nature.
Doc: A fluid?
La Fluer: Yes, a fluid — which is — a — fluid — and you know, doctor, that this fluid — generally called a fluid, is the most subtle of all that is most subtle — Do you understand me?
Doc: Yes, yes —
La Fluer: It ascends on high, [looking down] and descends on low, [looking up] penetrates all substances, from the hardest metal, to the softest bosom — you understand me, I perceive?
Doc: Not very well.

Later in the play it is revealed that practitioners of mesmerism have an uncanny romantic influence over women, an example of what has survived as the only vestigial meaning left for the phrase, "animal magnetism." See Elizabeth Inchbald, *Animal Magnetism: A Farce in Three Acts* (New York: Publisher unknown, 1809).

In his study of mesmerism in prerevolutionary France, Robert Darnton argues that animal magnetism, along with many other fantastic theories, fed a growing public fascination for popular science at the end of the century. "The reading public of that era was intoxicated with the power of science," writes Darnton, "and it was bewildered by the real and imaginary forces with which scientists peopled that universe. Because the public could not distinguish the real from the imaginary, it seized on any invisible fluid, any scientific-sounding hypothesis, that promised to explain the wonders of nature." See Robert Darnton, *Mesmerism and the End of the Enlightenment in France* (Cambridge: Harvard University Press, 1968), 23.

26 Braude, *Radical Spirits,* 5.

27 Leo Marx, *The Machine in the Garden* (New York: Oxford University Press, 1964), 195.

28 James Carey and John J. Quirk, "The Mythos of the Electronic Revolution," *Communication as Culture* (Boston: Unwin Hyman, 1989), 121.

29 Hardinge, *Modern American Spiritualism,* 29.

30 Ibid., 39.

31 For an account of Morse's contact with the mundane world, see "The Skeleton in the Fox Cottage," by P. L. O. A. Keeler, in *Hydesville in History,* edited by M. E. Cadwallader (Chicago: Progressive Thinker Publishing House, 1917), 53.

32 Reverend H. Mattison, *Spirit-Rapping Unveiled! An Expose of the Origin, History, Theology, and Philosophy of Certain Alleged Communications from the Spirit World by Means of "Spirit Rapping," "Medium-Writing," "Physical Demonstrations," Etc.* (New York: J. C. Derby, 1855), 67.

33 *The Shekinah* 1 (1852): 303.

34 Ibid., 304.

35 Neil Lehman, "The Life of John Murray Spear: Spiritualism and Reform in Antebellum America" (Ph.D. diss., Ohio State University, 1973), 147.

36 Hardinge, *Modern American Spiritualism,* 220. This was not Spear's first contact with otherworldly electricians. On his way to an abolitionist convention years earlier, Spear was given the following message by another medium: "I want J. M. Spear to call on that poor woman who has been struck by lightning." This message was attributed once again to the late Benjamin Franklin. For a more detailed account, see Adin Ballou, *An Exposition of Views Respecting the Principal Facts, Causes, and Peculiarities Involved in Spirit Manifestations: Together with Interesting Phenomenal Statements and Communications* (Boston: Bela Marsh, 1853), 209–211.

37 Hardinge, *Modern American Spiritualism,* 222.

38 Ibid.

39 Spear, *Educator,* 244.

40 Andrew Jackson Davis, "The New Motive Power," in *Telegraph Papers* 5 (May–Aug. 1854): n.p. Quoted in Hardinge, *Modern American Spiritualism,* 223.

41 Spear, *Educator,* 245.

42 Ibid. Despite Spear's personal efforts to animate the machine, the "new motor" still would not run. Finally, a Boston woman with mediumistic powers and known only as the "Mary of the New Dispensation" was introduced to the machine. There followed an extraordinary crisis, a "hysterical pregnancy" described by Andrew Jackson Davis where, "by means of a spiritual overshadowing, *a la* Virgin Mary, the maternal functions were brought into active operation; a few of the usual physiological symptoms followed; the crisis arrived; and being in the presence of the mechanism, the first living motion was communicated to it; in other words, that then the new motive power was born, which was therefore regarded as 'heaven's best, last gift to man' " (Davis, quoted in Hardinge, *Modern American Spiritualism,* 225). As Spear himself wrote, "In this comprehensive sense this mechanism is a child, — a male and female have been used for the impregnation of thought, and from that there has come forth the newly-constructed child, whose name is the ELECTRIC MOTOR" (Spear, *Educator,* 238). Within Spiritualist cir-

cles, stories began to circulate about the intervention of the "Mary of the New Dispensation" and the miraculous "birth" of the "electric infant." In her history of the movement, Hardinge complained that the "prurient mind, stimulated by the awkward and most injudicious claims of a human parentage of a material machine, indulged in scandalous and even atrocious rumors," apparently suggesting an adulterous affair between the two mediums (see Hardinge, *Modern American Spiritualism,* 221). Eventually, to continue his work on the machine in a new and presumably less hostile environment, Spear moved the apparatus from Massachusetts to a small town in western New York. However, Spear and his followers met with considerable resistance in New York, and it was not long until an angry mob broke into the building where the machine was housed and "tore out the heart of the mechanism, trampled [it] beneath their feet, and scattered it to the four winds" (Spear, quoted in Hardinge, *Modern American Spiritualism,* 229).

43 Robert Milne, "A Mysterious Twilight; Being a Dip into the Doings of the Four-Dimensional World," *Argonaut,* 27 June 1885, n.p.

44 Robert Milne, "An Experience in Telepathy; in which Clairvoyance and Spiritual Telegraphy Play a Part," *Argonaut,* 23 December 1889, n.p.

45 Robert Milne, "The Great Electric Diaphragm: Some Account of the Telegraphic System of the Baron O–," *Argonaut,* 24 May 1879, n.p.

46 Robert Milne, "Professor Vehr's Electrical Experiment," *Argonaut,* 24 January 1885; reprinted in *Into the Sun and Other Stories: Science Fiction in Old San Francisco,* edited by Sam Moskowitz (West Kingston, R.I.: Donald M. Grant, 1980), 87 (all page citations are to the reprint). Another tale of telegraphic teleportation from the period is J. E. O'Brien, "An Electric Flash," *Belford's Magazine,* October 1889, n.p.

47 Milne, "Professor Vehr's Electrical Experiment," 89.

48 Robert Hare, *Experimental Investigation of the Spirit Manifestations, Demonstrating the Existence of Spirits and Their Communion with Mortals* (New York: Partridge and Brittan, 1855), 393.

49 R. P. Ambler, "The Science of the Soul; Its Unfoldings and Results," *Spirit Messenger and Harmonial Advocate* 1, no. 1 (16 October 1852): 3.

50 William Fishbough, "Laws and Phenomena of the Soul. Number One," *Spirit Messenger and Harmonial Advocate* 1, no. 6 (20 November 1852): 1.

51 Ibid.

52 Frank J. Tipler, *The Physics of Immortality: Modern Cosmology, God, and the Resurrection of the Dead* (New York: Doubleday, 1994), ix.

53 Ibid., xi.

54 James S. Olcott, *Animal Electricity; or the Electrical Science; an Application of the Primary Laws of Nature, Never Before Discovered and Demonstrated; to a Solution of All the Physical and Intellectual Phenomena That Exist* (Boston: N. S. Magoon, 1844), 87.

55 Ibid., 91.

56 Charles Von Reichenbach, *Physico-Physiological Researches in the Dynamics of Magnetism, Electricity, Heat, Light, Crystallization, and Chemism, in Their Relations to Vital Force* (New York: Partridge and Brittan, 1851), 34.

57 Cynthia Russett, *Sexual Science: The Victorian Construction of Womanhood* (Cambridge: Harvard University Press, 1989), 40.

58 Judith Walkowitz, "Science and Séance: Transgressions of Gender and Genre in Late Victorian London," *Representations* 22 (spring 1988): 9.

59 Traverse Oldfield, *"To Daimonion," or the Spiritual Medium. Its Nature Illustrated by the History of Its Uniform Mysterious Manifestation When Unduly Excited.* In *Twelve Familiar Letters to an Inquiring Friend* (Boston: Gould and Lincoln, 1852), 24–25.

60 George W. Samson, *Spiritualism Tested; or, the Facts of Its History Classified, and Their Cause in Nature Verified from Ancient and Modern Testimonies* (Boston: Gould and Lincoln, 1860), 33.

61 Such "authority" was of particular importance and appeal in relation to the era's reigning discourses on gender and technology. As Carolyn Marvin notes, women of the late nineteenth century were often ridiculed for their lack of electrical knowledge, making them the subject of jokes about the inability to understand the "practical" workings of the telegraph (and, later, the telephone). "Technical ignorance as a form of worldly ignorance was a virtue of 'good' women," writes Marvin. Humor based on women and telecommunications often reaffirmed "the more important and even insistent point that women's use of men's technology would come to no good end." See Carolyn Marvin, *When Old Technologies Were New* (London: Oxford University Press, 1988), 23.

62 Braude, *Radical Spirits,* 57.

63 Emma Hardinge, *America and Her Destiny: An Inspirational Discourse* (New York: Robert M. DeWitt, 1861), 12.

64 Braude, *Radical Spirits,* 56.

65 Braude writes that "mediumship gave women a public leadership role that allowed them to remain compliant with the complex values of the period that have come to be known as the cult of true womanhood." The "cult of true womanhood," as described by Braude and others, asserted that women were characterized by "purity, piety, passivity, and domesticity" and were thus particularly suited for religious and spiritual matters (see Braude, *Radical Spirits,* 82). See also Barbara Welter, "The Cult of True Womanhood: 1820–1860," *American Quarterly* 18 (summer 1966): 151–174.

66 Braude, *Radical Spirits,* 85.

67 O. A. Brownson, *The Spirit Rapper; An Autobiography* (Boston: Little, Brown, 1854), vi.

68 Mattison, *Spirit-Rapping Unveiled!* 58.

69 Walkowitz, "Science and Séance," 5.

70 J. M. Charcot, "Hysteria and Spiritism," *Medical and Surgical Reporter* 59, no. 3 (21 July 1888): 65.

71 Walkowitz, "Science and Séance," 9.

72 S. E. D. Shortt, "Physicians and Psychics: The Anglo-American Medical Response to Spiritualism, 1870–1890," *Journal of the History of Medicine and Allied Sciences* 39: 339–355; Edward M. Brown, "Neurology and Spiritualism in the 1870s," *Bulletin of the History of Medicine* 57 (winter 1983): 563–577.

73 John S. Haller and Robin M. Haller, *The Physician and Sexuality in Victorian America* (New York: Norton, 1974), 11–12.

74 Ibid., 27–28.

75 A. H. Newth, "The Galvanic Current Applied in the Treatment of Insanity," *Journal of Mental Science* 19 (April 1873): 79–86.

76 A. H. Newth, "The Electro-Neural Pathology of Insanity," *Journal of Mental Science* 24 (April 1878): 78.

77 For a more detailed discussion of this field, see A. W. Beveridge and E. B. Renvoize, "Electricity: A History of Its Use in the Treatment of Mental Illness in Britain during the Second Half of the Nineteenth Century," *British Journal of Psychiatry* 153: 157–162; and Lisa Rosner, "The Professional Context of Electrotherapeutics," *Journal of the History of Medicine and Allied Sciences* 43: 64–82.

78 Haller and Haller, *Physician and Sexuality,* 13.

79 George M. Beard, "The Treatment of Insanity by Electricity," *Journal of Mental Science* 19 (October 1873): 356.

80 Charcot, "Hysteria and Spiritism," 68.

81 Matthew D. Field, "Is Belief in Spiritualism Ever Evidence of Insanity Per Se?" *Medico-Legal Journal* 6 (1888): 197.

82 "Case of Mania with the Delusions and Phenomena of Spiritualism," *American Journal of Insanity* 16, no. 3 (1859–1860): 324.

83 Ibid., 336–337.

84 Charles Richet, "Hysteria and Demonism: A Study in Morbid Psychology," *Popular Science Monthly,* May 1880, 90.

85 See Frank Podmore, *Mediums of the 19th Century* (New Hyde Park: University Books, 1963), 185–188.

2 The Voice from the Void

1 *Biographical Dictionary of Parapsychology* (New York: Helix Press, 1964), 68–69.

2 Ibid., 189–190.

3 B. C. Forbes, "Edison Working on How to Communicate with the Next World," *American Magazine,* October 1920, 10. A short story from 1902 is of interest in that it features fictionalized appearances by both Edison and Nikolas Tesla in a tale about "thought broadcasting." See George Justus Frederick, "The Dupe of the Realist," *Argosy,* March 1902, n.p.

4 "Plan Wireless Talks with Spirit World: Delegates at Paris Convention Aim for a Device to Eliminate Mediums," *New York Times,* 10 September 1925, 26.

5 Even before the age of wireless, Alexander Graham Bell's partner in research, Thomas Watson, developed an interest in using telephone technology to contact the dead. See Avital Ronel, *The Telephone Book: Technology, Schizophrenia, Electric Speech* (Lincoln: University of Nebraska Press, 1989).

6 Roy Stemman, *Spirits and the Spirit World* (London: Aldus Books, 1975), 97.

7 Daniel Czitrom, *Media and the American Mind* (Chapel Hill: University of North Carolina Press, 1982), 65.

8 Susan Douglas, *Inventing American Broadcasting, 1899–1922* (Baltimore: Johns Hopkins University Press, 1987), 23.

9 Catherine L. Covert, "We May Hear Too Much: American Sensibility and the Response to Radio, 1919–1924," in *Mass Media between the Wars: Perception of Cultural Tension, 1918–1941,* edited by Catherine L. Covert and John D. Stevens (Syracuse: Syracuse University Press, 1984), 206.

10 Ibid., 210.

11 Stephen Kern, *The Culture of Time and Space, 1880–1918* (Cambridge: Harvard University Press, 1983).

12 See T. Jackson Lears, *No Place of Grace: Antimodernism and the Transformation of American Culture, 1880–1920* (New York: Pantheon, 1981).

13 See John Higham, *Strangers in the Land* (New York: Atheneum, 1965).

14 Howard Vincent O'Brien, "It's Great to Be a Radio Maniac," *Collier's,* 13 September 1924, 15.

15 "Man Who Heard Washington in Hawaii," *Scientific American,* 15 May 1915, 450.

16 O'Brien, "Radio Maniac," 15.

17 "The Persistent Mysteries of Wireless Telegraphy and Telephony," *Current Literature* 49 (December 1910): 638.

18 Howard Orange McMeans, "Eavesdropping on the World," *Scribner's Magazine* 72, no. 15 (April 1923): 232.

19 Ibid.

20 Covert, "We May Hear Too Much," 199.

21 Ibid., 210.

22 P. T. McGrath, "The Future of Wireless Telegraphy," *North American Review* 175 (August 1902): 782.

23 "Human Radio Receivers," *Literary Digest,* 22 September 1928, 23.

24 "Electric Radio Ghosts," *Literary Digest,* 4 August 1922, 21.

25 Alden Armagnac, "Weird Electrical Freaks Traced to Runaway Radio Waves," *Popular Science Monthly,* June 1935, 11.

26 Ibid.

27 Rudyard Kipling, "Wireless," in *Traffics and Discoveries* (London: Macmillan, 1904). Originally published in 1902 (page citations are to the reprint).

28 Ibid., 235–236.

29 John Fleming Wilson, "Sparks," *McClure's Magazine,* June 1911, 149–154.

30 Ibid., 154.

31 Tom Gunning, "Heard Over the Phone: *The Lonely Villa* and the de Lorde Tradition of the Terrors of Technology," *Screen* 32, no. 2 (1991): 184–196.

32 Kern, *Culture of Time and Space,* 107.

33 Douglas, *Inventing American Broadcasting,* 230.

34 Ibid., 227.

35 See in particular Hereward Carrington, *Psychical Phenomena and the War* (New York: Dodd, Mead, 1918).

36 Sir Oliver Lodge, *Raymond; or Life and Death* (New York: George H. Doran, 1916).

37 *Thy Son Liveth: Messages from a Soldier to His Mother* (Boston: Little, Brown, 1918).

38 Kern, *Culture of Time and Space,* 309.

39 Carl Dreher, "Putting Freak Broadcasting in Its Place," *Radio Broadcast,* November 1927, 50.

40 Buckner Speed, "Voices of the Universe," *Harper's,* April 1919, 613.

41 Upton Sinclair, *Mental Radio* (New York: Collier Books, 1930), x.

42 "Sir William Crookes's Provisional Explanation of Telepathy — Harmony with Natural Law," in *The Widow's Mite and Other Psychic Phenomena,* edited by Isaac K. Funk (New York: Funk and Wagnalls, 1904), 519.

43 "Analogy between Wireless Telegraphy and Waves from Brain to Brain," *Current Opinion,* October 1914, 253.

44 Frank Podmore, *Telepathic Hallucinations: The New View of Ghosts* (Halifax: Milner, 1921), 39.

45 Frances Rockefeller King, "The Personality behind the Ghost Hour," *Radio News,* October 1929, 316.

46 Ellis Butler, "The Celebrated Pilkey Radio Case," *Radio News,* October 1923, n.p.

47 Ellis Butler, "The Voice of the People," *Radio News,* November 1927, n.p.

48 Lee Foster Hartmann, "Out of the Air," *Harper's,* September 1922, 499.

49 Ibid.

50 Sewall Peaslee Wright, "The Experiment of Erich Weigert," *Weird Tales,* May 1926, 683.

51 Clinton Dangerfield, "The Message," *Weird Tales,* September 1931, 170–175.

52 It is rather ironic, but perhaps typical of clumsy pulp story plotting, that in this tale of extraordinary communications, no one thinks of using the telephone to notify the prison of the governor's pardon.

53 Aline Kilmer, "Wicked Wireless," *Hunting a Hair Shirt and Other Spiritual Adventures* (New York: George H. Doran, 1923), 21.

54 Forbes, "Edison Working," 11.

55 Wainright Evans, "Scientists Research Machine to Contact the Dead," *Fate,* April 1963, 38–43. Near the time of Edison's death in 1930, meanwhile, a Belgian father worked to complete an electronic device that he claimed had been conceived by the spirit of his dead son and communicated to the father through a Ouija board. The "Vandermeulen Signaling Device," patented on 1 January 1931, was a spiritualist alarm clock of sorts. The sensitive device allowed the vapory incarnations of spirits to complete an electrical circuit and thus ring a small electrical bell. "The purpose of the signaling device," according to the patent, "lies in informing persons who are busy otherwise that an entity desires to make communication." The owner of the device, on hearing the bell, was to use the Ouija board or automatic writing to receive the spirit's message. See Evans, "Scientists Research Machine to Contact the Dead," 40.

56 Ibid., 43.

57 Susy Smith, *Voices of the Dead* (New York: Signet, 1977), 46–47.

58 Ibid., 11.

59 Ibid., 9.

60 Konstantin Raudive, *Break Through: Electronic Communication with the Dead May Be Possible* (New York: Zebra Books, 1971). An interesting account of the publication and reaction to *Break Through* can be found in Peter Bander, *Voices from the Tapes* (New York: Drake, 1973).

61 An overview of this work can be found in Smith's *Voices of the Dead.* See also William Welch, *Talks with the Dead* (New York: Pinnacle Books, 1975). Finally, a brief history of EVP can be found in Jurgen Heinzerling, "All about EVP," *Fortean Times,* December 1997, 26–30.

62 Raudive, *Break Through,* 23.

63 Susy Smith notes that a method using a germanium diode and devised in collaboration with Swedish physicist Alex Schneider "gave the most dramatic results." See Smith, *Voices of the Dead,* 18.

64 Raudive, *Break Through,* 24.

65 Samuel Beckett, *The Unnameable* (New York: Grove Press, 1958), 3.

66 Ibid., 179.

67 Raudive, *Break Through,* 157.

68 See Freud's discussion of religion in *The Future of an Illusion* (New York: Norton, 1961).

69 Following Raudive's experiments in radio, other psychic researchers employed new electronic telecommunications technologies in ever more elaborate efforts to transcend our mortal world. Building on Raudive's work, a former soldier and radio operator in the United States Army, Bill O'Neil, claimed in the 1970s to have perfected a two-way radio system with the afterlife. His efforts to make contact were assisted by investor George Meek and the spirit of George Jeffries Muller (known as "Doc Nick"), a former scientist for NASA who had died in 1967. Meek and O'Neil called their device "Spiricom." The apparatus is said to have achieved remarkable results until 1981, when the mechanism went permanently silent. At the time of Spiricom's demise, however, the two researchers were also working on "Vidicom," a device that would make it possible to videotape the dead. German experimenters Hans Otto Konig and Klaus Schreiber, meanwhile, claimed in 1987 to have received paranormal still video images by pointing their camera at a monitoring screen (resulting in a form of optical feedback). Finally and perhaps inevitably, British schoolteacher Ken Webster reported in 1984 to have found a mysterious file on a computer disk. When opened, the file contained a message from a "Lukas Wainman," who claimed to have lived in 1546. Webster also received on his computer a series of seemingly paranormal and increasingly hostile messages from a "Group 2109." Although Webster's desktop ghosts finally left, other EVP researchers are said to maintain frequent communications with the dead through their computers. Webster's "discovery," of course, only literalized one of the most common expressions of the computer age: "ghost in the machine." See Heinzerling, "All about EVP."

70 Raudive, *Break Through,* 157.

3 Alien Ether

1 A. G. Birch, *The Moon Terror* (Indianapolis: Popular Fiction Publishing, 1927), 5–6. This story appeared originally in serial form in *Weird Tales* (1922).

2 The "alien" source of these signals is finally revealed to be the Chinese. In both the era of radio and television, the mysteries of electronic contact were often associated with the "Orient." See also the scene in *International House* (1933) where the master of the new television technology is an elderly Chinese man.

3 Bertolt Brecht, "Notes on Radio," in *Wireless Imagination: Sound, Radio,*

and the Avant-Garde, edited by Douglas Kahn and Gregory Whitehead (Cambridge, Mass: MIT Press, 1992).

4   M. Camille Flammarion, "Shall We Talk With the Men in the Moon?" *Review of Reviews* 5 (February 1890): 90.

5   Ibid.

6   For an idea of speculation concerning these questions, see "Are Other Worlds Alive?" *Review of Reviews* 12 (July 1895): 69; "Life in Other Worlds," *Popular Science Monthly,* November 1903, 26–31; "Life on Other Worlds," *Forum* 27 (March 1899): 71–77.

7   Francis Galton, "Intelligible Signals between Neighbouring Stars," *Fortnightly Review* 66 (November 1896): 657.

8   Ibid., 663.

9   M. Amedee Guillemin, "Communication with the Planets," *Popular Science Monthly,* January 1892, 361. It is not known if this award still exists.

10 James G. Thompson, "Sending a Message to Mars," *Illustrated World,* December 1917, 578.

11 Ibid., 579.

12 See John B. Flowers, "Signaling to the Planets with a Cloth Reflector," *Illustrated World,* March 1921, 84–85; "Signaling to Mars," *Scientific American,* 8 May 1909, 346.

13 H. W. Nieman and C. Wells Nieman, "What Shall We Say to Mars? A System for Opening Communication despite the Absence of Any Common Basis of Language," *Scientific American,* 20 March 1920, 312.

14 "Professor David Todd's Plan of Receiving Martian Messages," *Scientific American,* 5 June 1909, 423.

15 Later investigation proved these transmissions to be from Schenectady. See "From Schenectady, Not Mars," *Literary Digest,* 5 August 1922, 33.

16 "That Perspective Communication with Another Planet," *Current Opinion,* March 1919, 170–171.

17 Thomas Waller, "Can We Radio a Message to Mars?" *Illustrated World,* April 1920, 240–242.

18 "Radio Messages from Mars?" *Literary Digest,* 6 September 1924, 28.

19 Ellis Butler, "The Great Radio Message from Mars," *Radio News,* November 1923, n.p. For a more unsettling account of radio contact with Mars, see Jan Dirk's "Radio V-Rays," *Weird Tales,* March 1925, n.p. A story by Hugo Gernsback, finally, combined wireless interest in both telepathy and Martian contact. See "Thought Transmission on Mars," *Electrical Experimenter,* January 1916, n.p.

20 H. G. Wells, "The Things That Live on Mars," *Cosmopolitan,* March 1908, 340–342.

21 Ibid., 342.

22 Carey and Quirk, "Mythos."

23 "Why the Dwellers on Mars Do Not Make War," *Current Literature* 42 (1907): 214.

24 Ibid.

25 Susan J. Douglas, "Amateur Operators and American Broadcasting: Shaping the Future of Radio," in *Imagining Tomorrow: History, Technology, and the American Future,* edited by Joseph J. Corn (Cambridge: MIT Press, 1986), 47.

26 "How Two Girls Made a Receiving Radiophone," *Literary Digest,* 10 June 1922, 29.

27 Jack Binns, *The Radio Boy's First Wireless* (New York: Grosset and Dunlap, 1922), v.

28 Ibid., vi.

29 Douglas, "Amateur Operators," 45.

30 Science forged a further link between space and radio in the early thirties when Bell Telephone Laboratories began an investigation of persistent high-frequency static interfering with transatlantic communications. Karl Jansky was given the task of discovering the source of this static and eliminating it. At a meeting of the international Scientific Radio Union, Jansky announced that it was his finding that the static emanated from a source beyond our solar system. Jansky's discovery demonstrated that the entire Milky Way pulsated with radio waves, a realization that founded what is now the predominant line of research in contacting other planets, radio astronomy.

31 Douglas, *Inventing American Broadcasting,* 300.

32 McMeans, "Eavesdropping on the World," 228.

33 "Is the Radio Amateur Doomed?" *Literary Digest,* 2 December 1922, 28.

34 For a more complete analysis of radio advertising during this period, see Thomas Volek, "Examining Radio Receiver Technology through Magazine Advertising in the 1920s and 1930s" (Ph.D. diss., University of Minnesota, 1991).

35 Susan J. Douglas, "Technology, Media, and the Idea of Progress," *Massachusetts Review* 25 (winter 1984): 655–656.

36 Robert W. McChesney, "The Battle for the U.S. Airwaves, 1928–1935," *Journal of Communication* 40, no. 4 (autumn 1990): 29.

37 Paul Lazarfeld, *The People Look at Radio* (Chapel Hill: University of North Carolina Press, 1945), 101.

38 Kenneth M. Goode, *What about Radio?* (New York: Harper and Brothers, 1937), 207.

39 John R. Speer, "Symphony of the Damned," *Weird Tales,* April 1934, 386–411.

40 H. F. Arnold, "The Night Wire," *Weird Tales,* September 1926, 380–384.

41 An interesting antecedent to Welles's strategy can be found in A. M. Low's short story "Raiders from Space," *Science Wonder Stories,* March 1930. In

this futuristic tale a couple buys a new experimental television set. When they activate the device, they see scenes of worldwide destruction at the hands of alien invaders. They are terrified until discovering that they have actually just seen a preview for a science fiction film broadcasting in Germany!

42 "Dialed Hysteria," *Time,* 7 November 1938, 13.

43 "Panic from Mars," *The Nation,* 12 November 1938, 498.

44 James McBride Dabbs, "Thin Air," *Christian Century,* 26 April 1939, 542.

45 Hadley Cantril, *The Invasion from Mars: A Study in the Psychology of Panic* (Princeton, N.J.: Princeton University Press, 1940), 70.

46 Jean Baudrillard, "Requiem for the Media," in *For a Critique of the Political Economy of the Sign* (St. Louis: Telos Press, 1981), 169–170.

47 Doane, "Information, Crisis, Catastrophe," 229.

48 Howard Koch, *The Panic Broadcast: The Whole Story of Orson Welles' Legendary Radio Show "Invasion from Mars"* (New York: Avon Books, 1970), 80.

49 Ibid.

50 Nick Browne, "The Political Economy of the Television (Super)text," in *Television: The Critical View,* edited by Horace Newcomb (New York: Oxford University Press, 1986), 585–599.

51 Doane, "Information, Crisis, Catastrophe," 232–233.

52 Patricia Mellencamp, "TV Time and Catastophe," in *Logics of Television,* edited by Patricia Mellencamp (Bloomington: Indiana University Press, 1990), 244.

53 Koch, *Panic Broadcast,* 97.

54 Cantril, *Invasion from Mars,* 96.

55 Ibid., 162.

56 " 'Strays' from the Laboratory," *Radio Broadcast,* April 1928, 427. By 1930 RCA built theremins and advertised them as a musical instrument for the home. See "The R.C.A. Theremin," *Radio Broadcast,* February 1930, 202.

57 Professor Theremin himself made this connection on the instrument's debut. "This is not a plaything for me. . . . To prove . . . that science can render the greatest services in the development of the arts, to demonstrate . . . the fertility of an intimate collaboration of the arts and sciences, is my aim." See " 'Strays' from the Laboratory," 427–428.

58 Kurt Vonnegut, *The Sirens of Titan* (New York: Dell, 1959), 102.

4 Static and Stasis

1 John Markus, *How to Make More Money in Your TV Servicing Business* (New York: McGraw-Hill, 1962), 152.

2 *Television Digest,* 18 September 1954, 11.

3 J. B. Priestley, "Uncle Phil on TV," *The Other Place* (New York: Harper and Brothers, 1953), 70–102.

4 Harry Stephen Keeler, *The Box from Japan* (New York: E. P. Dutton, 1932), 145. Many other short stories of the period trade in predictions about television's incredible ability "to see." George Stratton's humorous tale, "Sam Graves' Electric Mind Reader," imagines electricity being used to telecast a person's thoughts on a screen. See Stratton, "Sam Graves' Electric Mind Reader," *Practical Electrics,* February 1924, n.p. Another story, meanwhile, features a television experimenter using the "uncanny" powers of the new medium to terrify religious fundamentalists opposed to new electrical experimentation. See H. P. Clay, "The Radio Vision," *Practical Electrics,* October 1924, n.p.

5 William C. Eddy, *Television: The Eyes of Tomorrow* (New York: Prentice-Hall, 1945).

6 See in particular chapter 9 of Luther S. H. Grable's book, *The Miracle of Television* (Chicago: Wilcox and Follett, 1949).

7 Richard Hubbell, *Television Programming and Production* (New York: Rinehart, 1950), 13. Early commentators anticipated these uses of television, some with suspicion. A short story from 1929 concerns a man's disgust on discovering that his alma mater's football team consists entirely of robots and that supporters of the team no longer come to the stadium but stay home to watch the games on television. He recruits a human team to play and defeat the robots and in the process reintroduces people to the pleasures of actually attending the games. See David H. Keller, "The Threat of the Robot," *Science Wonder Stories,* June 1929, n.p.

8 See chapter 5 of William Boddy's *Fifties Television* (Chicago: University of Illinois Press, 1990).

9 Thomas H. Hutchinson, *Here Is Television, Your Window on the World* (New York: Hastings House, 1948).

10 Lynn Spigel, *Make Room for TV: Television and the Family Ideal in Postwar America* (Chicago: University of Chicago Press, 1992), 133.

11 Hubbell, *Television Programming and Production,* 13–14.

12 Williams, *Television,* 20.

13 Leo Bogart, *The Age of Television* (New York: Frederick Ungar, 1972), 268.

14 Oscar Handlin, "Comments on Mass and Popular Culture," in *Culture for the Millions? Mass Media in Modern Society,* edited by Norman Jacobs (Boston: Beacon Press, 1964), 70.

15 Ernst Van Den Haag, "A Dissent from the Consensual Society," in *Culture for the Millions? Mass Media in Modern Society,* edited by Norman Jacobs (Boston: Beacon Press, 1964), 59–60.

16 Irving Kristol, "The Mass Media," in *Culture for the Millions? Mass Media*

in Modern Society, edited by Norman Jacobs (Boston: Beacon Press, 1964), 168.

17 Lynn Spigel, "From Domestic Space to Outer Space: The 1960s Fantastic Family Sit-Com," in *Close Encounters: Film, Feminism, and Science-Fiction,* edited by Elizabeth Lyon, Constance Penley, and Lynn Spigel (Minneapolis: University of Minnesota Press, 1991), 209.

18 Ibid., 214.

19 In their own way, UHF and color each presented new "dimensions" in broadcasting, an association encouraged by accounts of radio astronomers and commercial broadcasters battling for control over these bandwidths and frequencies. See D. S. Greenberg, "Radio Astronomy: TV's Rush for UHF Threatens Use of Channel," *Science,* 1 February 1963, 393; and D. S. Greenberg, "Radio Astronomy: FCC Proposes Compromise to Share Frequencies with UHF Broadcasters," *Science,* 12 April 1963, 164.

20 "To get to know each other on a worldwide scale is the human race's most urgent need today; and this is where Telstar can help us," wrote one commentator. "It can make it possible for each section of the human race to become familiar with every other section's way of living; and, once this mutual familiarity is established, there is some hope that we may all become aware of the common humanity underlying the differences in our local manners and customs." See Arnold J. Toynbee, "A Message for Mankind from Telstar," *New York Times Magazine,* 12 August 1962, 31.

21 "TV's Biggest Mystery," *TV Guide,* 30 April 1954, 23.

22 Curtis Fuller, "KLEE . . . Still Calling," *Fate,* April 1964, 39.

23 Ibid., 40.

24 *The Outer Limits* was undoubtedly the medium's most vocal commentator on its own powers of discorporation and alienation. But so dominant was this theme that even within the narrative universe of *Star Trek,* the most utopian of all television's explorations into space, one episode featured a disembodied Captain Kirk dissolved and abandoned in the translucent energy stream of the transporter. Having been transformed into an other-dimensional ghost by this now most familiar technology for the discorporation and "telecasting" of human beings, Kirk's electronic body floats eerily across the mirrors, halls, and viewscreens of the *Enterprise* until his eventual rescue and reconstitution, a cogent reminder that even in the twenty-fourth century television transmission would remain the most immediate gateway to the terrifying voids of the universe. See "The Tholian Web," *Star Trek* (NBC 1967).

25 Spigel, *Make Room for TV,* 117.

26 "Telstar, Telstar — Burning Bright," *Life,* 3 August 1962, 4.

27 "A Watch Truck Is Watching You," *Life,* 25 September 1964, 38.

28 For a detailed examination of this transition, see Elaine Tyler May, *Home-*

ward Bound: American Families in the Cold War Era (New York: Basic Books, 1988).

29 Within the period many psychologists explicitly defined the family in such disciplinary terms as "a process of reciprocal roles perceived, expected, and performed by family members." According to this model, the "happiness" of any given family was "assumed to be reflected in the extent to which roles are accepted and shared among its members." See A. R. Mangus, "Family Impacts on Mental Health," *Marriage and Family Living,* August 1957, 261.

30 Mary Beth Haralovich, "Sit-coms and Suburbs: Positioning the 1950s Homemaker," in *Private Screenings: Television and the Female Consumer,* edited by Lynn Spigel and Denise Mann (Minneapolis: University of Minnesota Press, 1992), 111.

31 May, *Homeward Bound,* 36.

32 Harold Sampson, Sheldon L. Messinger, and Robert Towne, *Schizophrenic Women: Studies in Marital Crisis* (New York: Atherton Press, 1964), 21, 128.

33 Carol A. B. Warren, *Madwives: Schizophrenic Women in the 1950s* (New Brunswick: Rutgers University Press, 1991), 58.

34 Sampson et al., *Schizophrenic Women,* 158.

35 Spigel, *Make Room for TV,* 129.

36 Preceding this broadcast, an article entitled "TV Transmission on Laser Beam Demonstrated by North American" appeared in *Aviation Weekly,* 18 March 1963, 83.

37 Psychological studies of the period, after all, demonstrated that a married woman's sense of self-worth was most often bound to her "feminine" role of housekeeper and care provider. See Robert S. Weiss and Nancy Morse Samelson, "Social Roles of American Women: Their Contribution to a Sense of Usefulness and Importance," *Marriage and Family Living,* November 1958, 358–366.

38 Of course, neither *The Outer Limits* nor the genre of science fiction maintained an absolute monopoly over dystopic critiques of the family or of television's function within the family. As Spigel observes throughout *Make Room for TV,* anxiety over television and its "effects" on the family circulated through a variety of popular texts from the earliest days of the technology. All one has to do is recall the stunning scene in Douglas Sirk's 1955 film, *All That Heaven Allows,* in which a young brother and sister present their widowed, middle-aged mother with a monolithic television set in the hopes of curbing her sexual appetite and keeping her away from Rock Hudson.

39 Keith Laumer, "The Walls," *Nine by Laumer* (New York: Doubleday, 1967), 58.

40 Bogart, *Age of Television,* 73.

41 Ibid., 67.

42 Andres Huyssen, "Mass Culture as Woman: Modernism's Other," in *After the Great Divide: Modernism, Mass Culture, Postmodernism* (Bloomington: Indiana University Press, 1986), 50–51.

43 Spigel, *Make Room for TV,* 62.

44 Howard Nemerov, "Beyond the Screen," *A Commodity of Dreams and Other Stories* (New York: Simon and Schuster, 1959), 141.

45 Laumer, "The Walls," 67.

46 Spigel, "Domestic Space," 214.

47 "It Better Be Good," *Newsweek,* 9 May 1955, 84.

48 "Mouse at Yucca Flat: Televising Atomic Bomb Test," *Newsweek,* 16 May 1955, 63.

49 See "Victims at Yucca Flats: Mannequins," *Life,* 16 May 1955, 58; and "Close-up to the Blast," *Life,* 30 May 1955, 39–42.

50 R. J. Kerry, "Phobia of Outer Space," *Journal of Mental Science* 106 (1960): 1386.

5 Simulation and Psychosis

1 Lewis K. Parker, *Channel 10 from Nowhere* (Middletown: Weekly Reader Books, 1985), 13.

2 Guy Debord, *Society of the Spectacle* (Detroit: Black and Red, 1983), thesis 1.

3 Baudrillard, *Simulations,* 146.

4 Scott Bukatman, *Terminal Identity: The Virtual Subject in Post-Modern Science-Fiction* (Durham: Duke University Press, 1993), 8.

5 See Spigel, *Make Room For TV,* 136–140; and William Boddy, "The Shining Center of the Home: Ontologies of Television in the 'Golden Age,' " in *Television in Transition,* edited by Phillip Drummond and Richard Paterson (London: BFI, 1985), 125–133.

6 Feuer, "Concept of Live Television," 14.

7 Stephen Heath and Gillian Skirrow, "Television: A World in Action," *Screen* 18, no. 2 (summer 1977): 53.

8 Examples of this operation can be found in Margaret Morse's "Talk, Talk, Talk," *Screen* 26, no. 2 (March–April 1985): 2–15.

9 Heath and Skirrow, "Television," 54.

10 Williams, *Television,* 84.

11 See, for example, Beverle Houston, "Viewing Television: The Metapsychology of Endless Consumption," *Quarterly Review of Film Studies* 9, no. 3 (summer 1984): 183–195.

12 Heath and Skirrow, "Television," 54.

13 For a more detailed examination of this narrative quality, see Horace New-comb's discussion of soap operas in *TV: The Most Popular Art* (New York: Anchor Books, 1974), 161–182.

14 See Cassandra Amesley, "How to Watch *Star Trek*," *Cultural Studies* 3, no. 3 (October 1989): 323–339.

15 One of the most interesting pop artifacts of this phenomenon is Mark Bennett's book, *TV Sets: Fantasy Blueprints of Classic TV Homes* (New York: TV Books, 1996). Bennett provides blueprint layouts of some of television's most famous residences and communities, a geography culled from details gathered during his repeated viewings of TV reruns.

16 John Storey, *An Introductory Guide to Cultural Theory and Popular Culture* (Athens, Ga.: University of Georgia Press, 1993), 163.

17 Baudrillard, *Simulations,* 55.

18 Jean Baudrillard, *The Perfect Crime* (New York: Verso, 1986), 2.

19 Baudrillard, *Simulations,* 54.

20 Christian Metz, *The Imaginary Signifier* (Bloomington: Indiana University Press, 1982), 96.

21 Sandy Flitterman-Lewis, "Psychoanalysis, Film, and Television," in *Channels of Discourse,* edited by Robert Allen (Chapel Hill: University of North Carolina Press, 1987), 216.

22 John Ellis, *Visible Fictions* (London: Routledge and Kegan Paul, 1982), 138.

23 John Caughie, "The 'World' of Television," *Edinburgh '77 Magazine,* no. 2 (1977): 81.

24 Mimi White, "Crossing Wavelengths: The Diegetic and Referential Imaginary of American Commercial Television," *Cinema Journal* 25, no. 2 (winter 1986): 43.

25 Fredric Jameson, *Postmodernism, or, the Cultural Logic of Late Capitalism* (Durham: Duke University Press, 1991), 26–28.

26 John Caldwell, *Televisuality: Style, Crisis, and Authority in American Television* (New Brunswick: Rutgers University Press, 1995), 196.

27 Vivian Sobchack, "The Scene of the Screen: Envisioning Cinematic and Electronic 'Presence,' " in *Film and Theory,* edited by Robert Stam and Toby Miller (Malden, Mass.: Blackwell, 2000), 80.

28 Bruce Jay Friedman, "For Your Viewing Entertainment," *Far from the City of Class* (New York: Frommer-Pasmantier, 1963), 14–15.

29 Jameson, *Postmodernism,* 12.

30 L. Sprague de Camp, "Corzan the Mighty," in *A Gun for Dinosaur* (New York: Doubleday, 1963), 137.

31 Kate Wilhelm, "Baby, You Were Great," in *Orbit 2: The Best New Science-Fiction of the Year,* edited by Damon Knight (New York: G. P. Putnam's Sons, 1967), 26.

32 John MacDonald, "Spectator Sport," *Science-Fiction of the Fifties,* edited by Martin Harry Greenberg and Joseph Olander (New York: Avon Books, 1979), 6–7. Originally published in the February 1950 issue of *Thrilling Wonder Stories.*

33 Baudrillard, *Ecstasy,* 18.

34 Michael Benedikt, introduction to *Cyberspace: First Steps,* edited by Michael Benedikt (Cambridge: MIT Press, 1991), 3.

35 Nicole Stenger, "Mind Is a Leaking Rainbow," in *Cyberspace: First Steps,* edited by Michael Benedikt (Cambridge: MIT Press, 1991), 49–50.

36 Tom Standage, *The Victorian Internet* (New York: Walker, 1998), xiii.

37 John Durham Peters, *Speaking into the Air: A History of the Idea of Communication* (Chicago: University of Chicago Press, 1999).

38 Sarah Walters, "Ghosting the Interface: Cyberspace and Spiritualism," *Science as Culture* 6 (part 3), no. 28: 414–443.

39 Tom Gunning, "Phantom Images and Modern Manifestations: Spirit Photography, Magic Theatre, Trick Films, and Photography's Uncanny," in *Fugitive Images: From Photography to Video,* edited by Patrice Petro (Bloomington: Indiana University Press, 1995), 68.

40 Walters, "Ghosting the Interface," 438.

41 Bukatman, *Terminal Identity,* 9.

42 Ibid., 105.

43 See in particular Stone's discussion of Gibson in *The War of Desire and Technology at the Close of the Mechanical Age* (Cambridge: MIT Press, 1996).

44 Jameson, *Postmodernism,* 15.

Bibliography

Abbot, Mabel. "Those Fatal Filaments." *Argosy,* January 1903, n.p.

Ambler, R. P. "The Science of the Soul; Its Unfoldings and Results." *Spirit Messenger and Harmonial Advocate* 1, no. 1 (16 October 1852): 1–3.

Amesley, Cassandra. "How to Watch *Star Trek.*" *Cultural Studies* 3, no. 3 (October 1989): 323–339.

"Analogy between Wireless Telegraphy and Waves from Brain to Brain." *Current Opinion,* October 1914, 253.

Anderson, Betty Baxter. *Four Girls and a Radio.* New York: Cupples and Leon, 1944.

Apjohn, James. "Spontaneous Combustion." In *Cyclopaedia of Practical Medicine,* edited by John Forbes, Alexander Tweedie, and John Conolly, 474–475. Philadelphia: Lea and Blanchard, 1849.

Appleton, Victor. *Tom Swift and his Wireless Message: or, The Castaways of Earthquake Island.* New York: Grosset & Dunlap, c1911.

"Are Martians People?" *Scientific American,* 20 March 1920, 301.

"Are Other Worlds Alive?" *Review of Reviews* 12 (July 1895): 68–69.

Armagnac, Alden. "Weird Electrical Freaks Traced to Runaway Radio Waves." *Popular Science Monthly,* June 1935, 11–13, 101.

Arnold, H. F. "The Night Wire." *Weird Tales,* September 1926, 380–384.

Asquith, Lady Cynthia. "The Lord in Waiting." *Shudders: A Collection of New Nightmare Tales.* New York: Scribner, 1929.

Ballou, Adin. *An Exposition of Views Respecting the Principal Facts, Causes, and Peculiarities Involved in Spirit Manifestations: Together with Interesting Phenomenal Statements and Communications.* Boston: Bela Marsh, 1853.

Bander, Peter. *Voices from the Tapes.* New York: Drake, 1973.

Bangs, John Kendrick. "The Imp of the Telephone." *Bikey the Skicycle and Other Tales.* New York: Riggs Publishing, 1902.

Baudrillard, Jean. *The Ecstasy of Communication.* New York: Semiotext(e), 1987.

———. *The Perfect Crime.* New York: Verso, 1986.

———. "Requiem for the Media." In *For a Critique of the Political Economy of the Sign,* 164–184. St. Louis: Telos Press, 1981.

———. *Simulations.* New York: Semiotext(e), 1983.

Beard, George. *American Nervousness, Its Causes and Consequences, a Supplement to Nervous Exhaustion (neurasthenia).* New York: G. P. Putnam, 1881.

———. "The Treatment of Insanity by Electricity." *Journal of Mental Science* 19 (October 1873): 355–360.

Beckett, Samuel. *The Unnameable.* New York: Grove Press, 1958.

Bednarowki, Mary Farrell. "Women in Occult America." In *The Occult in America: New Historical Perspectives,* edited by Howard Kerr and Charles L. Crow, 177–195. Chicago: University of Illinois Press, 1983.

Benedikt, Michael. Introduction to *Cyberspace: First Steps,* edited by Michael Benedikt, 3–25. Cambridge: MIT Press, 1991.

Bennett, Mark. *TV Sets: Fantasy Blueprints of Classic TV Homes.* New York: TV Books, 1996.

Benson, Edward Frederic. "And the Dead Spake —." In *Visible and Invisible.* New York: George H. Doran, 1923.

Benz, Ernst. *The Theology of Electricity: On the Encounter and Explanation of Theology and Science in the Seventeenth and Eighteenth Centuries.* Translated by Wolgang Taraba. Allison Park, Penn.: Pickwick Publications, 1989.

Beveridge, A. W., and E. B. Renvoize. "Electricity: A History of Its Use in the Treatment of Mental Illness in Britain during the Second Half of the Nineteenth Century." *British Journal of Psychiatry* 153 (1988): 157–162.

Binns, Jack. *The Radio Boy's First Wireless.* New York: Grosset and Dunlap, 1922.

Biographical Dictionary of Parapsychology. New York: Helix Press, 1964.

Birch, A. G. *The Moon Terror.* Indianapolis: Popular Fiction Publishing, 1927.

Boddy, William. "Entering the 'Twilight Zone' — Transition to Hollywood Television." *Screen* 25, no. 4–5 (1984): 98–108.

———. *Fifties Television.* Chicago: University of Illinois Press, 1990.

———. "The Shining Center of the Home: Ontologies of Television in the 'Golden Age.'" In *Television in Transition,* edited by Phillip Drummond and Richard Paterson, 125–133. London: BFI, 1985.

Bogart, Leo. *The Age of Television.* New York: Frederick Ungar, 1972.

Bostock, John. *An Account of the History and Present State of Galvanism.* London: Baldwin, Cradock, and Joy, 1818.

Braude, Ann. *Radical Spirits: Spiritualism and Women's Rights in Nineteenth Century America.* Boston: Beacon Press, 1989.

Brecht, Bertolt. "Notes on Radio." In *Wireless Imagination: Sound, Radio, and the Avant-Garde,* edited by Douglas Kahn and Gregory Whitehead. Cambridge, Mass.: MIT Press, 1992.

Brennan, Martin S. *A Popular Exposition of Electricity.* New York: D. Appleton, 1885.

Brown, Edward M. "Neurology and Spiritualism in the 1870s." *Bulletin of the History of Medicine* 57 (winter 1983): 563–577.

Brown, John. *Mediumistic Experiences of John Brown: The Medium of the Rockies.* San Franciso: Office of the Philosophical Journal, 1897.

Browne, Nick. "The Political Economy of the Television (Super)text." In *Tele-*

vision: The Critical View, edited by Horace Newcomb, 585–599. New York: Oxford University Press, 1986.

Brownson, O. A. *The Spirit Rapper; An Autobiography.* Boston: Little, Brown, 1854.

Bukatman, Scott. *Terminal Identity: The Virtual Subject in Post-Modern Science-Fiction.* Durham: Duke University Press, 1993.

Butler, Ellis. "The Celebrated Pilkey Radio Case." *Radio News,* October 1923, n.p.

——. "The Great Radio Message from Mars." *Radio News,* November 1923, n.p.

——. "The Voice of the People." *Radio News,* November 1927, n.p.

Cadwallader, M. E. *Hydesville in History.* Chicago: Progressive Thinker Publishing House, 1917.

Cahagnet, Louis Alphonse. *The Celestial Telegraph; or, Secrets of the Life to Come, Revealed through Magnetism.* New York: J. S. Redfield, 1851.

Caldwell, John. *Televisuality: Style, Crisis, and Authority in American Television.* New Brunswick: Rutgers University Press, 1995.

"Camille Flammarion's Latest Views on Martian Signaling." *Scientific American Supplement,* 31 August 1907, 137.

Canby, Edward Tatnall. *A History of Electricity: The New Illustrated Library of Science and Invention.* New York: Hawthorn Books, 1963.

Cantril, Hadley. *The Invasion from Mars: A Study in the Psychology of Panic.* Princeton, N.J.: Princeton University Press, 1940.

Carey, James. "Technology and Ideology: The Case of the Telegraph." In *Communication as Culture,* edited by James Carey, 201–230. Boston: Unwin Hyman, 1989.

Carey, James, and John J. Quirk. "The Mythos of the Electronic Revolution." In *Communication as Culture,* edited by James Carey, 113–141. Boston: Unwin Hyman, 1989.

Carrington, Hereward. *Psychical Phenomena and the War.* New York: Dodd, Mead, 1918.

"Case of Mania with the Delusions and Phenomena of Spiritualism." *American Journal of Insanity* 16, no. 3 (1859–1860): 323–324.

"Cases of Hysteria and Hysteromania." *American Journal of Insanity* 17, no. 1 (October 1860): 127–152.

Caughie, John. "The 'World' of Television." *Edinburgh '77 Magazine,* no. 2 (1977): 80–85.

Charcot, J. M. "Hysteria and Spiritism." *Medical and Surgical Reporter* 59, no. 3 (21 July 1888): 65.

Clay, H. P. "The Radio Vision." *Practical Electrics,* October 1924, 686–687.

"Close-up to the Blast." *Life,* 30 May 1955, 39–42.

"Conan Doyle Gives Reasons for His Belief in Spiritualism." *Current Opinion,* January 1917, 39–40.

Cooter, Roger. *The Cultural Meaning of Popular Science: Phrenology and the Organization of Consent in Nineteenth-Century Britain.* Cambridge: Cambridge University Press, 1984.

Covert, Catherine L. "We May Hear Too Much: American Sensibility and the Response to Radio, 1919–1924." In *Mass Media between the Wars: Perception of Cultural Tension, 1918–1941,* edited by Catherine L. Covert and John D. Stevens, 199–219. Syracuse: Syracuse University Press, 1984.

"Crazed Knife-Wielder Invades a TV Studio, Stabs Cameraman, Fells Actor with Pitcher." *New York Times,* 1 July 1953, 39.

Crookes, Sir William. *Psychic Force and Modern Spiritualism: A Reply to the "Quarterly Review" and Other Critics.* London : Longmans, Green, 1871.

———. *Researches in the Phenomena of Spiritualism, by William Crookes; together with a portion of his presidential address given before the British Association, 1898; and an appendix by Sir A. Conan Doyle.* London: Psychic Bookshop, 1926.

———. "Sir William Crookes's Provisional Explanation of Telepathy — Harmony with Natural Law." In *The Widow's Mite and Other Psychic Phenomena,* edited by Isaac K. Funk. New York: Funk and Wagnalls, 1904.

Cummings, Raymond. "The Thought Machine." *Argosy All-Story,* 26 May 1923, n.p.

Czitrom, Daniel. *Media and the American Mind.* Chapel Hill: University of North Carolina Press, 1982.

Dabbs, James McBride. "Thin Air." *Christian Century,* 26 April 1939, 540–542.

Dangerfield, Clinton. "The Message." *Weird Tales,* September 1931, 170–175.

Darnton, Robert. *Mesmerism and the End of the Enlightenment in France.* Cambridge: Harvard University Press, 1968.

Davis, Andrew Jackson. "The New Motive Power." *Telegraph Papers* 5 (May–August 1854).

———. *The Present Age and Inner Life: Ancient and Modern Spirit Mysteries Classified and Explained. A Sequel to Spiritual Intercourse Revised and Enlarged.* 1853. Reprint, Rochester: Austin Publishing, 1910.

Debord, Guy. *Society of the Spectacle.* Detroit: Black and Red, 1983.

de Camp, L. Sprague. "Corzan the Mighty." *A Gun for Dinosaur.* New York: Doubleday, 1963.

Derleth, August W. "The Telephone in the Library." *Weird Tales,* June 1936, 710–719.

"Dialed Hysteria." *Time,* 7 November 1938, 13.

Dinsdale, A. "Television Needs New Ideas — and Less Ballyhoo." *Scientific American,* November 1930, 366–368.

Bibliography

Dirk, Jan. "Radio V-Rays." *Weird Tales,* March 1925, n.p.

Doane, Mary Ann. "Information, Crisis, Catastrophe." In *Logics of Television,* edited by Patricia Mellencamp, 222–239. Bloomington: Indiana University Press, 1990.

Douglas, Susan J. "Amateur Operators and American Broadcasting: Shaping the Future of Radio." In *Imagining Tomorrow: History, Technology, and the American Future,* edited by Joseph J. Corn. Cambridge: MIT Press, 1986.

——. *Inventing American Broadcasting, 1899–1922.* Baltimore: Johns Hopkins University Press, 1987.

——. "Technology, Media, and the Idea of Progress." *Massachusetts Review* 25 (winter 1984): 655–656.

Dreher, Carl. "Putting Freak Broadcasting in Its Place." *Radio Broadcast,* November 1927, 50.

Eddy, William C. *Television: The Eyes of Tomorrow.* New York: Prentice-Hall, 1945.

"Electric Radio Ghosts." *Literary Digest,* 4 August 1922, 21.

Ellis, David J. *The Mediumship of the Tape Recorder: A Detailed Examination of the (Jürgenson, Raudive) Phenomenon of Voice Extras on Tape Recordings.* Pulborough, West Sussex: the author, 1978.

Ellis, John. *Visible Fictions.* London: Routledge & Kegan Paul, 1982.

Evans, Wainright. "Scientists Research Machine to Contact the Dead." *Fate,* April 1963, 38–43.

"Evidence of Life on Mars." *Scientific American,* 26 October 1927, 287.

"Face on TV Set Goes, Mystery Lingers On." *New York Times,* 12 December 1953, 16.

Feuer, Jane. "The Concept of Live Television: Ontology as Ideology." In *Regarding Television,* edited by E. Ann Kaplan, 12–22. Los Angeles: AFI, 1983.

Fezandie, Clement. "The Secret of Television." *Science and Invention,* October 1922, n.p.

Field, Matthew. "Is Belief in Spiritualism Ever Evidence of Insanity Per Se?" *Medico-Legal Journal* 6 (1888): 194–202.

Fishbough, William. "Laws and Phenomena of the Soul. Number One." *Spirit Messenger and Harmonial Advocate* 1, no. 6 (20 November 1852): 1–4.

——. "Laws and Phenomena of the Soul. Number Two." *Spirit Messenger and Harmonial Advocate* 1, no. 7 (27 November 1852): 97–99.

——. "Laws and Phenomena of the Soul. Number Three." *Spirit Messenger and Harmonial Advocate* 1, no. 8 (4 December 1852): 113–114.

——. "Laws and Phenomena of the Soul. Number Four." *Spirit Messenger and Harmonial Advocate* 1, no. 9 (11 December 1852): 129–133.

Flammarion, M. Camille. "Shall We Talk with the Men in the Moon?" *Review of Reviews* 5 (February 1890): 90.

Flitterman-Lewis, Sandy. "Psychoanalysis, Film, and Television." In *Channels of Discourse,* edited by Robert Allen, 203–246. Chapel Hill: University of North Carolina Press, 1987.

Flowers, John B. "Signaling to the Planets with a Cloth Reflector." *Illustrated World,* March 1921, 84–85.

Forbes, B. C. "Edison Working on How to Communicate with the Next World." *American Magazine,* October 1920, 10–11.

Fox, Russell. "The Thoughtograph." *Royal Magazine,* November 1906, n.p.

Frederick, George Justus. "The Dupe of the Realist." *Argosy,* March 1902, n.p.

Free, E. E. "The Secrets of the Radio Hypnotist." *Popular Radio,* June 1927, 528–529.

Freud, Sigmund. *The Future of an Illusion.* New York: Norton, 1961.

———. "The Uncanny." In *Psychological Writings and Letters,* edited by Sander L. Gilman, 120–153. New York: Continuum, 1995.

Friedman, Bruce Jay. "For Your Viewing Entertainment." In *Far from the City of Class,* 11–23. New York: Frommer-Pasmantier, 1963.

"Frog Legs as Wireless Receivers." *Literary Digest,* 2 November 1912, 785.

"From Schenectady, Not Mars." *Literary Digest,* 5 August 1922, 33.

Fuller, Curtis. "KLEE . . . Still Calling." *Fate,* April 1964, 37–41.

Futrelle, Jacques. "The Interrupted Wireless." *Great Cases of the Thinking Machine.* New York: Dover, 1976.

Galton, Francis. "Intelligible Signals between Neighbouring Stars." *Fortnightly Review* 66 (November 1896): 657.

Galvani, Luigi. *Commentary on the Effects of Electricity on Muscular Motion.* Translated by Margaret Glover Foley. Norwalk, Conn.: Burndy Library, 1953.

Gannett, Ezra. *The Atlantic Telegraph: A Discourse Delivered in the First Church, August 8, 1858.* Boston: Crosby, Nichols, 1858.

Gernsback, Hugo. "Thought Transmission on Mars." *Electrical Experimenter,* January 1916, n.p.

"Ghosts That Talk — by Radio." *Literary Digest,* 21 October 1922, 28–29.

Goode, Kenneth M. *What about Radio?* New York: Harper and Brothers, 1937.

Grable, Luther S. H. *The Miracle of Television.* Chicago: Wilcox and Follett, 1949.

Greenberg, D. S. "Radio Astronomy: FCC Proposes Compromise to Share Frequencies with UHF Broadcasters." *Science,* 12 April 1963, 164.

———. "Radio Astronomy: TV's Rush for UHF Threatens Use of Channel." *Science,* 1 February 1963, 393.

Grubb, D. "Radio." *Twelve Tales of Suspense and the Supernatural.* New York: Scribner, 1964.

Guillemin, M. Amedee. "Communication with the Planets." *Popular Science Monthly,* January 1892, 361–363.

Gunning, Tom. "Heard Over the Phone: *The Lonely Villa* and the de Lorde Tradition of the Terrors of Technology." *Screen* 32, no. 2 (1991): 184–196.

———. "Phantom Images and Modern Manifestations: Spirit Photography, Magic Theatre, Trick Films, and Photography's Uncanny." In *Fugitive Images: From Photography to Video,* edited by Patrice Petro, 42–71. Bloomington: Indiana University Press, 1995.

Haller, John S., and Robin M. Haller. *The Physician and Sexuality in Victorian America.* New York: Norton, 1974.

Handlin, Oscar. "Comments on Mass and Popular Culture." In *Culture for the Millions? Mass Media in Modern Society,* edited by Norman Jacobs, 63–70. Boston: Beacon Press, 1964.

Hanson, O. B. "Here Comes Television!" *Scientific American,* April 1939, 207–209.

Haralovich, Mary Beth. "Sit-coms and Suburbs: Positioning the 1950s Homemaker." In *Private Screenings: Television and the Female Consumer,* edited by Lynn Spigel and Denise Mann, 111–142. Minneapolis: University of Minnesota Press, 1992.

Haraway, Donna. "A Cyborg Manifesto: Science, Technology, and Socialist-Feminism in the Late Twentieth Century." *Simians, Cyborgs, and Women: The Re-Invention of Nature.* New York: Routledge, 1991.

Hardinge, Emma. *America and Her Destiny: An Inspirational Discourse.* New York: Robert M. DeWitt, 1861.

———. *Modern American Spiritualism.* 1869. Reprint, New Hyde Park, N.Y.: University Books, 1970.

———. *Rules to Be Observed When Forming Spiritual Circles.* Boston: William White, 1870.

Hare, Robert. *Experimental Investigation of the Spirit Manifestations, Demonstrating the Existence of Spirits and Their Communion with Mortals.* New York: Partridge and Brittan, 1855.

Hartmann, Lee Foster. "Out of the Air." *Harper's,* September 1922, 490–500.

"Haunted TV Is Punished; Set with Face That Won't Go Away Must Stare at the Wall." *New York Times,* 11 December 1953, 33.

Heath, Stephen, and Gillian Skirrow. "Television: A World in Action." *Screen* 18, no. 2 (summer 1977): 7–59.

Heinzerling, Jurgen. "All about EVP." *Fortean Times,* December 1997, 26–30.

Higham, John. *Strangers in the Land.* New York: Atheneum, 1965.

Hoss, Glanville. "Dr. Jerbot's Last Experiment." *Weird Tales,* March 1926, n.p.

Houston, Beverle. "Viewing Television: The Metapsychology of Endless Consumption." *Quarterly Review of Film Studies* 9, no. 3 (summer 1984): 183–195.

Houston, E. J. "Shall We Have a Thought Machine?" *Review of Reviews* 6 (September 1892): 191.

Howitt, William. *Spirit Manifestations.* Boston: American Liberal Tract Society, 1862.

"How Two Girls Made a Receiving Radiophone." *Literary Digest,* 10 June 1922, 29.

Hubbell, Richard. *Television Programming and Production.* New York: Rinehart, 1950.

"Human Radio: Man Has to Be Grounded to Enjoy Broadcasts." *Newsweek,* 23 September 1933, 26.

"Human Radio Receivers." *Literary Digest,* 22 September 1928, 23–24.

Hutchinson, Thomas H. *Here Is Television, Your Window on the World.* New York: Hastings House, 1948.

Huyssen, Andres. "Mass Culture as Woman: Modernism's Other." In *After the Great Divide: Modernism, Mass Culture, Postmodernism.* Bloomington: Indiana University Press, 1986.

Impola, John. "Whispering Death." *Weird Tales,* November 1929, 683–694.

Inchbald, Elizabeth. *Animal Magnetism: A Farce in Three Acts.* New York: Publisher unknown, 1809.

"An Irate Video Owner Has Come Up with an Unusual Solution to Your Chief TV Bete Noir." *New York Times,* 22 October 1952, 37.

Isaacs, Ernest. "The Fox Sisters and American Spiritualism." In *The Occult in America: New Historical Perspectives,* edited by Howard Kerr and Charles L. Crow, 79–110. Chicago: University of Illinois Press, 1983.

"Is Radio Earthbound?" *Literary Digest,* 21 March 1925, 23–25.

"Is the Radio Amateur Doomed?" *Literary Digest,* 2 December 1922, 28.

"It Better Be Good." *Newsweek,* 9 May 1955, 84.

James, William. *Principles of Psychology.* New York: H. Holt, 1890.

Jameson, Fredric. *Postmodernism, or, the Cultural Logic of Late Capitalism.* Durham: Duke University Press, 1991.

Jürgenson, Friedrich. *Sprechfunk mit Verstorbenen: Eine dem Atomzeitalter gemeasse Form der praktischen technisch-physikalischen Kontaktherstellung mit dem Jenseits.* Freiburg: H. Bauer, 1967.

Keeler, Harry Stephen. *The Box from Japan.* New York: E. P. Dutton, 1932.

Keeler, P. L. O. A. "The Skeleton in the Fox Cottage." In *Hydesville in History,* edited by M. E. Cadwallader. Chicago: Progressive Thinker Publishing House, 1917.

Keller, David H. "The Threat of the Robot." *Science Wonder Stories,* June 1929, n.p.

Kern, Stephen. *The Culture of Time and Space, 1880–1918.* Cambridge: Harvard University Press, 1983.

Kerry, R. J. "Phobia of Outer Space." *Journal of Mental Science* 106 (1960): 1383–1387.

Kilmer, Aline. "Wicked Wireless." In *Hunting a Hair Shirt and Other Spiritual Adventures.* New York: George H. Doran, 1923.

King, Frances Rockefeller. "The Personality behind the Ghost Hour." *Radio News,* October 1929, 316.

Kipling, Rudyard. "Wireless." In *Traffics and Discoveries.* London: Macmillan, 1904.

Koch, Howard. *The Panic Broadcast: The Whole Story of Orson Welles' Legendary Radio Show "Invasion from Mars."* New York: Avon Books, 1970.

Kristol, Irving. "The Mass Media." A panel discussion in *Culture for the Millions? Mass Media in Modern Society,* edited by Norman Jacobs, 166–175. Boston: Beacon Press, 1964.

"The Latest Theory Regarding Life on the Planet Mars." *Current Opinion,* October 1917, 254.

Laumer, Keith. "The Walls." *Nine by Laumer.* New York: Doubleday, 1967.

Lazarfeld, Paul. *The People Look at Radio.* Chapel Hill: University of North Carolina Press, 1945.

Lears, T. Jackson. *No Place of Grace: Antimodernism and the Transformation of American Culture, 1880–1920.* New York: Pantheon, 1981.

Lehman, Neil. "The Life of John Murray Spear: Spiritualism and Reform in Antebellum America." Ph.D. diss., Ohio State University, 1973.

"Letters." *Journal of the American Society for Psychical Research* (January 1959): 2.

Lewis, E. E. *A Report of the Mysterious Noises Heard in the House of Mr. John D. Fox.* Canandaigua, N.Y.: the author, 1848.

"Life in Other Worlds." *Popular Science Monthly,* November 1903, 26–31.

"Life on Other Worlds." *Forum* 27 (March 1899): 71–77.

Lodge, Sir Oliver. "A Broadcast Experiment in Sending Thought-Waves via Ether." *Popular Radio,* September 1927, 111–113.

———. *Ether and Reality: A Series of Discourses on the Many Functions of the Ether of Space.* London: Hodder and Stoughton, 1925.

———. *Man and the Universe: A Study of the Influence of the Advance in Scientific Knowledge upon Our Understanding of Christianity.* London: Methuen, 1908.

———. *Raymond; or Life and Death.* New York: George H. Doran, 1916.

———. "The Reality of the Spiritual World." *Radio Digest,* December 1930, 49–50.

Low, A. M. "Raiders from Space." *Science Wonder Stories,* March 1930, n.p.

Lowell, Percival. *Mars and Its Canals.* New York: Macmillan, 1906.

———. *Mars as the Abode of Life.* New York: Macmillan, 1908.

MacDonald, John. "Spectator Sport." In *Science-Fiction of the Fifties,* edited by Martin Harry Greenberg and Joseph Olander. New York: Avon Books, 1979. Originally published in the February 1950 issue of *Thrilling Wonder Stories.*

Mangus, A. R. "Family Impacts on Mental Health." *Marriage and Family Living,* August 1957, 261.

"Man Who Heard Washington in Hawaii." *Scientific American,* 15 May 1915, 450.

"Marconi on the Curiosities of Wireless Telegraphy." *Current Literature* 48 (February 1910): 165.

Markus, John. *How to Make More Money in Your TV Servicing Business.* New York: McGraw-Hill, 1962.

Marvin, Carolyn. *When Old Technologies Were New.* London: Oxford University Press, 1988.

Marx, Leo. *The Machine in the Garden.* New York: Oxford University Press, 1964.

Matheson, Richard. "Through Channels." *Science Fiction Terror Tales,* edited by Groff Conklin. New York: Collier, 1962.

Mattison, Reverend H. *Spirit-Rapping Unveiled! An Expose of the Origin, History, Theology, and Philosophy of Certain Alleged Communications from the Spirit World by Means of "Spirit Rapping," "Medium-Writing," "Physical Demonstrations," Etc.* New York: J. C. Derby, 1855.

May, Elaine Tyler. *Homeward Bound: American Families in the Cold War Era.* New York: Basic Books, 1988.

McChesney, Robert W. "The Battle for the U.S. Airwaves, 1928–1935." *Journal of Communication* 40, no. 4 (autumn 1990): 29–52.

McGrath, P. T. "The Future of Wireless Telegraphy." *North American Review* 175 (August 1902): 782.

McMeans, Orange Howard. "Eavesdropping on the World." *Scribner's Magazine* 72, no. 15 (April 1923): 228–232.

Mellencamp, Patricia. "TV Time and Catastophe." In *Logics of Television,* edited by Patricia Mellencamp, 240–266. Bloomington: Indiana University Press, 1990.

"Mental Telegraphy." *Harper's,* December 1891, 95–104.

"Mental Telegraphy Again." *Harper's,* September 1895, 521–524.

Metz, Christian. *The Imaginary Signifier.* Bloomington: Indiana University Press, 1982.

Millingen, J. G. *Curiosities of Medical Experience.* London: R. Bentley, 1839.

Milne, Robert. "An Experience in Telepathy; in which Clairvoyance and Spiritual Telegraphy Play a Part." *Argonaut,* 23 December 1889, n.p.

———. "The Great Electric Diaphragm: Some Account of the Telegraphic System of the Baron O —." *Argonaut,* 24 May 1879, n.p.

———. "A Mysterious Twilight; Being a Dip into the Doings of the Four-Dimensional World." *Argonaut,* 27 June 1885, n.p.

———. "Professor Vehr's Electrical Experiment." *Argonaut,* 24 January 1885, n.p. Reprinted in *Into the Sun and Other Stories: Science Fiction in Old San Francisco,* edited by Sam Moskowitz. West Kingston, R.I.: Donald M. Grant, 1980.

Morse, Margaret. "Talk, Talk, Talk." *Screen* 26, no. 2 (March–April 1985): 2–15.

Moskowitz, Sam, ed. *Into the Sun and Other Stories: Science Fiction in Old San Francisco.* West Kingston, R.I.: Donald M. Grant, 1980.

"Mouse at Yucca Flat: Televising Atomic Bomb Test." *Newsweek,* 16 May 1955, 63.

Nemerov, Howard. "Beyond the Screen." *A Commodity of Dreams and Other Stories.* New York: Simon and Schuster, 1959.

Newcomb, Horace. *TV: The Most Popular Art.* New York: Anchor Books, 1974.

Newth, A. H. "The Electro-Neural Pathology of Insanity." *Journal of Mental Science* 24 (April 1878): 76–82.

———. "The Galvanic Current Applied in the Treatment of Insanity." *Journal of Mental Science* 19 (April 1873): 79–86.

Nieman, H. W., and C. Wells Nieman. "What Shall We Say to Mars? A System for Opening Communication despite the Absence of Any Common Basis of Language." *Scientific American,* 20 March 1920, 298, 312.

"A Note on the Meaning of Television to a Psychotic Woman." *Bulletin of the Menninger Clinic* 23 (1959): 202–203.

O'Brien, Howard Vincent. "It's Great to Be a Radio Maniac." *Collier's,* 13 September 1924, 15–16.

O'Brien, J. E. "An Electric Flash." *Belford's Magazine,* October 1889, n.p.

"Obviously Self-Defense: Long Islander Puts Bullet into TV Set as 7 Watch." *New York Times,* 21 October 1952, 31.

"The Oceanic Telegraph." *North American Review* 87 (October 1858): 532–544.

Olcott, James S. *Animal Electricity; or the Electrical Science; an Application of the Primary Laws of Nature, Never Before Discovered and Demonstrated; to a Solution of All the Physical and Intellectual Phenomena That Exist.* Boston: N. S. Magoon, 1844.

Oldfield, Traverse. *"To Daimonion," or the Spiritual Medium. Its Nature Illustrated by the History of Its Uniform Mysterious Manifestation When Unduly Excited.* In *Twelve Familiar Letters to an Inquiring Friend,* 24–25. Boston: Gould and Lincoln, 1852.

"Panic from Mars." *The Nation,* 12 November 1938, 498.

Papillon, Fernand. "Electricity and Life." *Popular Science Monthly,* March 1873, 526–541.

Parker, Lewis K. *Channel 10 from Nowhere.* Middletown: Weekly Reader Books, 1985.

Peck, A. P. "Television's Progress." *Scientific American,* December 1929, 487.

"The Persistent Mysteries of Wireless Telegraphy and Telephony." *Current Literature* 49 (December 1910): 636–638.

Peters, John Durham. *Speaking into the Air: A History of the Idea of Communication.* Chicago: University of Chicago Press, 1999.

Pevey, James. "The Man Who Saw Beyond." *Practical Electrics,* May 1924, 398–400, 404–406.

"Plan Wireless Talks with Spirit World: Delegates at Paris Convention Aim for a Device to Eliminate Mediums." *New York Times,* 10 September 1925, 26.

Podmore, Frank. *Mediums of the 19th Century.* New Hyde Park: University Books, 1963.

——. *Telepathic Hallucinations: The New View of Ghosts.* Halifax: Milner, 1921.

Poirier, Suzanne. "The Weir Mitchell Rest Cure: Doctor and Patient." *Women's Studies* 10 (1983): 15–40.

Powell, J. H. *Mediumship: Its Laws and Conditions; with Brief Instructions for the Formation of Spirit Circles.* Boston: William White, 1868.

Priestley, J. B. "Uncle Phil on TV." *The Other Place.* New York: Harper and Brothers, 1953.

"Professor David Todd's Plan of Receiving Martian Messages." *Scientific American,* 5 June 1909, 423.

"Quiz Shows." *New York Times,* 29 October 1952, 41.

"Radio Messages from Mars?" *Literary Digest,* 6 September 1924, 28.

"Radio 'Spooks' All Over the House!" *Popular Radio,* December 1927, 416–417.

The Rappers: or, the Mysteries, Fallacies, and Absurdities of Spirit Rapping, Table-Tipping, and Entrancement, by a Searcher after Truth. New York: Long, 1854.

Raudive, Konstantin. *Break Through: Electronic Communication with the Dead May Be Possible.* New York: Zebra Books, 1971.

"The R.C.A. Theremin." *Radio Broadcast,* February 1930, 202–203.

Richet, Charles. "Hysteria and Demonism: A Study in Morbid Psychology." *Popular Science Monthly,* May 1880, 86–93.

Rochester Knockings! Discovery and Explanation of the Source of the Phenomena Generally Known as the Rochester Knockings, reprinted from *Buffalo Medical Journal* (March 1851): n.p.

Ronel, Avital. *The Telephone Book: Technology, Schizophrenia, Electric Speech.* Lincoln: University of Nebraska Press, 1989.

Rosner, Lisa. "The Professional Context of Electrotherapeutics." *Journal of the History of Medicine and Allied Sciences* 43 (1988): 64–82.

Russett, Cynthia. *Sexual Science: The Victorian Construction of Womanhood.* Cambridge: Harvard University Press, 1989.

Bibliography

Sampson, Harold, Sheldon L. Messinger, and Robert Towne. *Schizophrenic Women: Studies in Marital Crisis.* New York: Atherton Press, 1964.

Samson, George W. *Spiritualism Tested; or, the Facts of Its History Classified, and Their Cause in Nature Verified from Ancient and Modern Testimonies.* Boston: Gould and Lincoln, 1860.

Sargent, Epes. *The Scientific Basis of Spiritualism.* 1880. Reprint, Boston: Colby and Rich, 1891.

Schivo, Erald. "The Wireless Girl." *Overland Monthly,* November 1922, 29–33.

Schlossel, J. "A Message from Space." *Weird Tales,* March 1926, n.p.

Schow, David J., and Jeffrey Frentzen. *The Outer Limits: The Official Companion.* New York: Ace Science Fiction Books, 1986.

"Scientific Standing of the Theory of Intelligent Life on Mars." *Current Opinion,* January 1917, 36–37.

The Shekinah 1 (1852), edited by S. B. Brittan.

Shelley, Mary. *Frankenstein.* In *Three Gothic Novels.* New York: Penguin, 1968.

Shortt, S. E. D. "Physicians and Psychics: The Anglo-American Medical Response to Spiritualism, 1870–1890." *Journal of the History of Medicine and Allied Sciences* 39 (1984): 339–355.

"Signaling to Mars." *Scientific American,* 8 May 1909, 346.

Sinclair, Upton. *Mental Radio.* New York: Collier, 1930.

"Sir Oliver Lodge on Marconi's Latest Dream." *Current Opinion,* September 1919, 174.

Smith, Susy. *Voices of the Dead.* New York: Signet, 1977.

Sobchack, Vivian. "The Scene of the Screen: Envisioning Cinematic and Electronic 'Presence.' " In *Film and Theory,* edited by Robert Stam and Toby Miller, 66–84. Malden, Mass.: Blackwell, 2000.

Spear, John Murray. *The Educator: Being Suggestions, Theoretical and Practical, Designed to Promote Man-Culture and Integral Reform, with a View to the Ultimate Establishment of a Divine Social State on Earth,* edited by A. E. Newton. Boston: Office of Practical Spiritualists, 1857.

Speed, Buckner. "Voices of the Universe." *Harper's,* April, 1919, 613–615.

Speer, John R. "Symphony of the Damned." *Weird Tales,* April 1934, 386–411.

Spigel, Lynn. "From Domestic Space to Outer Space: The 1960s Fantastic Family Sit-Com." In *Close Encounters: Film, Feminism, and Science-Fiction,* edited by Elizabeth Lyon, Constance Penley, and Lynn Spigel, 205–236. Minneapolis: University of Minnesota Press, 1991.

——. *Make Room for TV: Television and the Family Ideal in Postwar America.* Chicago: University of Chicago Press, 1992.

The Spirit World, Its Locality and Conditions, by the Spirit of Judge John Worth Edmonds, Late a Prominent Citizen of New York, Given through the Mediumship of Wash. A. Danskin, and Published at the Request of the First Spir-

itualist Congregation, of Baltimore. Baltimore: Steam Press of Frederick A. Hanzsche, 1874.

Standage, Tom. *The Victorian Internet.* New York: Walker, 1998.

Steavenson, W. E., and Lewis Jones. *Medical Electricity: A Practical Handbook for Students and Practitioners.* London: H. K. Lewis, 1892.

Stemman, Roy. *Spirits and the Spirit World.* London: Aldus Books, 1975.

Stenger, Nicole. "Mind Is a Leaking Rainbow." In *Cyberspace: First Steps,* edited by Michael Benedikt, 49–58. Cambridge: MIT Press, 1991.

Stone, Allucquère Rosanne. *The War of Desire and Technology at the Close of the Mechanical Age.* Cambridge: MIT Press, 1996.

Storey, John. *An Introductory Guide to Cultural Theory and Popular Culture.* Athens: University of Georgia Press, 1993.

Stratton, George. "Sam Graves' Electric Mind Reader." *Practical Electrics,* February 1924, 174–175, 210–211.

Strauss, Stuart. "The Soul Tube." *Weird Tales,* December 1928, n.p.

" 'Strays' from the Laboratory." *Radio Broadcast,* April 1928, 427–428.

"Telegraphic Meeting." *Tiffany's Monthly* 3 (1857): 142–143.

"Telepathy and Radio." *Scientific American,* June 1924, 382.

Television Digest, 12 December 1953, 11.

Television Digest, 18 September 1954, 11.

"Telstar, Telstar — Burning Bright." *Life,* 3 August 1962, 4–5.

"That Perspective Communication with Another Planet." *Current Opinion,* March 1919, 170–171.

Thompson, James G. "Sending a Message to Mars." *Illustrated World,* December 1917, 577–579.

"Those Martian Radio Signals." *Scientific American,* 14 February 1920, 156.

Thy Son Liveth: Messages from a Soldier to His Mother. Boston: Little, Brown, 1918.

Tipler, Frank J. *The Physics of Immortality: Modern Cosmology, God, and the Resurrection of the Dead.* New York: Doubleday, 1994.

Toynbee, Arnold J. "A Message for Mankind from Telstar." *New York Times Magazine,* 12 August 1962, 16, 26, 28, 31, 36.

Turkle, Sherry. *Life on the Screen: Identity in the Age of the Internet.* New York: Simon and Schuster, 1995.

"TV's Biggest Mystery." *TV Guide,* 30 April 1954, 23.

"TV Transmission on Laser Beam Demonstrated by North American." *Aviation Weekly,* 18 March 1963, 83.

Vail, Alfred, and J. Cummings Vail. *Eyewitness to Early American Telegraphy.* New York: Arno Press, 1974.

Van Den Haag, Ernst. "A Dissent from the Consensual Society." In *Culture for the Millions? Mass Media in Modern Society,* edited by Norman Jacobs, 53–62. Boston: Beacon Press, 1964.

Bibliography

"Victims at Yucca Flats: Mannequins." *Life,* 16 May 1955, 58.

Volek, Thomas. "Examining Radio Receiver Technology through Magazine Advertising in the 1920s and 1930s." Ph.D. diss., University of Minnesota, 1991.

Vonnegut, Kurt. *The Sirens of Titan.* New York: Dell, 1959.

Von Reichenbach, Charles. *Physico-Physiological Researches in the Dynamics of Magnetism, Electricity, Heat, Light, Crystallization, and Chemism, in Their Relations to Vital Force.* New York: Partridge and Brittan, 1851.

Walkowitz, Judith. "Science and Séance: Transgressions of Gender and Genre in Late Victorian London." *Representations* 22 (spring 1988): 3–37.

Waller, Thomas. "Can We Radio a Message to Mars?" *Illustrated World,* April 1920, 240–242.

Walters, Sarah. "Ghosting the Interface: Cyberspace and Spiritualism." *Science as Culture* 6:3, no. 28 (1997): 414–443.

Warren, Carol A. B. *Madwives: Schizophrenic Women in the 1950s.* New Brunswick: Rutgers University Press, 1991.

"A Watch Truck Is Watching You." *Life,* 25 September 1964, 37–40.

Weiss, Robert S., and Nancy Morse Samelson. "Social Roles of American Women: Their Contribution to a Sense of Usefulness and Importance." *Marriage and Family Living,* November 1958, 358–366.

Welch, William. *Talks with the Dead.* New York: Pinnacle Books, 1975.

Wells, H. G. "The Things That Live on Mars." *Cosmopolitan,* March 1908, 340–342.

Welter, Barbara. "The Cult of True Womanhood: 1820–1860." *American Quarterly* 18 (summer 1966): 151–174.

White, Mimi. "Crossing Wavelengths: The Diegetic and Referential Imaginary of American Commercial Television." *Cinema Journal* 25, no. 2 (winter 1986): 43.

Whiting, John. "Old Clothes." *Weird Tales,* August 1932, 265–266.

"Why the Dwellers on Mars Do Not Make War." *Current Literature* 42 (1907): 211–214.

Wilhelm, Kate. "Baby, You Were Great." In *Orbit 2: The Best New Science-Fiction of the Year,* edited by Damon Knight. New York: G. P. Putnam's Sons, 1967.

Williams, Raymond. *Television: Technology and Cultural Form.* London: Wesleyan University Press, 1992.

Wilson, David. "The Thought of Late Victorian Physicists: Oliver Lodge's Ethereal Body." *Victorian Studies* (September 1971): 29–48.

Wilson, John Fleming. "Sparks." *McClure's Magazine,* June 1911, 149–154.

Winsor, George McLeod. *Station X.* Boston: Gregg Press, 1975.

"Wireless Elopement." *New Englander,* March 1907, 95–102.

"Wooed by Wireless." *Cosmopolitan,* April 1908, 497–501.

Wright, Sewall Peaslee. "The Experiment of Erich Weigert." *Weird Tales,* May 1926, 683.

Index

Jeffrey Sconce is Assistant Professor
in the School of Cinema-Television at the
University of Southern California.

Library of Congress Cataloging-in-Publication Data

Sconce, Jeffrey
Haunted media : electronic presence from telegraphy to
television / Jeffrey Sconce.
p. cm. — (Console-ing passions)
Includes bibliographical references and index.
ISBN 0-8223-2553-5 (cloth : alk. paper)
ISBN 0-8223-2572-1 (pbk. : alk. paper)
1. Mass media — Technological innovations — History.
2. Telecommunications — History.   3. Mass media and
culture — History.   I. Title.   II. Series.
P96.T42 S37 2000
302.23'09 — dc21   00-029387

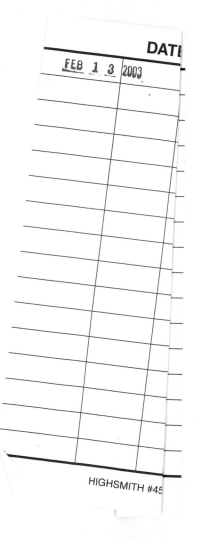

DATE

FEB 1 3 2003

HIGHSMITH #45